THE
LAST
CAMPAIGN

THE LAST CAMPAIGN

HOW PRESIDENTS REWRITE HISTORY, RUN FOR POSTERITY & ENSHRINE THEIR LEGACIES

ANTHONY CLARK

THE
LAST
CAMPAIGN
HOW PRESIDENTS REWRITE HISTORY, RUN FOR POSTERITY & ENSHRINE THEIR LEGACIES

Please refer all questions to: publisher@anthony-clark.com.

Front cover photograph (top): official White House Photo by Pete Souza, courtesy of the White House Photo Office. Front cover photograph (bottom): official White House Photo by David Valdez, courtesy of the George Bush Presidential Library. Unless otherwise indicated, all internal and back cover photographs are courtesy of the author.

Portions of the Introduction originally appeared on
History News Network, a website located at http://hnn.us.

Portions of Chapter 2 first appeared in Salon,
a Web site located at http://www.salon.com.

ISBN: 1508409749
ISBN-13: 978-1508409748

DEDICATION

In memory of my father, Tom Clark,
a funny, kind, hard-working man
who gave me my love of words.

"I told President Obama that this was the latest, grandest example of the eternal struggle of former presidents to rewrite history."

President Bill Clinton, at the dedication of the George W. Bush Presidential Library in Dallas, Texas, April 25, 2013.

CONTENTS

INTRODUCTION

I WAS A LITTLE NERVOUS. IT WAS MY THIRD WEEK ON THE job and things were moving quickly. Until the previous month, I worked in a classroom at a D.C. law firm teaching attorneys and administrative staff how to use legal software. Now I was standing behind the dais in the main hearing room of the Committee on Oversight and Government Reform, in the Rayburn House Office Building, about to run my first Congressional hearing. We were all waiting for my boss, the chairman of the Subcommittee on Information Policy, Census, and National Archives, to arrive and call the Members to order. Using my script.

The script I had written after my careful review of years of earlier hearings. After poring over the committee handbook and the Rules of the House and considering the issues as I understood them. The script I had finished a week earlier so there would be time for someone above me to read it. To scrutinize it carefully. To shepherd it through several layers of political, governmental, and legislative review, and, no doubt, revisions.

As it turned out, no one but me – including the chairman – had yet read the script. He would see it for the first time in a few minutes when he opened the binder and gaveled the hearing to order.

Preparing for the hearing, waiting for the chairman – whom, I would learn, never was on time – and getting more and more nervous, I forced myself to stop a moment to take it all in. I knew how difficult it had been for me to get to that point, and how easily it could all go away. I was optimistic – then, at least, at that early stage – about what I might accomplish. Just in case it didn't last, I wanted to remember what it looked like, and what it felt like, to be there, then.

1

The view from behind the chairman's seat was quite different from how a hearing looks on C-SPAN. And I don't just mean the imposing height, the trappings of office or the glare of the lights, the cameras, the witnesses, the audience. As I wrote the script, I had imagined it would be like the view of a special visitor to the dugout at a baseball stadium, watching as the "pros" readied themselves. In the hearing room, though, it felt more like I was standing on the first base line, ready to play in a major league game. That may sound odd, as staff have no official voice in Congressional proceedings. But as I would soon discover, staff play a much larger role in what happens on the Hill than most people realize. But at that point, I was more than a bit in awe at how it had all happened.

Six years earlier I had written a term paper about presidential libraries in a political science course. That paper led, through a series of twists and turns, to my position on the subcommittee. It was a remarkable experience, and promised to be an even greater challenge now that I had "made it." I couldn't have imagined that a simple class paper would change my life in any way, but my research and writing of this book completely transformed it, and at that point, resulted in my conducting official oversight of the presidential libraries, and the federal agency that administers them, the National Archives and Records Administration (NARA), for the United States House of Representatives.

The inspiration for a book about how presidents try to re-write history and campaign for posterity was my review of earlier visits to these attractions, and my desire to understand their purpose and explain what they were and what they mean to the country. As a tourist, I had been to four of the libraries, and while each one was different, my impression generally was the same for each. For a graduate class in American politics at Appalachian State University, in Boone, North Carolina, I wrote about the exhibits in presidential library museums, calling them "the last campaign."

It wasn't just about the effort to raise money and build their library. The president, his family, his advisors – and, unfortunately, a taxpayer-funded federal agency – all campaign to burnish a legacy. They campaign to rehabilitate, repair, and rationalize, that, with the proper planning and funding, will go on long after the president, his immediate family, and senior members of his administration have passed away. While the libraries were begun with a very different purpose, I had suspected that this is what they had become.

My professor encouraged me to explore the issues I raised in the paper in a longer format, perhaps even a book. At the end of the semester, I had some time off before teaching at the local community college, and I owned a small recreational vehicle. Taking his advice, I traveled to the presidential libraries I had yet to visit. I spent days in each of the museums, taking photographs and video of the exhibits, and talking with staff and visitors. Much of what I had surmised in the paper was confirmed by what I found. But it wasn't until I went back for second (and sometimes third, and fourth) trips, and examined the records held in the presidential library archives, that the real story emerged.

Starting off, I read everything I could get my hands on about the libraries. I spent weeks with the records, combing through and photographing thousands of pages, most of which had never been used by another researcher (people research *at* libraries, not the libraries themselves). I spent months in the National Archives examining the development of presidential libraries from the late 1930s, when the Office of the Archivist was responsible for them.

At first, I was only interested in the museums and other public aspects. I had spent my first trip touring the exhibits, and I didn't perform archival research. I had thought I might want to briefly visit the research rooms at some point, out of curiosity; they were only open during the same time as the museums, and I was on a tight travel budget. I had no idea then how important the archives would become to my work. I wasn't aware of the importance of the records I would find – nor of the records I wouldn't be able, or allowed, to find.

After my first round of visits, and as I got into the database research – newspaper, magazine and journal articles and the like – I identified three major areas of interest: the "history" that is being exhibited and promoted in the libraries; the influence of the private foundations that build and support them; and the controversies surrounding their locations – what is known as the "site selection" process. A lot has been written about two or three of the libraries' site selections, but in truth each one has had problems to a certain degree. Most of my "finds" in the records have been about this process – including the previously-unreported story of a sitting president who violated federal law to try to build his library on prime federal land. This site-selection process included the creation of a new government program to cover up his actions, which almost succeeded. While clearly the most outrageous example of the politics of presidential libraries, this wasn't the only one I found. The key to understanding the system, I learned, is understanding and exposing the private organizations that raise money, build, and support the libraries.

The simple facts of how each began led me to examine not just how they told the history of the presidents, but the libraries' own histories and politics. Franklin D. Roosevelt donated his family's property (a decision with which his mother, who actually held the deed, disagreed, though she did later come around). Harry Truman's brother and sister didn't want him to use his family's farmland (he ended up building the library in Independence, down the block from his in-laws' home). A Dwight Eisenhower museum – complete with his preserved boyhood home – was dedicated before he was president. Herbert Hoover built two libraries for his papers, the second after seeing his successors create ever-larger public memorials to themselves (and getting upset with the politics at the Hoover Institution). I was determined to try to document the stories through archival records.

At the earlier libraries, as well as in the enormous NARA facility in College Park, Maryland, known as "Archives II," I found good information. I spent months there reviewing plans, designs, fund-raising materials, and other records. The documents revealed how each president put his own stamp on the institution. A system, not just individual libraries, was developing. In 1964, the National Archives created an Office of Presidential Libraries (NL) to oversee the growing organization. Coincidentally – or perhaps not – 1964 is when I hit a brick wall.

I RECEIVED THE CALL IN THE LAW FIRM TRAINING ROOM. IT was a few weeks after Barack Obama had won the 2008 election. Darryl Piggee, the staff director of the Information Policy Subcommittee, had heard about my experiences with NARA and wanted to speak with me. We met a few times, discussing not only my concerns but the agency as a whole; the Archivist of the United States had recently resigned, and NARA would be without a leader until the new president nominated a replacement. This, combined with all of the controversies and unhappiness at the Archives – there was trouble brewing with archival security; many high-ranking officials were universally disdained; and NARA consistently fared very poorly in federal employee satisfaction surveys – created a air of uncertainty about the nation's guardian of records. The opportunities for real Congressional oversight were significant.

After I gave the subcommittee staff a series of presentations about presidential libraries, federal records, and the National Archives, Piggee asked me to help plan hearings in the 111th Congress. Immediately, I suggested that they hold one on the nomination of a new Archivist of the United States. While the Senate has the Constitutional responsibilities to advise and consent on whomever the president's nominee would be, the House wasn't prohibited from discussing what issues the president should consider when selecting the new archivist. More importantly, I felt that the House should hear from those who make use of the records in the Archives. That May, the subcommittee convened a hearing, "Stakeholders' Views on the National Archives and Records Administration"; I suggested three witnesses – all of whom were invited and testified – and I wrote questions for the chairman to ask during the hearing. By all accounts, it went well, and was a rare opportunity for experts to weigh in before the nomination process began.

After I helped plan a second successful hearing about security problems and other organizational problems at the agency, Piggee called to ask me to join the subcommittee as a professional staffer. Standing in that darkened training room, among computers and projectors and software and manuals, I took just over a second to consider and accept.

IT WAS NOW PAST TIME FOR THE CHAIRMAN TO ARRIVE. THE witnesses milled near their table, some with gaggles, others alone. The staff assistant set nameplates around the gently curved platform and neatly laid out pencils, writing pads, and bottles of water at the Members' places. Senior staff from both sides of the aisle sat behind their bosses' chairs (junior staff would stand along the broad side wall of the hearing room). The cameras were ready. Things were moving quickly.

A few weeks before, on my very first day – the same, coincidentally, as the Senate confirmation hearing for David Ferriero, President Obama's nominee for Archivist of the United States – the staff director told me to choose the next hearing topic.

Over the previous two years, the subcommittee had been heavily active in oversight of the 2010 Census (which was at that point only six months away) and the director was now looking to explore other areas of jurisdiction, particularly of the National Archives.

"What do you want to do?" Piggee asked me.

"Me?" I answered, somewhat taken aback.

"Yes, you. What should the next hearing be about?"

He had recruited me to expand the hearings and investigations of the National Archives ("expand" being a relative term, since before I started consulting, the subcommittee hadn't done much in the way of hearings and investigations of NARA – nor had, in fact, most of the previous several Congresses). As someone who knew about presidential libraries, federal records, and the agency – but not the mechanics of running a hearing – I had imagined I would, at least at first, advise. I would recommend. I would guide the other professionals in their work so they would have a better understanding of NARA and its challenges. I would identify opportunities for improvement and suggest solutions. All of which I had done for other hearings, as a consultant. At that point, I had no notion of the level of responsibility I would hold, right from the start.

Arriving with many ideas, I hadn't yet prepared any formal proposals (after all, it was still my first day, and I had spent part of it at the Senate confirmation hearing for the new archivist). As a brand-new employee, I couldn't just tell him I had no ideas, and I couldn't just offer a vague – or worse, bad – suggestion. I knew that one area of the subcommittee's jurisdiction was the Federal Advisory Committee Act (FACA). The law seeks to ensure all groups that agencies form to give counsel and make recommendations, advisory committees, are open, transparent, and, most importantly, represent a balanced, wide range of interests.

I told Piggee that NARA had an advisory committee on presidential libraries that was anything but balanced – it was comprised solely of representatives of the private foundations that build the libraries – and that the committee's operations were pretty well hidden, despite the law.

"OK, do that," he ordered.

"Do what – a hearing on NARA's advisory committees?"

"Yep. That'll be a good one."

And with that, he left. I was now charged to organize, prepare, write, and run a Congressional oversight hearing, for the most powerful investigative committee in the House, about the federal agency that had fought my attempts to access their records about presidential libraries for three years. The agency whose Congressional liaison had protested my appointment to the Oversight Committee just days earlier. The agency whose senior officials, simply because I had requested records they should already have made public and then criticized those who had inappropriately withheld them, considered me to be their enemy.

One of those officials, with whom I had clashed repeatedly, was responsible for NARA's Advisory Committee on Presidential Libraries.

AFTER GOING THROUGH MORE THAN TWENTY YEARS OF records, by October, 2006, I was up to the creation of the Office of Presidential Libraries, in 1964 – but the records of the office after that were nowhere to be found. They weren't described in the finding aids. NARA staff even brought me into the stacks to show me that the specific shelves on which we should have been able to find the records were empty. No one seemed to know where they were.

It wasn't until almost a year later – after some National Archives officials had ignored, delayed and misled me – that I found out that office considered every single record they had ever held or created to be "operational" (as defined by them, "necessary for their daily needs") and therefore unavailable.

Despite the law, regulations and common archival practice, forty-two years worth of records about the creation and operation of presidential libraries, amounting to more than three-quarters of a million pages, were being kept secret.

It took me two more years to gain access to the records, primarily by using the Freedom of Information Act (FOIA), but also, some public pressure; it was during this long struggle that I decided to tell my story, in an attempt to embarrass the agency to release the records.

Even after being ignored, or, worse, purposely blocked from access to NARA's records, writing about how the agency was treating me was something I didn't want to do (and, I learned from historians experienced in dealing with NARA, something "one didn't do").

My plan had been to research quietly and not reveal anything until I published a book; I was working in an area that was virtually untouched, and at any minute, established writers could have beaten me to the story.

But two years became too long, and I needed a way to push the agency toward action. I decided to risk airing the roadblocks I had encountered in order to make something happen. I wrote about some of these experiences in an article on History News Network, a popular web site for historians, and presented some lectures to interested individuals at some schools and a professional organization.

During my attempt to gain access to their records about presidential libraries, NARA officials delayed producing documents by ignoring my

FOIA requests, using subtle administrative tricks, and through outright obstruction – including, incredibly, denying that they held any records about the site selection process for presidential libraries – the institutions that they operated and maintained.

One Archives official – the one also responsible for the advisory committee – resorted to what I believe to have been direct deceit. I had long sought an interview with Sharon Fawcett, NARA's Assistant Archivist for Presidential Libraries. When finally I interviewed her in June, 2008 – an interview she agreed to allow me to record – I asked why she and others kept insisting that they held no records about the process by which presidents select the site for their libraries. Fawcett told me that the reason why NARA had not produced anything responsive to my FOIA requests for documents relating to the site selection process was that NARA has *never had a role to play* in the process, and therefore would hold no documents. She told me that NARA "finds out where a presidential library will be located the same day that the public does."

This not only strained credulity, but it contradicted a memo written by a NARA official dated January 11, 1997 to then-Archivist John Carlin, in advance of an early meeting with President Bill Clinton regarding his proposed library. The author of the memo urges the archivist to remind the president that "NARA can play a key role in assisting the President in making the site decision...Provide evaluation criteria and assess the viability of competing sites...Provide the rejection for sites not selected in accordance with the President's wishes...NARA through the Office of Presidential Libraries has a long history of assisting Presidents with the planning, development, and establishment of Presidential Libraries."

One might argue that Sharon Fawcett, in the summer of 2008, should not be expected to have known specific agency policy and history from eleven years earlier; one could argue that, perhaps, but Fawcett – in 1997, serving then as Deputy Assistant Archivist for Presidential Libraries – was the author of that memo.

I contacted NARA's general counsel, cited the memo as evidence of improper withholding of records, and insisted that NARA release the records in question; shortly thereafter I received hundreds of pages about the site selection process for the Reagan, Bush and Clinton libraries (though that was just a small portion of the documents I sought). It took more than a year after that incident for NARA to agree to release the complete record of the Office of Presidential Libraries – more than

750,000 pages – that Fawcett and other officials had been trying to keep hidden.

From: Sharon Fawcett
To: ARCH2D2.A2D2P1.jcarlin, ARCH2D2.A2D2P1.lbellard
Date: 1/11/97 5:12pm
Subject: Briefing paper for meeting with the President

Attached is my draft of the briefing paper. I apologize for exceeding one page. The first page, especially the first section on "Immediate Decisions" includes all the major points John wanted to make in this meeting. If you get into any of the remaining, we'd consider it a bonus.

BRIEFING POINTS FOR THE CLINTON PRESIDENTIAL LIBRARY

Immediate decisions and actions needed
- The Archivist recommends the President designate a contact person to work with NARA to facilitate early and coordinated planning for the development of the Clinton Presidential Library.

    ◦ The President makes a decision on the site for the Library
        ◦ Early decision allows fundraising to begin in earnest
        ◦ NARA can play a key role in assisting the President in making the site decision.
            › Provide evaluation criteria and assess the viability of competing sites and the level of commitment of the individuals and institutions involved in offering the site. A questionnaire for site selection could include questions that examine what the university can do for the Library, related academic programs, the depth of staff support, environmental conditions and regulations, and transportation and lodging.
            › Provide the rejection for sites not selected in accordance with the President's wishes.
            › Provide the President or his designee with a suggested time-line for site selection.

- NARA through the Office of Presidential Libraries has a long history of assisting Presidents with the planning, development, and establishment of Presidential Libraries. In addition

Portions of briefing document, Office of Presidential Libraries, NARA.

This large release of records came about only through the direct intervention of the archivist at the time, Allen Weinstein. Ironically, I finally received full access just before I started working for the Oversight Committee. Ironic, as I had agreed to postpone my research at NARA while working for the committee that had oversight of the agency, and so did not have the immediate opportunity to review the records.

In fact, I did more than postpone my research. I left my career as a technology trainer, closed my blog about my experiences researching at NARA, and stopped writing this book. The work could have been, or could even have created the appearance of, a conflict.

I canceled a journal article I had arranged to write about the agency, stopped giving lectures, and put the book on hold indefinitely to focus exclusively on my official duties. It was difficult, after so much time and effort, to get so close and then have to put it aside. While in retrospect I feel it was well worth it, that first day in the Oversight Committee room I was concerned I had made the wrong choice.

I HAD A LOT RIDING ON THIS FIRST HEARING. I HAD changed my life and what had been my main pursuit for six years. I was been appointed because of what was believed to be my expertise about not only the agency in general but the specific problems facing presidential libraries. And here was my first test: a hearing I created on my own, concerning an agency the Congress rarely examined. About an issue of which few off the Hill – or even most on it – had ever heard. Its obscurity, and the relative lack of attention paid to the agency, however, didn't match the growing concern in Washington that the subcommittee was beginning to look into things that were better left unexamined. Some didn't like what it meant that the chairman had brought me on board.

The National Archives formally had complained about my appointment before I started working on the committee. Senior officials in the agency weren't the only ones who were unhappy. Also on my first day, the then-ranking member of the Oversight Committee, Rep. Darrell Issa (R-California) complained to my boss. On the Floor of the House of Representatives. During legislative business.

Crossing the aisle – literally – Issa approached the chairman, Rep. Lacy Clay (D-Missouri), saying he was upset that I had been hired.

"He's an expert in presidential libraries!" Issa said.

"Yes. Does that disqualify him to work in Congress?" Clay asked.

"But he's writing a book!" Issa protested.

I had been – and continue to be – more critical of the Reagan Library Foundation than any other in the system. As the Keeper of the Supply Side Flame, the Sacred Altar upon which all of their candidates must be anointed before seeking the presidency, Republicans can be particularly sensitive to any criticisms of that holy shrine.

Apparently, my work didn't sit well with the gentleman from California, nor, I assume, those for whom he did favors (such as protesting a staffer's appointment to a committee on which he served).

"Yes," Clay said. "And I hear it'll be a good book; what's your point?"

His message delivered, and without an actual argument to make, Issa instantly was deflated. The ranking member of the most powerful House committee, carrying water for the largest, best-funded, and most powerful presidential library foundation, simply shrugged and walked away.

It was no coincidence, then, that I chose to investigate how these private foundations work with NARA, which had been mostly in secret. Congress had tried for decades, without much success, to learn about and improve the way the libraries are created, funded and operated. Despite several revisions in the law, the private foundations do pretty much what they want. And they have received considerable assistance from NARA officials in bending, circumventing or even violating the law.

I wanted to change that. Working on the Oversight Committee, I was determined not only to increase the transparency of the system but to reform it, to make it more accountable, and to remove the politics from what should be nonpartisan presidential archives.

I JUST WANTED TO WRITE A BOOK ABOUT PRESIDENTIAL libraries. I wanted to tell people about them: what they are, how they started, why they're important. When I started my research, I thought the result would be a simple history of the libraries, and of presidential records – like a reference book, including all "sides" of the story: the public, academic, and private. I wanted to get all of the facts and figures and the basic stories into one volume. There is not a lot published about the libraries, and what is available isn't comprehensive (and often inaccurate).

The libraries are a major source of twentieth-century American history: authors, documentary and dramatic filmmakers, historians, journalists, academics and students get much of their material from these institutions. We spend close to a hundred million taxpayer dollars a year on the library system. Yet the average American couldn't tell you what a presidential library is, nor is it likely that they have ever visited or will ever visit one.

This has turned out to be a different book. It's not an unabridged history of each of the libraries nor the system in general. While some have compiled their own histories (for example, the Roosevelt Library has created an excellent "artificial collection" of the records that document their history, as well as a good narrative on their web site), only half have enough records that are opened to write such a history.

But that's not why the book is different from what I planned. When I began, I didn't think about examining the political aspects, which turned out to be considerable. It was because I became caught up in the politics – became, in a way, part of the story – that I realized I had to write a different book; my experiences with NARA, and then participating in oversight of the agency and the libraries, altered the direction of my research.

Twelve years ago, I didn't know this process would make me some powerful enemies, many close friends, introduce me to an amazing group of scholars and archivists and historians and educators, and lead me to a dream job. I had no idea that it would change my life.

The irony is that if some NARA officials hadn't done so much to keep me from the records, I probably wouldn't have found myself standing in the committee room that day waiting for Chairman Clay to call to order the hearing about the NARA's Advisory Committees that I planned and wrote, including inviting witnesses; the first of which would be Assistant Archivist for Presidential Libraries, Sharon Fawcett.

NATIONAL ARCHIVES: ADVISORY COMMITTEES AND THEIR EFFECTIVENESS

TUESDAY, OCTOBER 20, 2009

House of Representatives,
Subcommittee on Information Policy, Census, and
National Archives,
Committee on Oversight and Government Reform,
Washington, DC.

The subcommittee met, pursuant to notice, at 2 p.m. in room 2154, Rayburn House Office Building, Hon. Wm. Lacy Clay (chairman of the subcommittee) presiding.

Present: Representatives Clay and McHenry.

Staff present: Darryl Piggee, staff director/counsel; Jean Gosa, clerk; Frank Davis, professional staff; Yvette Cravins, counsel; Charisma Williams, staff assistant; Anthony Clark, professional staff member; Leneal Scott, information systems manager (full committee); Adam Hodge, deputy press secretary (full committee); Gerri Willis, special assistant (full committee); Adam Fromm, minority chief clerk and Member liaison; Howard Denis, minority senior counsel; and Chapin Fay and Jonathan Skladany, minority counsels.

Mr. Clay. Good afternoon. The Information Policy, Census, and National Archives Subcommittee of the Oversight and Government Reform Committee will come to order.

Hearing record, House Committee on Oversight and Government Reform, Government Printing Office.

IN MY OPINION, THE THREE MOST IMPORTANT PROBLEMS facing presidential libraries are the well-meaning but ultimately problematic Presidential Records Act (PRA) of 1978; the biased "history" in the library museums; and the unchecked power of the private foundations that build (and then use, for political purposes) the libraries. I detail my concerns about the exhibits, and the failures of the law and these organizations – and offer suggestions for reform – in the following pages.

The effect of these failures can be seen in the presidential libraries that have come into the federal system since the reforms were enacted. With the exception of the Johnson Library, I have not been critical of those that were created or accepted prior to these reforms, whether for Democratic or Republican presidents.

My criticism (and I'm not the only one to offer it) has been focused on the laws, and the ways that National Archives officials – and the private foundations that run build and support the modern libraries – interpret and apply them (or not). Regardless of the party of the president whose library I am discussing.

When I point out how the law, and the ways that NARA has implemented it, have created more problems than it was intended to solve – and how the foundations exploit the truck-sized loopholes in it for political gain – I mostly refer to libraries dedicated to Republican presidents; this is not, however, a result of my bias.

I'm not suggesting that I don't have one; any writer who does isn't being honest. The reason it may appear to some that my bias has led me only to criticize one party one is simple: of the four libraries that have been built since the PRA took effect, three of them are for Republican presidents. A fifth came into the federal system during this time period; while subject to a different statute (one with its own challenges), this, too, is a library for a Republican president.

Even if my concerns were equally distributed among these five libraries – those for Richard Nixon, Ronald Reagan, George H.W. Bush, Bill Clinton and George W. Bush (and they're not, in part because of the very different ways each library foundation approaches these issues, and how NARA administers each library) – eighty percent of those concerns would cover Republican presidential libraries. I didn't stack that deck, and I don't indulge in the "equal treatment" fallacy that some in the media believe allows them to appear balanced. If each organization acts differently, each deserves to be examined individually. That I determined Republican presidential library foundations have acted more egregiously, skirted more of the law, and made more political use of presidential libraries than have Democratic foundations was not a foregone conclusion based on my politics, but a consequence of timing. In the coming years, without significant reform (and with enough Democratic presidential victories) I have no doubt that the parties will be more balanced in their distribution of using the libraries inappropriately.

Given the great distance that Barack Obama has traveled from candidate to president on money issues (fund-raising for super PACs, public financing of presidential campaigns, lobbyists serving in his administration, use of soft money); on transparency and the Freedom of Information Act (record number of FOIA lawsuits and denials, increased delays and use of exemptions); and, most importantly, on "probably not even building" an actual library (and instead digitizing his records), it seems likely that the Barack Obama Foundation will make great strides in closing the gap with its Republican counterparts.

In contrast to his explanation as to why he would not prosecute those responsible for authorizing and committing extreme interrogation tactics (that had a "belief that we need to look forward as opposed to looking backwards"), that's exactly what he'll be doing with his library.

As of this writing, the conventional wisdom has it that, sometime in late 2029, we'll see the opening of either the second Clinton, or the third Bush, presidential library. The odds aren't good that future presidents and their foundations voluntarily will reform and rein in the excesses of their predecessors.

Parties aside, for many reasons, more recent presidential libraries tend to be more political, and push against the restraints of the laws and regulations in order to, for lack of a better phrase, make hay while the sun shines. Presidents and their supporters have a finite amount of time in which to raise enough money to ensure they can write their own history and control their legacy for decades to come, and they do everything they can to take advantage of that time.

Once it's over, today's new, exciting and dynamic library – one that hosts presidential nominees, international leaders, and celebrities, and generates headlines, controversy, and a lot of cash – becomes tomorrow's underutilized, mostly-forgotten local gathering place that hosts square dances, war re-enactors, and community awards ceremonies. And that no longer rakes in the cash.

I would simply ask readers to evaluate the problems I describe (and my suggested solutions) not as if they applied to "good" or "bad" – or "your" – presidents, but to any and all presidential libraries operated by the federal government. If you have a negative reaction to my criticisms of your favorite president, think about how you would feel if your least-favorite president were allowed to get away with the same loophole or dodge or evasion. Over the last forty years each party has come to believe that their opponents, once in the Oval Office, act as if they are above the law; presidents from both parties seem to continue that belief as they use their libraries. If they are to have meaning, the laws, and the criticisms of those who abuse them – must apply to all.

YOU WILL READ IN THESE PAGES ABOUT A PRESIDENT OF THE United States who violates the law. For some – many, even – that simple fact might not be surprising. What may be, though, is that this president violated the law to try to build his library on a spectacular piece of prime federal property, which was, and is, prohibited. What may be even more surprising is that the story has never been reported.

I discovered the information in the fall of 2006 thanks to two NARA archivists who assist researchers in Room 2000 at Archives II in College Park, Maryland. I would consult with them every day for weeks; at the end of each day I would ask, "Are you sure those are all of the records you have about the origins of that library?"

They would pretend to be exasperated with me asking the question one more time (at least, I think they were pretending), and answer, "Yes!"

It became a (bad) running joke. Finally, when we all thought I had exhausted the records in question that were then held there, I asked them one last time, literally as I was on the way out the door. Through the windows of the consultation room where they worked, I saw them exchange a look, shrug, and I heard one of them say, "Yes…well, except for those boxes marked 'Nixon Library at Camp Pendleton'…but he didn't end up building it there, so they won't be of any help to you."

That answer changed everything, and I'm grateful to both of them.

I'm also grateful to the fourteen individuals whom, in the eight years since I found out this secret, I "read into the program." Because I had no platform to immediately publish this book, I was concerned that some established historian or journalist would beat me to the punch. I therefore kept it to myself, only telling, for different but important reasons, these persons, asking for their word not to reveal the story. Each of them kept their promise – from which they are now released, with my thanks.

Once I came across this transgression – and the considerable ways that president and his administration covered up their actions – I did my best to examine the so-called "site selection" process for the other presidential libraries. That is, as they say, when all hell broke loose.

Uncovering this episode changed considerably the direction and theme of this book. Instead of how each library began and changed – a simple, comprehensive history of the libraries – what I hope instead is to illuminate how far presidents will go to ensure and enshrine their legacy…some during their terms, most after they have left office.

While I was successful at forcing certain records out of the National Archives about how other recent presidents have chosen the site for their libraries – and caught the then head of the presidential library system in what I believe to have been a lie about this process – I have no doubt that the whole story, indeed, the whole story of each presidential library, is yet to be discovered in the unprocessed, unreleased (and, in some cases, purposefully withheld), records. It is my hope that some intrepid future researchers soon will take up the challenge of bringing the rest of the records, and the rest of the stories, to light.

Detail of window, the William Clinton Library, Little Rock, Arkansas.

CHAPTER 1

THE LAST CAMPAIGN

I PROMISED MYSELF I WOULDN'T BEGIN WITH THAT QUOTE from Franklin D. Roosevelt. Just about every well-meaning, critical, or self-serving thing that's been written about presidential libraries begins with that quote from Franklin D. Roosevelt about presidential libraries.

The reason is clear: FDR was the first president to build a library for his papers and deed them, and the library, to the federal government. Rather than look at FDR, and how and why he began this particular institution; and how Harry Truman actually made it the tradition, following in FDR's footsteps; and how Dwight Eisenhower followed him, and so on, this book focuses on the politicization of modern presidential libraries. That didn't happen in a vacuum, or suddenly appear; it developed over time. And, where relevant, I will examine the past to understand its impact on the current system.

But this isn't a history of the presidential libraries. It's not a recitation of chronological facts.

Nor is it a polemical jeremiad.

I support the preservation of and open access to presidential papers; using federal tax dollars to do so; the idea that we have the right to know what presidents and their administrations do, and that we can come to know this, at least in part, through their records; the principle that, in order to understand what has happened so that we may shape what will happen, we must have open access to those records; the notion that, as FDR said (I suppose I am beginning with this quote after all):

> *"To bring together the records of the past and to house them in buildings where they will be preserved for the use of men and women in the future, a Nation must believe in three things. It must believe in the past. It must believe in the future. It must, above all, believe in the capacity of its own people so to learn from the past that they can gain in judgment in creating their own future."*

President Franklin D. Roosevelt, at the dedication of his presidential library in Hyde Park, New York, June 30, 1941.

This is why I changed my mind, and decided to open with Roosevelt: because I believe he fervently believed these things when he said them more than seventy years ago, I do not believe he would recognize – nor would he support – how presidential libraries have evolved in the twenty-first century.

The Franklin D. Roosevelt Library, Hyde Park, New York.

He would not support monumental shrines carefully and expensively designed to aggrandize while assiduously erasing all negative aspects from his life and administration – not only in his library, but in depictions of presidents in textbooks and history books and popular films and other media. How through our budgetary and policy choices we have almost lost the original – and, I believe, the only legitimate – purpose for presidential libraries. That the bringing together, preservation, and use of records of the past is now so ignored, so overlooked, so much worse than an afterthought that it's in danger of being forgotten altogether.

How, rather than believing in our capacity to learn from the past to create our own future, the partisan political organizations that build and write the histories in presidential libraries believe we must be told carefully-crafted, incomplete, and sometimes false narratives so we may be manipulated into creating the future that would most benefit them.

I believe that while Franklin Roosevelt the politician might have understood the inclination of his successors to campaign for posterity and rewrite history, Franklin Roosevelt the meticulous collector, ardent champion of archives, and zealous defender of self-determination would be ashamed of modern presidential libraries.

A PRESIDENT OF THE UNITED STATES BREAKS THE LAW SO HIS library could sit on prime federal real estate, creating a new bureaucracy to cover up his actions.

In his final months in office, a vice-president, who also serves as president of the Senate, claims to belong neither to the executive nor legislative branches, asserting that he alone should be allowed to determine which, if any, of his official records would go to the National Archives.

Just hours before his successor is sworn in, a president pardons an international fugitive whose ex-wife is a major contributor to, the president's party, and, more importantly, to his planned library.

A president – ever fearful of his status and mindful of his image – demands the builders of his library change the numbering on the elevator buttons, counting the sub-basement as "1" and the basement as "2," instantly creating a "ten-story" rather than an "eight-story" structure.

Late on his last night in office, a president signs an unlawful agreement with the Archivist of the United States to take control of electronic records that should, under the law, be turned over to the National Archives; after word gets out, the archivist retires – to run that president's private library foundation.

A small group of people, grieving over the death of their brother, friend, and employer two weeks earlier, gather in Boston to form a corporation dedicated to creating a library that was initially intended to serve as the nation's memorial to the assassinated president.

Congress seizes the papers and audio tapes of the only president to resign from office, in order to stop him from destroying evidence of his crimes and abuses of power.

Also on the last night of a presidency, a federal judge issues a temporary restraining order to stop a president from destroying backup tapes of the White House email system, including years of presidential records.

From violating federal law to fudging the number of building stories, presidential libraries demonstrate the extent to which presidents will go to run for posterity and shape the way history remembers them. When running for re-election, presidents often claim it will be "the last campaign" – because no more electoral contests await. However, they do engage in one last campaign: the fight to define and control their legacy. The title of this book comes from a rally during the 1996 election:

"You know, this is my last campaign…unless I run for the school board someday." – President Bill Clinton, Oakland, California October 31, 1996. Courtesy C-SPAN.

When I saw the video of that speech in 2003, immediately I thought: no, your last campaign will be when you build your presidential library, and try to construct your legacy by writing the story of your administration through what's in, and what's not in, the exhibits – just like so many of your predecessors have done. This book examines what presidents will do to insure their place in history is secured positively, by designing that history themselves while keeping historians, journalists and the rest of the public from seeing the records that document the actual history.

THE FOUR MOST RECENT PRESIDENTIAL LIBRARIES – FOR Ronald Reagan, George Bush, Bill Clinton, and George W. Bush – opened an average of four years after leaving office; the papers of their presidencies will not be fully opened for 100 years or more. That is not a consequence of the adoption of some reasonable pause in the release of records, to allow for the cooling down of emotions and the passing away of individuals involved in the activities described in the records. Nor is it due to the physical limitations of our universe.

That our history is being locked up for a century or more is the result of conscious choices – about our priorities, our budgets, and the sensitivities of powerful people – that our legislators and high-ranking federal officials have made and continue to make. Because the National Archives has failed to dedicate adequate resources, it will take these libraries more than 100 years to process and the records.

These decisions are not the only factors that ensure we don't know what presidents do. The laws that govern presidential documents, photographs, film, video and audiotape, and electronic records are flawed, and have had the opposite effect that their authors – who were well-meaning reformers – intended, which was prompt, open access for all.

In the libraries dedicated before the Presidential Records Act of 1978 (PRA) created the enormous backlogs that we see today, most records have been processed and are open. With the notable exception of the John F. Kennedy Library, though, only a fraction of what is available to in-person researchers has been digitized and placed online (the Kennedy Library recently undertook a project to digitize and post online a large percentage of its archival holdings).

In the PRA libraries, the decades-long processing delays resulting from compliance with the law, as well as not enough resources committed to ending those delays, mean that relatively few records are available and even fewer are online.

The consequence of these delays are serious and lasting. Students revise dissertation topics; authors abandon books; and reporters give up on writing newspaper and magazine articles. Journalism in particular is negatively impacted by these extreme delays. When current events necessitate a look back, reporters rely on being able to discover how earlier presidents handled similar events. Without access to this valuable perspective, those stories cannot be told.

Contrary to the common accusations of partisan critics from across the political spectrum, this is not a result of political choices made by staff-level archivists at the libraries. Instead of being able to process entire series of records – on broad subjects such as the environment, the economy, and education, or on specific matters such as the Clinton universal health care plan, the First Gulf War, and Iran-Contra – archivists at the PRA libraries must answer hundreds of requests for specific documents made through the Freedom of Information Act. This requires careful screening of the records, out of context, to remove sensitive or protected information, and takes considerably longer than what is known as "systematic processing" – reviewing a whole series of records in context.

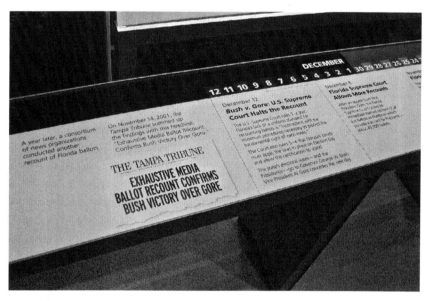

Exhibit on the 2000 election, the George W. Bush Library, Dallas, Texas.

The fact that the law has not turned out the way legislators intended is not only the fault of those who wrote and enacted it, though; NARA's decisions have significantly affected how the law has been implemented. The agency staffs libraries with archivists to process the records, but also employs museum curators and exhibit specialists and educators and museum registrars and public affairs specialists and events coordinators and communications directors and visitor services coordinators and volunteer managers and administrative officers and public program directors and gift shop clerks. Those positions take up funding that otherwise could be spent on records, if that were NARA's priority. But it isn't.

For organizations that Congress has authorized to – and provides funding for – first and foremost, preserve and provide access to records, that's an awful lot of people with responsibilities in areas other than preserving and providing access to records. In the newer libraries, the number of archival staff is inadequate to meet the demands of processing tens of millions of records, and so the delays mount. In the older libraries – where one might expect the emphasis on image management to decline over time, and give way to more archival pursuits – newly-invigorated foundations, inspired by success of the more recent libraries, seek out new ways to revitalize and rehabilitate their president's legacy through renovated exhibits, ambitious public events, and aggressively advertising and social media. Across the board, then, records are secondary – if that – priorities.

That works out just fine for former presidents and their foundations. While they would prefer that the most damaging, critical, accurate – the most dispositive – records of their presidency not come out while they are still alive (or while their spouses, siblings, and children are still viable candidates for high office), they wouldn't want to appear to be influencing the process inappropriately by actively, and publicly, demanding that millions and millions of documents be withheld.

They don't have to; NARA's decisions to emphasize tourism and public history (which is, technically, private history) over their legislative mandate to open records serves the purposes of former presidents quite conveniently.

By cooperating fully with their desire to open the museum exhibits in their libraries as quickly as possible – and not providing staffing and resources to quickly (or even relatively slowly) process and open records – NARA helps ensure that the public learns only what former chief executives and their supporters want them to learn, decades before we have access to the records, or what really happened.

Pundits, journalists, and other writers examine, analyze, and review sitting presidents in real time, but can know, even with sources and leaks, only a small percentage of the "real story" while the president is in office. The records of any administration – the memoranda, mail (physical and electronic), position papers, photographs, video and social media (even the artifacts, gifts of state, and the tens of thousands of objects sent to the White House) – help us to understand actions, context, and meaning, by revealing (among many other things) what we didn't know at the time.

Without free and open access to these records, we can only know and understand what each president allows us to know, and only from their perspective.

Most who view the exhibits in presidential library museums – which are operated by the United States government – trust that what they're learning is the full, documented truth; it hardly ever is. NARA claims, though, that presidents who pay for the exhibits should be allowed to control them – even if that means distorted history.

In addition to questions about what presidential libraries contain and what they do, there are serious concerns about the expense of the system. To defray the costs of operating presidential libraries, federal legislation specifies how they are to be built, and the amount of the financial endowment that the private organizations that build them are required to provide to NARA prior to acceptance by the archivist. This legislation is rife with loopholes and vague language open to interpretation.

Presidential libraries have been built without adequate space for educational programs, archival storage and processing, or temporary exhibits. The Reagan Library hosts patently political events, but claims to not violate the Hatch Act because the specific room in which the event takes place – inside the federal library – was not deeded to the government, and so is not subject to federal restrictions.

Many foundations have offices inside the library, and their staff have federal government e-mail addresses and use federal government equipment to carry out their private efforts at not only supporting the libraries but in furthering the goals of their respective political parties.

These private foundations operate money-making enterprises within the libraries but are not required to give any of that money to the government, to help with operation, maintenance, or programming.

Recent libraries have built or are planning to build large additions to the original buildings, but will not deed them to the government, in order to avoid the size restrictions and mandatory endowment requirements of the law; at some point in the future, when support for the private foundation has decreased significantly (as has happened to most library foundations), the federal government will have to step in and take responsibility for these structures. No law, regulation, or policy currently in effect – nor any seriously being contemplated – takes this into account.

PRESIDENTIAL LIBRARIES ARE INORDINATELY INTERESTING institutions with the great promise of making a significant impact on our society; that promise, though, for the most part, remains unrealized – particularly in the newer (and some of the newly-renovated) ones. I have been fascinated by them ever since the day I drove into the parking lot at Hyde Park, New York, paid my ticket at the small National Park Service ticket booth (which is no more, a casualty of progress), and visited the Franklin D. Roosevelt Presidential Library for the first time. Since then, I've made more than forty trips in total to the libraries of Herbert Hoover through George W. Bush.

I'm captivated by the libraries. I've often been thrilled by them. And I've always been challenged by them. I have favorite research rooms and collections and exhibits and educational programs and gift shops – in libraries for presidents on both sides of the aisle.

But I struggle with four major areas of concern: the influence of hundreds of millions of dollars of private, political donations on NARA's operation and administration of the law; that the government is hosting biased, factually-incorrect, legacy-polishing exhibits and partisan political events; that taxpayers are paying for them; and that records are languishing, unprocessed and unavailable – specifically because NARA allocates scarce resources to exhibits, education, and public programs, rather than to the core function of the libraries: records.

This last issue was reflected in the discussions about where the Barack Obama Presidential Center will be located: in neither the competing bids nor the request for proposals were records given more than a passing reference (and only then as to how much cubic feet they might take up), much less the consideration that is due their central place as the presidential libraries' reason for existence.

No wonder, though: no city, university, or organization will win the right to host a library on their promise of how quickly and thoroughly the records will be processed, how carefully they will be protected, and how fairly they will be served if their site is chosen. In modern presidential libraries, it's about tourism; the potential to awe, influence, and manipulate; and the ability of the "presidential center" to be "transformative."

The Chicago Architecture Club and the Chicago Architecture Foundation held a worldwide competition in 2014 to design a hypothetical Barack Obama Presidential Library.

Not connected to the official process of selecting a site and an architect conducted by the Obama Library Foundation, the contest asked entrants to "see what these buildings could do." The successful proposals, announced in early 2015, demonstrate some of the problems facing the presidential library system.

The two winners and the first honorable mention all contained renderings of buildings that contained rows and rows of library shelves, even though a presidential library isn't "that kind of library."

More than that, though, answering the charge to be radical and to expand on what the libraries could do simply resulted in bold architecture, with seemingly little care for the realities of what a library is and does – much less for expanding the concept of what the libraries could become.

The second honorable mention, however – from Drew Cowdrey and Trey Kirk – offered a truly radical design, in several ways: not only did they de-emphasize the magisterial nature of the presidential library that dominates everything in its immediate vicinity, but the core of their idea is to get out of the building, and into the community. Literally.

Cowdrey and Kirk posit that "As the production of architectural narrative intervenes and conditions the visitor's experience, we have chosen to liberate the archival core from its vernacular wrapper" – by placing the records and artifacts on a series of exhibit trucks that each day drive through the city, bringing the record of a presidency to the people.

Concerns about preservation and security aside, these two have hit upon on an urgent question facing the system: are the buildings archival depositories, or are they organizations that, as the Obama Library Foundation describes itself, "marshal resources to address present and future global and domestic challenges of interest to the president"?

To those who ask, "can't they be both?" the answer is no, they cannot; at least not without significant changes to the laws that govern them.

Presidential libraries have, over time, evolved beyond the limits of the law. The newer "presidential centers" showcase these roles, and more; the question is whether or not the people should pay for – and, by doing so, officially approve of – the operation of institutions that are far outside of their legislative purpose. If we are to accept and support this evolution, we should do so affirmatively…and, I hope, only after a new national discussion on their roles, functions, and limits.

This debate – or rather, the lack of it, as the question already seems to have been answered – is evident whenever a new library is dedicated, or a permanent exhibit renovated; during these celebrations, NARA and the libraries share links and photos and videos on social media, but very few of the links are about records. They're focused almost exclusively on what they consider to be the "public" side, and all but ignore the records.

To be sure, there have been some notable exceptions. But by and large, we're asked to "celebrate" the lives of these presidents and how their museums tell the stories of those lives. By the National Archives and Records Administration, the agency created to do something quite different: preserve and make available the permanently valuable records of our federal government.

Atrium of the John F. Kennedy Library, Boston, Massachusetts.

I GET THE ATTRACTION OF PRESIDENTIAL LIBRARIES. I GET the patriotic honor of visiting such a place. I don't mean that sarcastically; I honestly understand, and – to a certain extent – have shared it. The first three presidential libraries I visited were for Democratic presidents, and two of them were (at the time, at least) heroes of mine. I will not forget the feelings, the images – the excitement – of driving up and walking in and being in those libraries. It felt as if I were privy to some special, insider access. *Franklin Roosevelt worked here. This is a memorial to John F. Kennedy. Jimmy Carter is right next door, eradicating guinea worm and ensuring fair elections and working towards peace.*

I left each feeling proud of my country and full of hope for the future. I was excited to be there, so close to the artifacts of the history I had learned in school and of the stories I had read about in books and watched in movies and documentaries and television shows.

And while I was eager to visit the next two, those trips also brought me anxiety and grief. As I entered the Reagan and Nixon libraries, paid my admission fee, and looked at the gift shops, donor walls, and initial displays, I thought, "they'll find me out."

Listening to the docents speak lovingly, reverentially, in hushed tones, about these presidents, their great deeds, and awesome lives, I felt sure they would know. They would discover me. *A Democrat!* In our shrines! Call security!

Every time the guides said something I knew wasn't true, and each time I saw an exhibit that was egregiously slanted, my cheeks burned red. I mean that literally; I was simultaneously embarrassed by the fiction and anxious I would be discovered. Not simply as One Who Didn't Believe, but as someone who knew better.

I wasn't a True Believer. I wasn't *with the program*. I didn't nod along with the rest of the crowd when the guides explained how Richard Nixon actually was a great president whom Democrats railroaded out of office or that Ronald Reagan single-handedly ended the Cold War while never removing his jacket inside the Oval Office or, most importantly, that this country needs more leaders like Ronald Reagan and Richard Nixon.

I didn't even make half-hearted attempts to fit in with the tourists. I didn't ask anyone to take photographs of me with statues or in front of iconic images or beside historic artifacts (selfies weren't yet a big deal).

Certainly, I had been embarrassed by the lack of balance at the three Democratic presidential libraries I had visited, but – I thought then – at least they based their praise on actual accomplishments, and dealt with the negatives, even if while softening the blows. These two Republican libraries, however, were outright Spin Machines.

Unlike the three Democratic libraries, which had left visitors to wander the exhibits on their own, the Reagan and Nixon libraries had docents. Active, and activist, docents. Answering questions, though not always accurately. Providing "context" – which amounted to little more than anecdotes, tall tales, and outright myths. Telling us the Real Story.

I did not feel welcome. I felt put-upon. I felt as if I had better do what I could to hide who I was, and how I thought, and what I knew.

This is the bias I held when I began; little I experienced in the dozen years since has changed my opinion – except I now understand and acknowledge that the Democratic libraries spin, too. Boy, do they spin.

That opinion was bolstered during my time working on the House subcommittee. I knew, going in, that oversight of presidential libraries would be difficult. For decades, former presidents, their families and supporters, administration officials and others had successfully fought off any real examination. A lot of their success had to do with the information imbalance: the powerful interests who ran library foundations were no match for the overworked and underinformed Congressional staffers – to say nothing of the mostly-disengaged Members – among whose many responsibilities oversight of the libraries fell.

But it wasn't until the Archivist of the United States asked my boss to cancel an innocuous oversight hearing to be held at a presidential library that I knew I would fail. More on that story, and my efforts to restart professional oversight of the libraries, can be found in Chapter 3.

PRESIDENTIAL LIBRARIES HAVE A LOT IN COMMON WITH presidential campaigns, which also begin with records – including platform planks, position papers, speeches, and the rest of "the message." Campaign web sites, media kits, and other resources promote the candidate's biography, with a special emphasis on the "origin story."

Like a library, a campaign can't run without money, and so finance – targeting of donors, fund-raising events, and other outreach for cash – is crucial, not only to get the campaign started, but to sustain it until victory. Both presidential libraries and campaigns can garner more press about how much they have raised than about what the candidate stands for, and what they would do if elected.

Defining the candidate – a requirement of any campaign – is not just about highlighting their positive qualities, but showcasing their enormous success in all aspects of their life.

Like exhibits in presidential libraries, campaign commercials, social media, and activities must fundamentally adhere to a specific, tested, and narrow narrative; usually heroic, always positive, and never, ever negative – unless it's information about anyone who opposes the candidate.

Careful planning will only get you so far; campaigns must be agile, nimbly spinning events in real time and rigorously policing anything that might reflect poorly on the candidate. Supporters must be rallied, courted, and celebrated, and given opportunities to interact with the candidate and the family, in order to cement their commitment and their financial generosity.

When the candidate is not able to appear in-person, campaigns use surrogates to stand in and represent the candidate, at events, in the news, and in private sessions with potential donors.

Communicating – with the base, with reporters, and with undecideds – leads to greater margins of victory (and greater financial windfalls). Emails, emails, and more emails – and then, some more emails. With teasers. Tantalizers. And images. Lots and lots of images.

In fact, all media is important. Ads (both traditional and viral), the biography film, sound bites, photos, footage –image is primary; substance is very definitely not at work in campaigns.

Take-aways are key. Buttons, hats, bumper stickers, social media logos, and other memorabilia help spread the message – the right message.

Each of these main elements of a presidential campaign are main elements of the last campaign – the courting of money and support; the creation and maintenance of a strictly-enforced narrative; and the elevation of image over substance.

The modern presidential foundations go further, directly connecting the libraries with campaigns by hosting primary debates, politicians seeking to enter or raise their profile in the national arena, and anointing "chosen ones" to carry on the legacy of their predecessors.

THE RISE OF THE PRESIDENTIAL LIBRARY HAS FOLLOWED THE fall of the presidency. We once held the office of president, as well as its occupant, in high regard. As we have lowered our opinions of both, presidential libraries, consequently, have grown larger and more power-ful – and, not incidentally, less truthful.

As private information is revealed, taboos about what the press may report are discarded, and myths are shattered, the public learns more about the individuals who hold the office and the limitations of both. This leads to increased scrutiny of presidents, from major failures and scandals to peccadilloes, and to lower approval ratings. To counter these effects, the libraries make greater efforts to dispel the (mostly-negative) opinions that are formed by that knowledge.

Increased partisanship also plays a role in the increasingly myth-making presidential library. With fewer and fewer "undecideds" among the electorate, presidents leave office with only a small number of citi-zens feeling neither strongly positive nor strongly negative towards them. Rather than write the "history" of their administrations that is displayed in their libraries with gently persuasive techniques, presidents double down on the strident messaging employed during their terms and campaigns, and insist – as strongly as possible – that they were "right."

This reinforces not only their supporters' positive opinions but their opponents' negative views, which makes convincing the latter group of the president's greatness all the more difficult. But perhaps that is not the point. At least not when the library first opens.

Modern presidents leave office at an average age younger than earlier ones, and have longer ex-presidencies, but their ability to shape public opinion (and capitalize on it) begins to wane soon after their successor takes power. While they may continue to play elder statesman or party leader, their final opportunity to make a real impact on how they will be remembered is the first permanent exhibit in their library. Just like they do in their electoral campaigns, presidents write off trying to convince the dyed-in-the-wool adversaries, and concentrate on cementing their image among their faithful as successful, heroic, larger-than-life icons.

Against such a bulwark, constructed at the cost of hundreds of mil-lions of dollars, and with their actual records – which could contradict their narrative – closed for a hundred years or more, an honest account of the past has no chance. Within a generation, what appears to critics at the opening of a library as opportunistic, whitewashed hagiography be-comes accepted, even venerated, "history."

This approach pays off; many former presidents have seen their ap-proval ratings rise in the years after they leave office due to the aggressive, ongoing campaign waged at and by their library. But it wasn't always this way; some earlier presidents didn't use their libraries as a campaign.

Since Franklin D. Roosevelt established his archive at Hyde Park, New York, presidents have built larger and more expensive temples to themselves. At first the libraries were simple depositories with modest museums affixed, almost as an afterthought, to attract and delight a curious public. As the influence of big money – in political campaigns as well as in actual governing – has increased, the libraries have become important tools for national parties.

There are now thirteen federally-run presidential libraries in the United States; the most recent, for former President George W. Bush, was dedicated in 2013. President Barack Obama has begun plans for his own, and, as of this writing, in early 2015, sites in New York, Hawaii and Illinois are vying to be selected as the location.

All presidential libraries perform a certain amount of legacy-shaping, though the phenomenon of "the last campaign" belongs significantly more to Republicans than to Democrats. This is partly because only two of the last seven libraries have been for Democratic presidents, and both of them – Carter and Clinton – have had the most active post-presidencies in history. Rather than use their libraries as memorials or legacy-management devices, they have rehabilitated themselves through continuing engagement in the political and policy arenas. That may change – especially at the Clinton Library – as more Democrats (and more Clintons) run for and are elected to the presidency.

Republicans, however, employ presidential libraries both to repair a president's image, promote new GOP luminaries, and advance policy. The Nixon Library's speaker series is a *Who's Who* of ultra-conservative political media darlings and Tea Party favorites. The Reagan Library hosts presidential primary debates and campaign "launch" (and "bow out") events; the George Bush Library welcomes national candidates for major addresses; and the George W. Bush Library is undertaking serious efforts to force a revisionist view of his policies, protecting his legacy, as well as the future electoral viability of his administration's – and his family's – future stars.

No contender for the Republican nomination for the presidency can be considered "serious" without repeated visits to the Reagan Library, including at least one major address, and a public anointing by his widow or former top acolytes. This ritual has been dutifully performed by announced (or presumed) presidential candidates Jack Kemp, George W. Bush, John McCain, Mitt Romney, Newt Gingrich, Ron Paul, Mike Huckabee, Rudy Giuliani, Steve Forbes, Paul Ryan, Chris Christie, Jeb Bush, Scott Walker, Jon Huntsman, Rand Paul, Marco Rubio, Bobby Jindal, Rick Santorum, Ben Carson, and Rick Perry. There is no Democratic presidential library that plays an equivalent role, or anything near it.

Even something that is supposedly apolitical, such as access to the library's records, is fraught with campaign considerations. During John Roberts' Supreme Court nomination the Reagan Library temporarily "lost" thousands of pages from his tenure at the Department of Justice, "finding" them once he was confirmed by the Senate.

Congress only recently allowed the Nixon Library to house his presidential records as part of the government system, having been a private institution for almost two decades. Even so, it took the government three years of high-profile fights with the Nixon family and private foundation to renovate the Watergate exhibit (and three more years to name a replacement for the first federal director, who won those fights, but then resigned), beginning the now-stalled transformation of the entire permanent exhibit into something approaching factual accuracy.

The impact of presidential libraries – both in the records they hold (and withhold) and in the "history" they tell – is considerable. About two million people visit the presidential library museums each year, and over 250,000 attend and participate in their public programs. Millions watch programs on C-SPAN, PBS, History, and other channels that originate from the libraries or were created using their resources. Thousands of writers, journalists, students and other researchers use the over four hundred million pages of documents and tens of millions of photographs, feet of film, and audio and videotapes stored in their archives.

The federal government spends about $100 million a year administering and maintaining the libraries, and private organizations spend almost as much supporting them (though they are not required to use the money they raise at the libraries in support of the libraries). While some have relatively few visitors, others have become central to furthering their respective political party's goals.

Arguably, the presidential library system is the largest single source of popular American history of the last eighty years, through exhibits and educational and public programs, and the books, articles, theses and documentaries produced using their resources. Yet few understand the mechanisms that drive this system of taxpayer-funded legacy factories, particularly the role that national political parties and big, private money play in their planning, development, and operation. It is this ignorance, along with the benign neglect of Congress, that enables the worst offenders to operate unimpeded.

George W. Bush reportedly raised close to $500 million to build and endow his library, more than all twelve of his immediate predecessors combined. In late 2001, he ended decades of open-access law and practice with a controversial executive order severely restricting access to presidential records past and future. The order even extended the debatable power of "executive privilege" to former presidents and their heirs, in perpetuity. At the start of his term, Obama reversed that order, but it did not have the force of law until late 2014, when Congress amended the Presidential Records Act. The bill, while important, did not begin to address the real problems and loopholes in the law.

WHY AREN'T MORE HISTORIANS VOCAL ABOUT PRESIDENTIAL libraries? The majority of the historians, journalists and writers with whom I have spoken who have performed research in presidential libraries have done their work in the libraries for Hoover through Ford, and a few at Carter – but only a few at Reagan, Clinton, or the two Bush libraries (not much is open, relatively, for these newer ones). I mention this, because, I think, it influences their views.

Which are: most of these researchers love presidential libraries. Most of them are supporters of presidential libraries. Most of them have never set foot in a presidential library *museum*. Most couldn't care less what kind of exhibits are hosted there (they've told me so); all they want is access to the records. That's perfectly reasonable; typically, the museums and the research rooms are open at the same times, and researchers don't want to spend their valuable time away from the records. I've traveled to every presidential library – all but one on multiple trips – and I know how expensive they are for researchers.

It's rational to be fans of earlier libraries that don't operate under the PRA; at these non-PRA libraries, a lot of what researchers need is open and can be served immediately. High-quality facilities, knowledgeable and helpful staff, fairly open access, few restricted collections, and virtually non-existent political hurdles: what could be better for researchers?

I understand why these people may not know how bad things are in the presidential library system, particularly (but not only) at the newer libraries. They may not realize how skewed many of the exhibits are; they may not be aware of the partisan events hosted in the libraries – and therefore in the government's name; they may not have felt the impact of a years-long FOIA backlog or the decades-long estimates for processing records (to say nothing of records that mysteriously disappear when most needed, only to reappear once, say, a Court nominee is confirmed).

If they knew this, maybe they'd feel differently about presidential libraries. And, perhaps, they'd even help to reform them.

WHEN WE FOCUS ON MAKING IT SEEM THAT EVERYTHING A president did was successful – and had been planned to be so – we lose great opportunities to learn from the very real mistakes presidents make. Once, presidents benefitted from their predecessors' errors.

Now that, thanks to presidential libraries, it appears they no longer make mistakes, presidents – and the citizens who choose presidents – no longer learn from them, either.

What if the Kennedy Library had addressed what has become the conventional wisdom of the "stolen" 1960 election? Has a president not entered office under less than honest conditions since then?

What if the Nixon Library had been truthful about Watergate? In the last four decades, haven't we faced a growing list of questions about presidential secrecy, abuse of power, and extra-legal activities?

What if the Clinton Library had been more open about personal character and its impact on moral leadership? The presidency whose rhetorical nadir was "it depends on what the definition of 'is' is" ushered in one that gave us the specious "Clear Skies" and "Healthy Forests" initiatives (which led to the presidential promise, "if you like your health care plan, you can keep your health care plan").

What if the Reagan Library had examined Iran-Contra and the difficulties of maintaining national principles in the face of unprecedented security challenges? If the library had taught us about this succession of serious crimes, through discussion and debate, in an open and sincere process, would our journey to Abu Ghraib and Guantanamo and black sites and enhanced interrogation techniques have been so smooth? Or have seemed so inevitable?

What if the Johnson Library had been candid about Vietnam? What if it had been honest about how LBJ squandered the chance for real social and civil change on his quagmire in Southeast Asia?

In his quest for greatness, Johnson lost the wars in Vietnam and on poverty; he lost the best chance for social change in a generation; he lost the argument about the promise of the liberal agenda; and, ultimately, he lost the presidency. Over a war he escalated from 16,000 advisors when he took the oath of office aboard Air Force One in Dallas to more than half a million troops when he handed power to Richard Nixon on the East Front of the Capitol sixty-two months later.

We could have learned a great deal from an honest reckoning of what Vietnam cost the president and the country. And the world. Yet no presidential library offers us one; and so, Iraq, Afghanistan, and so on.

Until we – and the presidents we elect to lead us – learn.

Original Watergate exhibit, Richard Nixon Library, Yorba Linda, California.

CHAPTER 2

PRESIDENTIAL LIBRARIES

"Unlike the pyramids, [presidential libraries'] function is not to deify the dead but rather to distill from the past the essence of experience that may illuminate the dim path into the future."

President Gerald Ford, at the dedication of his presidential
library museum in Grand Rapids, Michigan, September 18, 1981.

MOST EVERYONE HAS HEARD OF A PRESIDENTIAL LIBRARY, but for the average person they're hard to define. Are they memorials? Places to store documents? Museums? Think tanks? Actual libraries, with books?

One reason it's hard to get a handle on them is that we have no archetype of what they are "supposed to" look like – no one prime example that everyone has followed or that stands in for the rest as that inclusive, comprehensive presidential library. When we think about a "monument" or "memorial" – even though there is wide variety of them – we have a general picture of what they mean; not so for presidential libraries.

Other nations are no help; the United States invented the presidential library. While some have tried to copy the idea, none have contributed to the creation of an archetypal building.

Of the thirteen here in the United States, some are modest, but not all of the newer ones are grander than the older libraries. They're scattered around the country, at colleges and in or near big cities and in small towns and out in the country. A few have reached for architectural prominence but many are plain, even utilitarian. Some are made up of multiple buildings (one is sort of on its own campus) while most are single structures.

If many can't picture what a presidential looks like, most don't understand what a presidential library is. Even those who have visited one or more of them often don't fully grasp that no matter how many hours they spent touring exhibits and watching videos and playing interactive games and gazing at treasures and sitting in the president's chair and purchasing mementos, they never came close to seeing the core mission, the prime (and, some think, only legitimate) reason for presidential libraries: to preserve and make available the records of the president.

Presidential libraries, from left, top: Hoover, Roosevelt, Truman, Eisenhower; middle: Kennedy, Johnson, Nixon, Ford; bottom: Carter, Reagan, Bush, Clinton.

Three libraries – the Johnson, Carter, and Clinton – make explicit attempts to display their archival storage within or in view of museum exhibits, and there are countless (mostly facsimile) documents displayed in all of the museums. But only a tiny fraction of those who enter presidential libraries actually enter presidential libraries: the archives portion, that is, as opposed to the museum. Relative to the total size of the buildings, the archives components are getting smaller and smaller. Even to describe the archives area of a presidential library as a "portion" is to in-dicate how much less important the records are in the modern libraries.

That works out well for those who build and support (and, sadly, even to some who operate) the libraries. Their goal isn't to allow us to form our own opinions based on a complete and accurate accounting of a presidency, through open access to records; it's to tell us as many tall tales as they can in the museum side for as long as they can, until the re-cords, languishing unprocessed for decades, finally (if ever) are open, and reveal the whole truth.

THESE UNIQUELY AMERICAN INSTITUTIONS RANGE FROM old-fashioned, document/artifact/photograph history museums to high-tech, cult-of-personality shrines.

The first federal presidential library was built by Franklin D. Roose-velt in Hyde Park, New York. Unlike the newer libraries, which are lo-cated on university campuses or where local governments provide the best incentives, the site is steeped in history.

Entering the grounds feels like stepping back in time. FDR placed the library next to his family home where he was born and raised. He and First Lady Eleanor Roosevelt, and their beloved Scottish terrier Fala, are buried there. Among the many exhibits, visitors can see the president's personal office in the library that he used while president.

A highlight of the Nixon Library is, after many years and much con-troversy, Watergate – complete with The Tapes, as well as video histories of participants, officials, and others.

When he renovated his library in 2007, George H.W. Bush included, in the expanded Gulf War exhibit, an "immersive environment" recreat-ing a military setting in Saudi Arabia – a tent full of visual imagery, video, and sounds of explosions.

In all of the discussion about presidential libraries and their impact, not much emphasis is placed on the museums. Community opposition, open access to papers, possible undue influence of donors, and the proper management of collections are all important.

For better or worse, though, the libraries have a far more direct and meaningful impact on the public through their museums. Much of the presidential history of the last eighty years reaches the average American through the filter of the presidential library museum.

A unique "public-private partnership" builds, equips, operates (and renovates) these institutions, but when it comes to exactly what goes into the exhibits (and what does not), the private foundation that supports the library has the last word.

And since the foundation is likely to be funded and operated by loyal supporters (even family members) of the president, that "last word" is a carefully-scripted history that more often than not emphasizes only the positive, omits inconvenient facts and events, and makes the case to "sell" the president one final time. When presidents retire, willingly or otherwise, they traditionally claim that their campaigning days are over, but they have one more to wage, and it's the longest and costliest of their careers. The presidential library is the last campaign.

PRESIDENTIAL LIBRARIES WERE CREATED TO PRESERVE PRESIdential records. The laws and regulations governing the libraries characterize records as their main mission. Over the last few decades, they've become a nationwide network of tourist attractions. Officially, they're a combination of the archives that house presidential records and museums that detail the life of the president. Unofficially, it can seem at times that many in the system wish not to have to deal with the records at all; that they would just go away (and as we will see, it's turning out that way, in legislative and tourism terms).

Overwhelmingly, people come for the museums. And while each is very popular at first, over time it gets more difficult to maintain visitor levels. That means more and more emphasis on making the exhibits interesting and unique, and "refreshing" and "renovating" them, as frequently as possible.

While all of the libraries' permanent exhibits are similar to a degree, some focus more on the president's childhood and others highlight pre- and post-presidential accomplishments. Each also has that singular detail that sets it apart from the others.

The exhibit on Hiroshima at the Truman Library offers a guest book to share reactions to the president's decision; the comments reveal, as well as add to, the emotional impact of the display.

The Ford and Clinton libraries re-create the Cabinet room, allowing visitors, using touch screens, to participate in real decisions that the presidents made.

In the "Decision Points Theater," the George W. Bush Library allows visitors to re-live three difficult crises. Faced with threats and given briefings on options, participants vote on how to handle the situation, viewing the changing opinions of their fellow visitors on a real-time graph.

Decision Points Theater, the George W. Bush Library, Dallas, Texas.

In the libraries for presidents Truman, Johnson, Ford, Carter, Reagan, George Bush, Clinton, and George W. Bush, full-(or almost) scale Oval Office replicas allow us to enter, if only for a few steps, that most iconic of rooms, that most powerful of settings. Visitors to either Bush library can even sit behind reproductions of the president's desk. Other exhibits allow one to stand at the president's podium at a nominating convention (Ford Library); walk through the president's helicopter (Nixon Library); and even climb aboard Air Force One.

That's right, the actual plane. The Oval Office replicas formerly were the most impressive part of a visit to a presidential library – until the Reagan Library added the Air Force One Pavilion: a 90,000 square foot room that houses, among other attractions, SAM 27000, the official aircraft used by seven presidents as "Air Force One." Visitors can walk through the plane and even have their photo taken (for a fee) while boarding, just like a president.

The most unusual feature in all of the presidential libraries is found in this room (no, not the plane; not the Marine One helicopter; not even a circa 1984 presidential motorcade, complete with a limousine, a California Highway Patrol car and motorcycle, and Secret Service Suburbans – all of which the pavilion showcases).

This unusual display grew out of – fittingly, for the Reagan Library – a presidential photo opportunity. On June 3, 1984, Ronald and Nancy Reagan toured Ireland, and stopped briefly at O'Farrell's Pub in Ballyporeen, the Reagan clan's ancestral home. Years later, the Reagan Foundation learned that the pub had closed, and bought it, lock, stock and beer glass. Shipped to California and re-created inside the Air Force One Pavilion, the "Reagan Pub" is now a snack shop.

Near the entrance, under protective glass – like holy relics – are the bar the Reagans touched, the glasses they used, and the bottle of Carolans Irish cream Mrs. Reagan sampled (the president chose a pint of Smithwick's).

The "reliquary" section of the bar from O'Farrell's Pub in the Ronald Reagan Library, Simi Valley, California.

PRESIDENTIAL MUSEUMS, HISTORICALLY AND LEGISLATIVELY, were, are (and should be) subordinate to the real reason that the libraries exist – to preserve and make available presidential and related records. Yet far more people visit the increasingly-touristy presidential museums than the libraries. Most of the small percentage of visitors who do make it into the research room, and who access records, are historians, journalists, or students, who aren't concerned with the exhibits. And the exhibits, as they say, are where the money is; and so that's, unfortunately, where NARA's focus is today.

The size, costs, and focus of presidential libraries aren't new concerns, for the public nor for Congress. Almost forty years ago, a report by the General Accounting Office determined:

> *"The primary purpose of archival depositories is preserving Presidential papers and making them available for research. However, since the greatest interest in libraries from the public view is not the library function but the museum aspect (researchers represent less than one percent of all visitors), we believe there is a tendency for management to direct much of its attention toward the museum function...the sizes and uses, and thus the costs, of most Presidential libraries exceed what was envisioned when the Presidential Libraries Act was being considered. In view of the increasing costs and the inevitable growth in the number and sizes of Presidential archival depositories since the act was passed, it seems highly advisable to carefully consider alternative methods of establishing depositories."*

This report was the result of a Congressional request to study alternative approaches to maintain presidential records and materials, and included recommendations on establishing a central presidential archival depository in place of creating separate libraries for each president. That same year, the National Archives submitted to Congress a report on such approaches, "The Presidential Libraries System: A Review."

In May, 1980, the General Services Administration (GSA) produced an examination of the costs and size increases of presidential libraries and "alternatives for future care of Presidential records."

Section 5 of the Presidential Libraries Act of 1986 – which sought to restrict the size, reduce the cost, and reframe the purpose of the libraries – mandated a study of establishing a central museum of the presidents, again, in place of creating separate library museums for each president.

With a few exceptions – size limitations, endowments, and authority to set and enforce building standards, all enacted in 1986 – these studies and reports did not produce substantive reforms of presidential libraries and museums, nor the process by which we build them.

Section 6 of the Presidential Historical Records Preservation Act of 2008 required NARA to produce a report providing one or more alternative models for presidential libraries that "reduce the financial burden on the Federal Government; improve the preservation of presidential records; and reduce the delay in public access to all presidential records."

NARA submitted their "Report on Alternative Models for Presidential Libraries" in 2009; Congress has not implemented, nor has it even seriously considered, adopting any of the possible alternatives. As we will see in Chapter 3, however, it's not as if no one considered such alternatives in the intervening years. It's just that they were blocked from trying.

UNDER CURRENT LAW, PRESIDENTIAL LIBRARIES ARE built by private foundations, using donations as well as funding from state and local governments. No federal funds may be used, and no presidential library may be built on federal land. There are restrictions on their size, and mandatory endowments (that increase with the size of the building).

Once they are completed and equipped, the libraries are handed over – some deeded, some jointly operated, some leased – to the United States government, which operates them on behalf of the American people. Though they initially were formed just to build the libraries, the foundations now continue to operate, most within the walls of each building (elegantly, or awkwardly, segregated from government space by ever more inventive deeds and operating agreements). Ostensibly there to "support" ongoing operations, the foundations are in fact political organizations whose goals not only often conflict with NARA's legislative requirements, they can prevent NARA from fulfilling them.

The three largest areas of potential concern regarding a foundation's continuing involvement (and, in some cases, enmeshment) with the government's operation of the libraries are in public programs, exhibits, and education. It wasn't always like this; earlier libraries were not only modest but offered modest programs in addition to their core mission.

As budget pressures caused the National Archives to become more and more focused on attendance statistics – not only to bring in the funds that ticket sales generated but to continue justifying ever-increasing outlays from Congress – library directors turned their attention to ways to bring in more of the public.

In a 1980 briefing book prepared for the new Archivist of the United States, Robert Warner, National Archives staff informed him of a then-ongoing study to "examine the nature, effectiveness and appropriateness of educational or public programs in Presidential Libraries." They continued,

> "While legislative authorities for Presidential libraries include little direct basis for educational or public programs, Presidential libraries over time have developed broad programs for the general public.
>
> "These programs include sponsoring conferences, developing activities for school groups, presenting film festivals, developing packets of educational materials, and providing other programs for casual researchers, members of the general public and students and teachers at elementary, secondary, and college levels.
>
> "Public programs in presidential libraries vary substantially in scope and size ranging from the ambitious approach at the Kennedy Library to more modest efforts at the Hoover and Roosevelt Libraries.
>
> "At the Presidential Libraries Directors' Conference in June, 1980, directors strongly supported a broad range of public programs as significant facets of Presidential library activities and requested that an open-ended mandate be added to the Presidential Libraries Handbook."

The growing emphasis on everything other than records naturally means that records are seen more and more each year as less and less important. And as NARA hires more library directors with no experience or training in archives, history, or preservation, the money and staff time that records require – and the political controversies that their opening engender – may begin to seem not only unimportant, but problematic.

Most current presidential library directors, rather than shy away from this overemphasis on legacy and tourism and "celebration," seem eager to work with a former president's foundation to find even more ways to bring in tourists (and their money) as well as to appease the foundation's concerns about how their president is portrayed.

And since NARA is putting more and more pressure on the libraries to increase attendance and make nice with the foundations, it's no wonder the directors are doing just that.

THE PEOPLE WHO FUND AND BUILD PRESIDENTIAL LIBRARIES – supporters, business owners, major donors, university officials, and members of the president's foundation – envision hundreds of thousands of tourists descending annually on their town to gawk at the artifacts, pore over the trophies, interact with the high-tech exhibits, marvel at the slickly-produced videos, and, of course, fork over their hard-earned money for admission tickets, gift shop trinkets, meals, hotel rooms, and other tourism-related spending. All drawn there, year in and year out, to pay unquestioning tribute to the person for whom the tens of millions, hundreds of millions – or, now, half a billion – dollars have been raised and spent building what should be an archive but which now is unquestionably a shrine. A shrine containing records that none of us alive ever will see, but for which we – and our children and grandchildren – will pay to keep closed, while also paying to commemorate a presidency whose real actions and motives remain hidden in those unseen records.

But to those who are planning a library, all they can see are the positives. And the crowds. The huge, promised crowds.

When a presidential library opens, admirers of the president bask in the museum's artificial glow, critics call the exhibits skewed or worse, and local boosters tout the economic benefits that supposedly will accrue to the area (or, as is happening more frequently, to the host university). The initial excitement – both positive and negative – wanes rather quickly, and the economic benefits most often don't quite materialize. And soon after the dedication ceremony, new fund-raising begins to underwrite temporary exhibits, school curricula, conferences, and expanded policy programs. Before you know it, a new capital campaign to renovate the "outdated" exhibits pulls in new money. None of this funding, however, goes to basic operations, or to archival processing (the entire reason for having official, government-run presidential libraries).

What really happens – at least after all of the initial fanfare and attention die down – is very different. Each library's supporters thinks theirs is going to be unique, that *this* one will be the one to break the mold. But for the most part they have all followed similar patterns. After a few years of the strong supporters, the school groups, and the look-in tourists, there won't be an unending flood of people lining up to get in.

The evolution normally begins either after a former president passes away or when his political era has passed. Exhibits are changed, sometimes gradually, sometimes radically, to reflect either a more balanced approach to the history (the norm, for libraries that have begun to fade early) or a more entrenched insistence on the president's greatness or how he was misunderstood or cheated by history (in the libraries that figure prominently in their political parties' ongoing agendas).

Either way, the library eventually must change into something more than a shrine to a particular president in order to keep people coming back. It's difficult to sell tickets to people who weren't alive when the president was in office, and especially if he didn't do much that people remember fondly today. The Herbert Hoover Library is the least-attended in the National Archives system but one of the biggest tourist attractions in Iowa; most people aren't going there to stand in awed silence at Hoover's record of accomplishment as president. He did serve a remarkably productive three-decade ex-presidency, but even for Iowans filled with favorite-son pride there are only so many times one can learn about Hoover's reorganization of the federal government.

At the most-attended library – the Reagan – a recent splashy, wildly-popular temporary exhibit wasn't on the Cold War or supply-side economics or "Dutch's Eternal Optimism" or "The Wit and Wisdom of the Great Communicator"; the exhibit celebrated "Treasures of the Walt Disney Archives." Twelve thousand square feet (only two thousand fewer than the entire permanent exhibit at the George W. Bush museum) of temporary space. Full of Disney treasures.

At the Ronald Reagan Presidential Library.

Yes, some libraries are still pulling them in. But are those visitors getting any benefit directly related to the reasons that we fund the libraries?

The decline in visitors happens to all libraries. For some of them, it only takes a few years, but for others, it could take a decade or more. Sooner or later we are left with the unrealized economic promises, and a politicized, highly partisan institution ostensibly operated by the government but in reality run by politics and politicians.

The museum – by far the more-attended of the two main parts of a library – has the stamp of approval of the government, but NARA has little to no say in the content of the exhibits or public programs, and absolutely no say in the operation of the adjoining "institutes." There have been examples of a library's private foundation stopping, or at least strongly trying to stop, guest speakers, temporary exhibits, and educational materials. The foundation has a strong say in NARA personnel decisions, particularly in the leadership roles. At several libraries, the staff of the private foundation work in the government-run building, using government resources, and even using government email addresses.

CONGRESS HAS TRIED OVER THE YEARS, HALF-HEARTEDLY, TO rein in the cost and other problems with the libraries. They tried a size limit on the buildings, but foundations get around that by creating an enormous structure and simply deeding to the government a portion of the building that does not exceed the statuary square footage limit.

What happens, though, when the foundation begins to lose supporters and money? Will the government take over the whole facility? At the Reagan Library, well over 100,000 square feet in the building is not deeded to the government...yet. The Eisenhower Library is made up of five separate buildings, including his tomb/chapel and boyhood home.

Congress tried to require the foundation to provide a monetary endowment when handing over the library to the government; foundations found creative ways to significantly decrease the amount they pay (in one case years ago, the then-archivist resigned, took the job of executive director of the foundation, and helped the foundation reduce the amount, skirting Congressional intent).

In any case, after all of the strong supporters, the local boosters, the regionally-curious and the what-the-heck-let's-stop-along-the-way tourists have had their fill – a lot sooner than both the lovers and the haters understand – the nation's newest presidential library begins a slow but steady decline. They try to drum up visitors with every gimmick, trick and hook they can think of – just like most of the other libraries, which struggle to attract visitors.

And they try everything. Adding touch-panel interactive exhibits. Displaying presidential limousines and aircraft. Featuring best-selling authors, whether or not the book has anything to do with the president, his administration, or even politics in general. And temporary exhibits. Lots of temporary and special exhibits. On every conceivable subject: the culture of wine, Chinese art, custom motorcycles, the traveling miniature White House – anything to boost attendance figures.

Whether or not a library is located in a major metropolitan area or if it's for a Republican or Democratic president or if it has the coolest exhibits, about the only determining factor that reliably predicts if, ten or twenty years down the line, people will still visit is the approval rating of the president when he left office. If it was high, like Reagan and Clinton, attendance will be high; if it was low, like Hoover and Nixon, attendance will be dismal. Using that method, the new George W. Bush Library will soon look a lot more like a Hooverville than a Shining City on a Hill.

TO VISIT A PRESIDENTIAL LIBRARY – EVEN ONE DEDICATED to a president for whom you didn't vote, or perhaps didn't particularly like – is a singular experience. Some are modest, and others are way, way over the top. This one chooses to ignore notorious topics, that one decides to spin controversies. From analog displays to high-tech exhibits, gifts of state to handmade objects, letters and recreated offices and theaters and photographs – thousands of photographs – presidential libraries are fascinating artifacts in and of themselves.

And they're distinctively American: proud, defensive, and a little self-absorbed. When they first open, they're full of promise and fanfare. A newly-minted library can seem, to supporters, destined to enthrall visitors for a hundred years.

But hard as it is to believe now, amidst all the celebrations and the protests, the new, fantastic presidential library – like most of the ones before it – will drop off, in attendance and fund-raising, precipitously. Not right away. They'll be a "re-dedication" ceremony in ten or fifteen years, a "re-design" of the exhibits to examine "newly-available material" and include "historical re-evaluations" of his presidency. The former president will invite national and international heavyweights to conferences, lectures and symposia.

If another presidential family member runs for the White House (if??), there will be a renewed interest in donors and funding sources. Many years from now, when the president and spouse pass away, the library will be the site of solemn ceremonies. And then it's all downhill – if it hasn't already reached that point.

In the year following the death of the nation's thirty-fourth president, Dwight D. Eisenhower, more than three quarters of a million people came to Abilene, Kansas to pay their respects at his presidential library, museum and place of burial. That's about twice as many as had ever visited any other library before (or, with the exception of some questionable visitor statistics in the Bicentennial year 1976, since).

But to focus on how many and how much and what does he say and what does he leave out and who visits and who doesn't misses a larger point. The libraries are supposed to be just that: libraries. Repositories of records. Guardians of history, of the documentary evidence. They're not supposed to be theme parks – or they didn't start out that way. All it took was the idea that by regulating access to those records, and carefully planning how he is evaluated and commemorated, a legacy wouldn't have to be left to historians; a president could write their own history. Once we passed that point, there was no looking back. But maybe there can be. Maybe we – the government, the taxpayers – can return to the libraries' original purpose, and let others operate grand memorials, on their own. Without public dollars. Or at least without federal dollars. The idea isn't so far-fetched. And it's closer to the original intent.

Franklin Roosevelt donated his presidential library at Hyde Park, New York to the people of the United States in 1940. Built with private funds at a cost of $376,000 (or 6.2 million in today's dollars), the modest fieldstone structure that he designed preserves his papers, books and memorabilia. While FDR's inspiration for building the library clearly was the records, he included a small public area for visitors to view his personal collections and what he called "oddities" – items that people had sent to him.

That FDR preserved his historic twelve-year presidency and made available the records of the Great Depression, the New Deal, and World War II has been an enormous gift to our country and the world. Congress approved this first presidential library, and then formalized the system with the passage of the Presidential Libraries Act in 1955.

But in the years since, these archival institutions have evolved to become enormous commemorative memorials. While the president's papers are still housed in them, the archives have become afterthoughts to state-of-the-art museum exhibits, in-depth educational curricula, often-controversial public programs, and in some cases, overtly political events.

It's natural that family and strong supporters would want to commemorate – even celebrate – a president's legacy. But the National Archives – the federal agency charged with operating and maintaining the libraries – often puts more resources into the museum and public events than it does on processing and opening records. The libraries opened decades ago haven't finished making all of their holdings available, or even completed inventorying their artifacts.

THE GEORGE W. BUSH LIBRARY BEGAN ACCEPTING FREEDOM of Information Act, or FOIA, requests for most of their records on January 20, 2014. But just because the documents are now subject to FOIA does not mean they're processed and available for release. Soon after the availability date, the backlog quickly became measured in years, as is the case with the most recent libraries. The Bush Library notified one requester in early 2015 that their request for unclassified electronic records would be completed in approximately twelve years.

The library also may withhold certain records, at the request of the former president, until January 20, 2021, at which time a new FOIA backlog for those documents would then begin. Many records journalists and historians are eager to see will not be released for decades.

In addition to the limits on access to records, presidential libraries are getting bigger and bigger – despite legislative attempts to rein in the size and costs. Presidents, and, in some cases, their allies in NARA, continue to find loopholes, far exceeding the restrictions without penalty.

And the libraries are getting pricier: the first Bush Library cost fifty percent more than the Reagan before it, and Bill Clinton's was built at twice the cost of Bush's. The total cost to build the George W. Bush Library wasn't quite twice that for the Clinton, but it was more than all twelve earlier libraries combined. Despite legislative efforts to make these foundations pay for operating the libraries, only a small fraction of the money raised will go to the government as an endowment.

If these institutions were maintained the same way they're built – privately – there wouldn't be a problem. But the National Archives has accepted responsibility to run the Bush Library and Museum, as they do the other twelve. The total cost to the taxpayers for all thirteen presidential libraries is approaching a billion dollars a decade – and is growing.

Even though the Archives operates the museums, the agency doesn't really have a say in the exhibits' content, scope or appearance. The president's supporters design, create and mostly pay for them, while enjoying the government's stamp of approval, and the (free, to them) services of government archivists, curators, exhibit specialists, technicians, and others. As one might expect, the history displayed in these museums is not terribly balanced; in fact, it's often quite skewed. Instead of fairly portraying a president's life and years in office, the newer libraries have become legacy-polishing temples that all but ignore controversy or criticism.

Meanwhile, at the current rate of processing, it will take over a hundred years for all the records, computer data, photographs, film, audio and videotape stored in the libraries to be opened to the public. Federal budget cuts and ever-increasing pressure to improve exhibits, increase attendance, and "pack them in" will continue to drain money and personnel from records.

Of the thirteen presidents for whom libraries have been built, nine either did not serve full terms; lost bids for re-election; did not serve as many terms as they set out to; or died in office. Only four – Eisenhower, Reagan, Clinton and George W. Bush – served their full terms. But each one since Herbert Hoover has built a library, and we operate all of them.

This is not is what our representatives, who enacted the laws governing presidential records and libraries, intended from the start, nor each time they amended the legislation over the last six decades. And it's not what FDR envisioned. He began the tradition to preserve and make available the historical record of the presidency. Congress should stop accepting these partisan shrines, only fund presidential archives, and leave the myth-making – by far more costly and problematic – to private organizations.

EARLIER PRESIDENTS WHO HAD THE MISFORTUNE OF NOT being memorialized by libraries (or grand monuments) left office with a reputation – positive or negative – and most could do little on their own to alter it. They had to suffer the fate of the judgment of history – that is to say, of historians. Rehabilitation, if it came at all, was granted by others, most of whom had no skin in the game, were working with limited sources, and likely weren't alive during the president's administration.

Those historians had much less to go by in terms of the historical record, what with presidents destroying – by act or neglect – most of their documents and their heirs selling much of the rest. While historians of modern presidents technically have more information on which to base their assessments, access to that information is so restricted by law (or by process) as to make it meaningless. Between that and the strong insistence by presidents to write the first draft themselves, many historians, particularly graduate students, are discouraged from starting projects, leaving the presidentially-written museum exhibits as the only publicly-available "history" for decades or more. Readers and consumers of history are left with, in regard to earlier presidents, more complete and balanced history based on less information, and in regard to modern presidents, less complete and more skewed history that may be balanced by access to much greater information, but not for many years to come.

This at least partially explains why high schoolers today don't know anything about Calvin Coolidge; barely know Herbert Hoover (but think he either "caused" or "did nothing to stop" the Great Depression); and who accept as absolute fact that Ronald Reagan was the Greatest President Since Abraham Lincoln, saving the United States from nuclear annihilation, Soviet domination, and the Bad Ol' Democrats.

Beginning with Truman, presidents were eager to get their documents processed and released; the idea being that historians, with the complete record available, would recast the president from the reputation with which he had been stuck while in office. And beginning with Truman, this worked – to a point. But as the first generation, regulated by the somewhat sparse Presidential Libraries Act (and no law controlling the disposition of their records), gave way to the second, a lot changed. As they have become not only tourist destinations but "economic engines" debate over how to build and pay for them has increased.

In 2014, controversy surrounded a plan put forth by some Democratic legislators in Illinois to offer $100 million of public funds to encourage the Obama Foundation to select Chicago as the site to build the nation's next presidential library. That controversy has centered on critics' assertion that this would be the first time that taxpayer money would go to build a presidential library.

Critics excoriated the president, Chicago politicians, university officials, and lawmakers for such an "unprecedented" move, one that they say demonstrates how unconscionable are Obama and his supporters.

Fine.

Except that, the use of taxpayer funds to build a presidential library is not unprecedented: the state of Texas built the Johnson Library and the attached School of Public Affairs. In 2014 dollars, the total cost of state money for the project amounts to just over $109,000,000 – more than the amount some in Illinois wanted to offer the Obama Foundation. And at least three other presidential libraries (those for Eisenhower, Ford and George H.W. Bush) were built partially with taxpayer funds.

While the Illinois plan was scrapped, no doubt the next "controversy" over the president's plans for his library is just around the corner. Some might argue that this is just "politics," but sadly, while these games are being played, "governance" is being neglected – the kind of governance that seriously could examine the presidential library system and lead to real and meaningful reforms – and the saving of hundreds of millions of taxpayer dollars.

NO PRESIDENTIAL LIBRARY FOUNDATION, BEFORE OR AFTER the 1986 amendments, has exploited the truck-sized legal loopholes, pushed the boundaries of propriety, and outright crossed the lines more than have the Reagan and Nixon foundations.

If the Clinton Library hosted the extreme, left-wing versions of the extreme, right-wing talk show hosts, failed candidates, authors, pundits, and media personalities that the Reagan and Nixon foundations – under the imprimatur of their respective, governmental libraries – regularly welcome to spout extreme political views and irresponsibly attack anyone they deem to be adversaries, I would be as critical.

And so, I presume, would every anchor, reporter, and guest on Fox News, as well as every conservative with Twitter feed.

If the Kennedy Library became the altar upon which Democratic candidates for national office were required to be baptized and approved by the extreme left, wealthy political elite before being allowed to announced their candidacy and receive the endorsement of a respected, governmental institution – as is the case with the Reagan Library, which, being used by the Reagan Foundation, has become this altar/proving ground for the extreme right's candidates, would-be candidates, might-be candidates and has-been candidates (yes, former New York Mayor and "Every-Third-Word-is-9/11"-celebrity Rudy Giuliani bowed out of the presidential race in 2008 and endorsed John McCain not in Manhattan at Ground Zero, nor City Hall, nor Gracie Mansion, but in Simi Valley, California, at the Ronald Reagan Library) – it would send the already-agitated right-wing blogosphere into heretofore unknown heights of unhinged disturbance. I, too, would be as critical as I have been with the Reagan and Nixon libraries.

If the Johnson Library museum opened exhibits that ignored the negative, and overly-promoted the positive as much as do the Reagan and Nixon libraries – well, actually, the Johnson Library did, in 2012. Their newly-renovated exhibits shift the "history" being showcased there away from the objective and complete (which they never had quite reached, but towards which they had been headed) to the subjective and selective. And the private foundation that supports the library rapidly is becoming as active in "reshaping legacy" as its Republican counterparts. Not nearly as much as those two California libraries, but certainly more than enough for me to admit I cannot use the Johnson Library as a counterpoint.

But the fact is, the Reagan and Nixon presidential libraries – their foundations particularly – currently have no equal, neither Democratic nor Republican. If you're thinking that it would be acceptable if the those libraries continued along their path, ask yourself how you'd feel about the Obama Library doing the same.

That's not to say that I think the Obama Library will be any different, given the initial reports I've been reading over the past few months. The first comment that the president made about his library – several years ago – led some to believe that he might forgo building the kind of shrine to his ego that other presidents relished, and instead focus on simply making his records available. Sadly, it appears that he has abandoned that notion.

If the Obama Presidential Library museum opens with the kind of overly-reverential, patently-false, adulatory, factually-incorrect, over-the-top exhibits that fill the Reagan and Nixon libraries, I will be as critical. As for whether or not Illinois should spend a dollar on the proposed Barack Obama Presidential Library museum – or whether any federal, state, or local government should commit tax dollars to constructing presidential libraries – my opinion is a simple but emphatic, "No."

Though the state appeared to be doing so in an appropriate manner – through decisions made in the open by democratically-elected officials (as opposed to, say, the manner in which some universities have welcomed and paid for some presidential libraries) – I believe the decision would have been a mistake. The promised economic gains never materialize – or if they do, they don't last – and they're not worth the trouble of a government getting into bed with a private political organization. The benefits eventually accrue solely to the library (or, more to the point, the president, and the unregulated political organization that builds and supports the library). It is not, in my judgment, a sound decision for a state government to make.

The federal government should pay to preserve and make available for research the presidential and federal records that the law requires the National Archives to care for. And that's it. If a state government wishes to support the preservation of and access to these records so that historians, journalists, students, writers and others may make use of them – and they do so in a fair, open, and democratic process – that is their decision to make. If a private organization wants to build a political shrine – and operate a political shrine – they can do so on their own. The Richard

Nixon Library and Birthplace got along as a private institution, without government assistance or approval, for seventeen years. But I believe that no government, at any level, should run a political organization.

No matter where the initial or subsequent money comes from, tax-payers – through the National Archives – should not be in the business of celebrating, commemorating, or promoting any political views. Which, if we're honest, we should admit is exactly what the National Archives is doing with modern presidential libraries.

The National Archives has tried to pass off the responsibility by saying that private donors pay for the exhibits or the renovations or the absolutely partisan political events that are held at what are, in fact, government institutions. But simply by hosting them, the government is granting their approval. Which means the people of the United States – we – are granting our approval. To every factless political exhibit, every tactless political event, and every hapless political hack.

Which, of course, we shouldn't. Whether it's for someone we supported or someone we tried to delegitimize didn't support.

The population density, infrastructure, and tourism of New York or Chicago would give the Obama Library an attendance edge over other recent ones, but no matter how popular a president when he leaves office, attendance declines on a predictable path.

Until the mid-2000s – when the National Archives began to encourage the libraries to get aggressive with their attempts to bring in visitors – attendance was declining across the board. Even the most-attended, the LBJ Library (which had been the only one that was free, and was very liberal in how they counted "visitors"), was averaging about 200,000 a year.

Around the same time, former President Reagan died, and his library, which had experienced a 31% drop in visitors, saw a resurgence; the following year, they opened the Air Force One Pavilion and other new attractions, and have experienced increasing attendance.

But what really packs them in at the most popular presidential museums – the ones that command the greatest number of visitors – usually is lacking in other presidents. Most do not inspire hero worship like Ronald Reagan; do not inflame passions – in every sense of the term – like Bill Clinton; nor provoke wistful, what-if reveries like John F. Kennedy.

Even if the president leaves office with low approval ratings, there is usually initial interest in what they have to say about themselves.

Air Force One Pavilion, Ronald Reagan Library, Simi Valley, California.

After the initial "look-in" visitor surge – which can last a few years after a library opens, as well as after a major event such as a president's death (as happened at the Gerald Ford Museum in Grand Rapids) – the novelty of the no-longer-new library fades (as do the initial controversies surrounding the exhibits, and therefore the press coverage as well), and attendance starts a slow but certain decline. That's when you start to see unrelated public programs and temporary exhibits, to draw back in at least the locals, if not the adventurous tourists from farther away.

A key factor is whether, like Jimmy Carter and Bill Clinton, a former president will spend more time on active engagement than on self-memorialization; if it's the former – if President Obama puts his energies not on touting his library, but on solving big problems – then attendance will wane more rapidly. If, like Richard Nixon and Ronald Reagan, he spends more time trying to rehabilitate his image and use his library's history-making machine to "set the record straight" then yes, I could see the high attendance numbers remaining steady for a longer period of time.

Given his few remarks about his library – even that he was reluctant to have one, instead wanting to spend the resources digitizing and making available his records – as well as his age and my expectation of what he will do with the rest of his life, I'd guess President Obama will follow more of the Carter/Clinton model, and spend less energy on his library.

CONTRARY TO WHAT ONE READS IN THE PRESS, THERE IS NO trend. Presidents are not all rushing to build their presidential libraries on a university campus, nor have they been. In fact, out of the thirteen libraries, only three are fully integrated into a campus: the Lyndon Johnson Library at the University of Texas, Austin; the George Bush Library at Texas A&M University; and the George W. Bush Library at Southern Methodist University.

A fourth, the Gerald Ford, is split between two cities in Michigan; the library is located on the Ann Arbor campus of the University of Michigan, and the museum is 132 miles away in Grand Rapids. While other libraries are affiliated in various ways with universities, mostly through programming agreements, none of those are hosted on a college campus. But it makes it easier to promote the idea of new libraries being built on university campuses, to call something a "trend."

The Johnson Library was the first to be located on a university campus; the second, the Bush Library, opened at Texas A&M twenty-five years later. The two libraries are associated with policy schools at their respective universities; the second Bush Library is associated with the private Bush Institute, on the Southern Methodist campus.

The Kennedy Library is adjacent to the University of Massachusetts, Boston; the Clinton Center partners with the University of Arkansas; and a few libraries and schools have agreements for program cooperation. Two others, the Nixon and Reagan, almost were built on university campuses but were rejected; the former by Duke and the latter by Stanford.

Is locating a library on a campus is a good idea – for the government, the university, or the foundation? Should the libraries collaborate with universities? How involved in the academics associated schools should the foundations, with their partisan and celebratory agendas, become?

While the cost to build the libraries is increasing, the majority of that cost has to do with the non-presidential-library aspects: the foundation's offices and public spaces, and the think tanks and policy shops and public programming functions and partisan support mechanisms. Even the museums, which had been the major driver of increased costs, are now secondary to these new "presidential center" additions.

Which poses a challenge for universities vying to host libraries: in the past, the student and faculty concern was over hosting museums of spin, which, though operated by NARA, still receive the university's stamp of approval. Today, the concerns would be more about the foundation's activities than the exhibits – which are getting smaller. The permanent exhibit at the most-recently opened library, the George W. Bush, is fourteen thousand square feet; the Clinton and George H.W. Bush are twenty thousand; and the Reagan is two hundred thousand square feet.

Presidential libraries allow presidents to write their own history, and for decades they used the museum exhibits to do so. If the museums are decreasing in size while the expense to build the libraries is increasing – and the "presidential center" components are growing – then these institutes, and the events and speakers they host and the works that they produce, are how presidents will now enshrine their legacies.

And that is – or should be – a problem for universities, institutions of higher learning that ought not be co-opted into participating in managing presidential legacies. And it is a problem for taxpayers, who must pay to operate and maintain presidential libraries.

The George W. Bush Institute, Southern Methodist University, Dallas, Texas.

The George Bush Library, Texas A&M University, College Station, Texas.

The Lyndon Johnson Library, University of Texas at Austin, Texas.

CHAPTER 3

NARA AND THE FOUNDATIONS

"So, my prayer is merely this: That all of us will be inspired...by the people who have thought it proper to preserve for America in a written form the record of the era through which this generation is passing."

President Dwight Eisenhower, at the dedication of his presidential library in Abilene, Kansas, May 1, 1962.

"AS I THINK THE CHAIRMAN KNOWS, THIS HAS BEEN A MOST successful public-private partnership and we greatly appreciate the opportunity to explain why our relationship with our foundations has been a large part of our success for 66 years and 12 presidential administrations."

In her testimony before Congress in 2007, Sharon Fawcett, Assistant Archivist for Presidential Libraries, defended the way in which the National Archives and private foundations work together in the presidential library system. She explained, "The contributions of these support organizations to the libraries spell the difference between static repositories and lively, vital centers of scholarship and service to the public."

Is that the only choice? Between stasis and vitality? Is the money of the private foundations – many of them politically-active – the only way to effect that difference? And why must the presidential libraries be centers of public service, especially when they are not currently fulfilling their basic archival responsibilities?

Congress has debated and passed legislation on the very idea of presidential libraries; reining in their growth in size and cost; ownership of presidential records; speeding access to those records; and disclosing donations to sitting presidents for their libraries. But neither Congress, nor the nation at large, have had substantive discussions on the history that is taught in the libraries – history that is paid for by the foundations – and the role that these private, political organizations play in the administration of government institutions. We need to have that discussion, and that debate. We need to decide, through the choices we make in authorizations and appropriations, what exactly we expect of the presidential library system. And of the federal agency that runs it.

Over the last forty years, the National Archives has experienced a slow (and, during the late 1980s/early 1990s, not-so-slow) decline: in managerial effectiveness; in employee morale; in responsiveness to stakeholders and customers; in the administration of its core function, preserving records and making them available; and in the speed and effectiveness of fulfilling Freedom of Information Act (FOIA) requests.

Perhaps nothing has contributed more to the negative image of the agency than its decline in – perceived or real – nonpartisanship, due to the increasing politicization of its administration of presidential records and libraries. The single greatest contributing factor to this growing politicization is the increasing influence of the partisan library foundations.

Initially, the foundation served the function of enabling the president to organize, raise funds, and construct the building, which upon completion is turned over to the government to operate. As former presidents began to think of new ways to utilize the libraries, these foundations grew, in some cases dwarfing the budgets and staffs of the libraries.

Earlier organizations created to build presidential libraries sponsored grants for academics to travel and research the collections in person; symposia on the administration; and efforts to publish the president's papers and scholarly works on related subjects. Modern foundations operate "presidential centers" with policy shops, think tanks, scholars in residence, speaker series, educational programs, social media presences, lucrative gift shops, major addresses by political figures, appearances by media celebrities, and awards, conferences, political events, and presidential primary debates. As these are held and conducted on government property, within government buildings (the deeds to which are now artfully cut up to exempt certain rooms, areas, and spaces from government control, and therefore laws and regulations governing their use), such activities pose real problems for NARA. Or they should.

But the agency has been unsuccessful in enforcing the federal records laws which they are charged with administering. And NARA has not been able to secure adequate federal funding for the libraries. Already on the defensive for years over major problems such as management failures; the Electronic Records Archives debacle; their inability to guarantee the security of veterans' and other electronic records; the years-long FOIA backlog; and their ever-decreasing morale and employee satisfaction, NARA has allowed the private foundations to overpower them, and use the libraries for purposes far beyond the law. And propriety.

Members of Congress faced with the prospect of allocating even more resources to the agency when it does not appear able to meet the demands of their core mission are right to be skeptical. And the concerns aren't just about finances or managing personnel. For an agency tasked with crucial responsibilities such as NARA's, credibility is key. The agency that determines who gets to see records, what records get released or withheld, what remains classified – even what is and isn't a record – lives or dies on trustworthiness. Beginning in the late nineteen eighties, NARA leaders eroded, jeopardized, and even destroyed that credibility. And once it's lost, with Congress and the people, it's difficult to get back.

"ALL ARCHIVES OR RECORDS BELONGING TO THE GOVernment of the United States (legislative, executive, judicial, and other) shall be under the charge and superintendance of the Archivist to this extent: He shall have full power to inspect personally or by deputy the records of any agency of the United States Government whatsoever and wheresoever located, and shall have the full cooperation of any and all persons in charge of such records in such inspections, and to requisition for transfer to the National Archives Establishment such archives...and he shall have authority to make regulations for the arrangement, custody, use, and withdrawal of materials deposited in the National Archives Building"
    – *Section 3 of the National Archives Act, June 19, 1934.*

In the eight decades since the creation of the National Archives, Congress has authorized the agency to do more – including creating and hosting public exhibits – but its basic responsibility hasn't changed. NARA must preserve and make available federal and presidential records. Whatever else it does, it if doesn't do that, it fails. And if it doesn't fulfill its primary duty *because of* the additional things it does, Congress should consider stepping in and limiting what NARA may do, unless and until is meets its basic responsibilities.

And it isn't. NARA won't open the records of the last five presidents (including Obama) for a century. Their FOIA backlog is up to twelve years long. They continue to have problems securing records. Agency after agency reports missing records, improperly preserved records, electronic records on inaccessible media, and lack of compliance with federal records laws. The revelation that, while Secretary of State, Hillary Clinton used only a private system for email communication was just the highest profile example of the ways in which officials consistently skirt the law and regulations. The National Archives is not meeting basic obligations. But they're opening up new presidential library museums on time. They're celebrating the renovation of biased history exhibits. And they're hosting nakedly partisan events.

NARA is not only failing in their intragovernmental and external responsibilities, they are failing their own employees. In the 2014 Best Places to Work in the Federal Government report, which included results from the Federal Employee Viewpoint Survey and other measures of employee satisfaction, the Archives staff ranked it among the worst agencies. In almost every category – Effective Leadership, Senior Leaders, Strategic Management, Training and Development – NARA failed their employees. Year after year, the agency's ranking gets worse.

Despite the challenges they face, NARA employees strive to do their jobs well, and without regard to politics. With a single notable exception, those whom I met at presidential libraries were scrupulously nonpartisan – in their approach, in their practice, and in their discussions with me.

Federal employees of the library archival programs are not given the resources – by NARA nor by Congress – they need to meet their responsibilities; the agency's focus is on public programs, not records. Federal employees of the library museums have an even more difficult task: they must work on creating exhibits designed and paid for by the private foundation that built, and supports, the library.

And federal employees must then use the exhibits; while at some libraries, the educational component is staffed by foundation employees – which is another major concern – in some cases the federal workers end up having to participate in completely rewritten history.

NARA officials have claimed that without the foundations' money, the libraries couldn't survive. What they really mean is that the museums wouldn't be renovated and public programs wouldn't expand. But Congress would still appropriate funds to operate presidential archives.

Granted, the legislative branch never provides enough funds for the executive branch to do what it is required to do. Every agency says that, but in this case it's true. However, on top of what NARA should be doing, the agency chooses – and, to a point, Congress has supported this – to do other things: create and host exhibits, public programs, and educational programs about their records. Congress has been explicit that such activities at presidential libraries should not be funded by the government. And yet they continue to be.

When faced with criticism that an exhibit may be skewed, or even historically inaccurate, the agency claims that all costs were borne by the foundation, that no taxpayer money was spent on it, and that, therefore, foundation officials get to create whatever they want. Leaving behind the problem of rewritten history hosted by the federal government – just think of how that would go over at the Smithsonian – federal employees who work in the libraries as museum curators, museum specialists, museum technicians, visual information specialists, exhibit specialists, education specialists, public program specialists, and public affairs staff work on creating, installing, and maintaining (and educating students and the public through the use of) those exhibits; taxpayer money is in fact spent on them.

In a time of shrinking appropriations and NARA's failure to meet its basic duties, if one part of NARA's mission is less urgent than any others – and that's an important question when you're cutting a budget – it's the exhibits and the public programs. And the largest part of NARA that hosts exhibits and programs is the presidential library system.

Exhibits are adjuncts of the archival mission, not a primary part of it. I don't think a museum exhibit qualifies as a "records access program" as NARA creatively claims. Public visitors to a museum aren't actually "exploring records" – not like researchers, historians, genealogists, journalists, and others, who share their explorations with the public. And we need to be able to explore *all* of the records, not just the ones in exhibits, chosen by the presidents' foundations for us to see. It's unacceptable that a private political organization is deciding what governmental records the public sees, and choosing the speakers and topics for public events, at a governmental institution.

When events are held at the libraries, which are operated by the government – but more importantly, are known to the public as being operated by the government – those events carry the seal of approval of not only the government, but of the *people* of the United States. Political events that could not possibly happen in other federal buildings – even those that engage in transparent public-private partnerships, such as the National Park Service, the Veterans Administration, or the Smithsonian Institution – occur frequently at some federal presidential libraries (most often the Reagan and Nixon). The libraries are too important, and federal financial support of them too fragile, to risk with improper, inappropriate political events.

In addition to the aforementioned presidential primary debates, the Reagan Library hosts political candidates seeking higher office. The speeches and "interviews" that take place within this government building (though, because of the deal the foundation worked out with NARA officials, within rooms not technically under the control of the government) could not take place inside the main National Archives Building in Washington. Because of their political content and lack of propriety, they would be deemed inappropriate for such a venerable, nonpartisan location. But inside a presidential library? Apparently, that's no problem.

These events – and the book signings, "Reagan Forum" panels, addresses, interviews, and discussions – serve a two-fold purpose: to promote the political agenda of a partisan organization, and to raise money. And they do raise a lot of money. Well, some of the foundations raise a lot of money.

In 2012, the Eisenhower Foundation had net assets of $820,508; the Reagan Foundation had net assets of $258,552,156.

Even though they use government institutions to raise money – soliciting contributions, hosting fee-based events, selling items in the gift shops, and even taking a portion of the government's admission fees – no presidential library foundation is required to share a single dollar with the government. While some do – some support NARA's ongoing programs, fund foundation employees who work under government supervisors, and pay for projects, such as digitizing records – others don't. Not, at least, without strings attached, such as controlling the content of exhibits.

NARA operates the twelve federal presidential libraries, including the Reagan; the private, hyper-political Reagan Foundation does not operate the library– even though they work very hard to make it appear as if they do. And even though the majority of your admission fee, which you think you are paying to the National Archives when you enter the National Archives' Reagan Library, actually goes to the Reagan Foundation. To fund their partisan activities, particularly their political events.

I've attended several of them. Through some intentionally-complicated lawyering and clever linguistics, the foundation gets away with what otherwise would be clear violations of the Hatch Act (which prohibits campaign and partisan events in government buildings and by government employees) by holding the events inside rooms that technically haven't been deeded to the government. However, the foundation still bills the events as being at "the Reagan Library." This is how the public gets to see Ann Coulter, Bill O'Reilly, and Newt Gingrich – as well as three election cycles' worth of Republican candidate debates – at the federal Ronald Reagan Presidential Library, with all of the cachet that comes along with such an appearance.

I've been paying close attention to what presidential library foundations do and say for more than a decade. I've seen examples of spin, whitewashing of history, and outright whoppers. I've seen foundations push the envelope of what's appropriate, what's ethical, and even what's legal. I've seen two of them cross those lines, regularly, and a few others come perilously close.

Not incidentally, at other library foundations for presidents from both parties, I've also seen humble, generous people working hard, more to continue the community institution that they support than to insist on and promote a particular adulatory narrative...though that's becoming more and more rare.

The Ronald Reagan Presidential Library is a federal government institution – and only a federal government institution. The foundation built the building, and then turned it over to the people of the United States. That's what the law allows.

Except, they didn't. They stuck around. In a big way. More than any other presidential library foundation, before or since. The Reagan Foundation's offices, private event space – which they use for private fund-raising, partisan political events, and even rent to outside groups – and gift shop, it's all intermingled with the federal government's presidential library. In a bad way.

The foundation's messaging, promotion, social media, and events all conflate the private organization with the government institution, not making clear to the public which events and programs are hosted by the library – the government – and which are hosted by the foundation.

Why? Why try to blur the line between private, political enterprise and nonpartisan government institution? First, because the government is footing the bill for running the library (ironic that a taxpayer-funded government program is paying to keep alive the legacy of Ronald Reagan).

But more importantly, it's because of that cachet. Because of that prestige. Because of that sense that a presidential library couldn't be biased, because it's run by the government. Just like the Smithsonian, right? So if the Reagan Library says it (or sells it), it must be true (or quality). No?

So it has been for the past quarter century, when the Reagan Foundation broke the mold (and a lot of the rules) and invented a new kind of inappropriateness. They engage not simply in the kind of backward-looking, legacy-managing revisionism that, say, the Johnson Library Foundation has increasingly embraced over the last few years. The Reagan Foundation's fund-raising emails use phrases like "Americans are searching for answers" and "confidence in Washington has never been lower" and "Americans are more troubled about our nation's direction than any time since just before Ronald Reagan was elected president." And then ask for our money to make sure they can effect a change in that direction. An electoral change.

The foundation preys upon their donors' worst fears about the direction in which the country is headed, and which, purportedly, only the Reagan Legacy can correct.

More troubling, though, is that this political fund-raising ploy – aimed squarely at anyone but Democrats – uses the honor and dignity of a federal institution to make a buck. That, too, is supposed to be illegal.

Congress needs to rein in this political use of government institutions. Any properly-registered private organization should be able to send this kind of email and engage in such politics...but not by using a taxpayer-funded resource as the platform and seal of approval.

WHILE THEIR PRESIDENTS MAY HAVE FOUGHT WITH EACH other, the presidential library foundations work closely together to make sure their rights and prerogatives are protected. As a group, they meet regularly both on their own and with NARA officials, and they support each other's programs.

In 1988, then-Archivist of the United States Don Wilson (an official about whom we will learn more in the next chapter) created the Advisory Committee on Presidential Libraries, to advise him and the agency on important issues. Given the broad range of stakeholders, customers, and the public that the libraries serve, one would think that such a committee would reflect that range, and include a wide variety of interested parties. Unfortunately, that was not – and is not – the case.

The Federal Advisory Committee Act of 1972 (FACA) was one of that era's "sunshine laws" designed to improve transparency and prevent the kind of insider, back-room deals that had characterized government for decades. Prior to FACA, groups advising the government were inefficient, inaccessible, and imbalanced; typically they were made up solely of the very organizations and special interests that would benefit the most if the government took their advice, with no one else weighing in.

The Act requires that committee membership be fairly balanced in terms of the points of view represented and the functions to be performed, and that the committee should not be inappropriately influenced by the appointing authority or by any special interest. Additionally, FACA mandates that nearly all committee meetings be open to the public.

The Advisory Committee on Presidential Libraries is very different in important ways from most federal advisory committees, including even other NARA advisory committees: only representatives of the private library foundations may serve on it.

NARA claims that the membership of the Advisory Committee on Presidential Libraries must be limited to representatives of the foundations that build the libraries because only they have been deeply involved in the development of the various libraries, and only they can speak with authority on issues that arise in connection with establishing new libraries or administering existing ones.

Obviously, the expertise of the foundation is valuable, given the rare world in which they live and work. There are currently only thirteen federal presidential libraries, and understanding how to prepare for, build, maintain, and support one requires a specific set of skills and experiences. However, that the membership is so narrowly limited is a big concern, especially given the legislative mandate that committees be fairly balanced in terms of the points of view represented.

The advisory committee does not include any other stakeholders, including historians, archivists, preservationists, curators, educators, researchers, or the general public, whose experience, perspectives, and skills could greatly assist the agency.

The challenges faced by new and existing libraries aren't limited to fund-raising and construction. There are serious questions of prompt access to presidential records; the records management policies and practices of presidential administrations and executive agencies; the care, preservation, and exhibition of artifacts; the security of presidential collections at the libraries and at other NARA facilities; education programs at the libraries; historical balance, or often lack of it, within permanent and temporary museum exhibits, just to name a few. But, apparently no one else's opinions, experiences, or ideas on these subjects matter.

THE BENEFITS OF PRESIDENTIAL LIBRARIES ARE, IN MY opinion, overstated and often misunderstood. They do bring jobs to a community, both directly and indirectly. Tourism adds, according to the National Archives, an estimated $100 to $200 per visitor. While I don't necessarily question those numbers, knowing how each library counts visitors in a variety of often creative ways, I do question whether the total economic impact is what people believe it to be.

Whatever the supposed dollars amounts, presidential libraries are not self-sustaining. It's not as if the argument is: the government pays for it now, and reaps the economic benefits once it's up and running. Right from the start, the libraries must be subsidized by taxpayers.

In 2014, an Illinois House committee voted to appropriate $100 million to attract the Obama Presidential Library to Chicago. The question as to whether public funds should be spent to build a presidential library (contrary to most commentators on this subject, public funds have in fact been spent to build as many as five of the presidential libraries currently in the federal system), the big questions are: who puts up the initial costs; who pays to operate them; who takes ultimate responsibility for the structure and its contents; and who really benefits the most?

But by and large, we're not asking those questions. When a controversy over the location of a presidential library arises, the issues that are discussed normally are political. In the case of Illinois' $100 million proposal, critics either attacked the president because the state might have spent taxpayer money to secure his library there, or supporters of the plan attacked critics – all for political reasons.

With all of the talk of economic impact and attendance numbers and community renewal and Oval Office replicas and Air Force One pavilions and interactive technology it's easy to forget: these are supposed to be presidential archives. We've debated how, and whether as a country, we would – whether we should – support the preservation of presidential records through taxpayer funds. We decided that for our history, for our understanding of ourselves, it's worth the time and effort and cost.

We've never really had a debate, though, over whether we should support presidential *museums*. And that question isn't just one of funding; should our government – in our name – operate partisan political shrines? Congress did decide that the libraries were getting too big, and too far afield from their function as archives, but their attempts to rein in size and cost backfired, and resulted in even larger, and even more political, memorials. As to the question of benefits and impact, it's helpful to think of this like a bankruptcy: who gets paid, and in what order?

The first and most important benefits accrue to the president. The modern library is the last campaign to rewrite history and enshrine a legacy. The library bypasses formal history to tells its own story.

Presidential family members, particularly those who seek to establish or advance their own political careers, receive benefits from a presidential library. Not only do they have their story told well, they have a ready-made platform for events, speeches, and other organizational needs.

And then, the mega-donors who build the library get their benefits. They may have been motivated to bring tourism to their region, or give their brand a boost, or by the general public relations benefits – or to position themselves as party kingmakers. Some of the bigger donors, though, may already have received their benefits while the president was still in office – since we allow unlimited, unregulated, and undisclosed contributions to the libraries, we can't really be sure.

After that come members of the administration, who at least want to look good for history, if not for their next – hopefully higher – appointment, or even their own electoral runs.

And then the national party, both to improve their image and to position themselves for future campaigns. Officials come out looking better, potential candidates have a forum, a place to receive approval from the faithful, and the "policy institutes" develop and test new initiatives.

And then the government benefits, at least initially; the law requires the National Archives preserve and make available the president's records. Without a donated archival facility, the government would have to build one – with taxpayer funds.

After all the other secured and unsecured creditors, we come to the shareholders: the people. It's only after everyone else reaps the rewards that the nation and the local community begin to see some benefits. Such as: they get a world-recognized (if not necessarily world-class) museum in their midst…for which they have to pay $16 to $21 each time they visit.

THE HEYDAY OF CONGRESSIONAL INTEREST IN RECORDS issues was the dozen years following Richard Nixon's resignation. That time period saw the enactment of sunshine laws to provide transparency and open up government to more public scrutiny; strong willingness to move – over presidential objections and vetoes – legislation about presidential and federal records; and major changes to both the Presidential Records and Presidential Libraries Acts. It was such a successful legislative period that no one saw how the laws would inadvertently lead to less access, more secrecy, and greater political influence within NARA.

There's no better time to try to get around a law than when right after Congress spends time and political capital reforming it; everyone thinks – or allows the public to think – that everything's "fixed."

In the years immediately following the last of these reforms, a new Archivist of the United States was confirmed; the Reagan Library began to be built; and the first Bush Administration came into office. And that's when the laws began to show their flaws.

But rather than be proactive, Congress, for the most part, was passive. Archivist Don Wilson was deferential – to a fault – to Republican Presidents Nixon, Reagan, and Bush, allowing them wide latitude in presidential records questions. The fight against the worst of these abuses didn't come from legislators, but from stakeholder organizations and private citizens, who filed lawsuits to protect presidential records and reverse illegal actions by presidents and the archivist. Years of court battles, the prospect of failed legislation, and other, more "popular" issues drew Congress' attention away from fixing the defects and closing the loopholes. The 1990s and 2000s were bad decades for open government, and great years for presidential library foundations, which operated with virtually no oversight. They found ways around the size limitations; decreased the required endowments; rewrote history on a massive scale through incredibly skewed exhibits; hosted more and more political events at the libraries; and found willing – even enthusiastic – partners in many NARA officials.

As just one glaring example of the need for oversight: journalists can pore over Internal Revenue Service forms and examine donor walls in the lobby of presidential libraries (how appropriate a place for them) and speculate about "foreign money" – but without adequate Congressional oversight, we have no idea who's giving money to build presidential libraries. And we have no idea what they're expecting in return.

FEDERAL AGENCY HEADS DON'T CALL COMMITTEE STAFF directly. And not at home. Not on a Saturday. But David Ferriero, the Archivist of the United States, needed to get in touch immediately with my supervisor, Darryl Piggee, the staff director for the Subcommittee on Information Policy, Census, and National Archives of the House Committee on Oversight and Government Reform. He couldn't wait until Monday, and he couldn't go through channels. Ferriero was calling with an urgent request.

Contact between a federal agency and Congressional committees is usually handled "staff to staff" – that is, personnel within the agency's Congressional Affairs department contact committee staffers; less common – though not unheard of – is contact between an agency head and a chairman or ranking member, though that, too, normally would be at least arranged by staff. An agency head contacting a committee staffer on a weekend, on the staffer's cell phone – even the staff director – is rare.

In 2010, the subcommittee had scheduled a hearing about the foundations – *at* a presidential library (the Reagan) – and Ferriero called to ask Piggee to cancel the hearing. There was great concern, not only at the Reagan Foundation, but among the other foundations, that the hearing would cause them problems. I suspect, too, that the optics of a Democratic committee chairman holding an official event within the walls of that Republican shrine had something to do with them pressuring the archivist. My bosses gave in and canceled the hearing.

It wasn't the only time NARA pushed back on our plans to oversee the libraries. In 2009, in response to a Congressional mandate, the agency had produced the "Report on Alternative Models for Presidential Libraries" examining ways to reduce costs and speed access to records. Using that as a blueprint, I had developed a series of hearings to explore the alternatives that NARA had proposed, in anticipation of creating legislation to reform the library system.

That didn't sit well with the foundations, nor their enablers within the agency. Even more than public hearings about the libraries, the foundations didn't want legislation reforming the system moving through Congress – legislation that would, in all likelihood, reduce their influence and ability to use the libraries for their own purposes.

I planned another hearing to review the George W. Bush Library, at the time under construction on the campus of Southern Methodist University (SMU) in Dallas, Texas. For every library up to the Carter, Congress had held individual hearings, and a vote, to accept each library into the system. After passage of the Presidential Libraries Act Amendments of 1986, acceptance was automatic; NARA would present Congress with a report on the proposed library, and if they took no action to prevent it, the archivist was pre-authorized to accept the library.

However, since we were examining NARA's own plans for alternative models, and they were in the process of creating a new library, I thought it would be a good opportunity to discuss and debate the issues. Darryl Piggee, the subcommittee staff director, and Lacy Clay, the chairman, agreed. I reached out to SMU officials responsible for the Bush Library, and they agreed to host a field hearing on campus. I began work, contacting potential witnesses and preparing the script and questions. Part of that process is notifying the agency of a pending hearing; soon after I did, SMU inexplicably retracted their invitation to host it. As I was seeking an alternative location, possibly a nearby NARA facility, we once again heard from the agency that, because of tremendous pressure from the foundations, they wanted us to cancel the hearing. Piggee and Clay again went along, not wanting to put Ferriero in a difficult situation.

I did not agree with the decisions to cancel the hearings. And while I strove to maintain good professional relationships with all of the agencies under the jurisdiction of the committee, we had an oversight responsibility that naturally created some tension. As long as they weren't inappropriately hiding anything and we weren't egregiously zealous, I felt that the committee could do its work cordially. We did so, successfully, with our oversight of the 2010 Census; there was no reason to think we couldn't do so with presidential libraries.

So why did Clay acquiesce? Perhaps part of his reasoning was that he serves as the representative from the First Congressional District of Missouri, in which is located the largest National Archives facility outside of the Washington, DC area, with nearly 800 employees. Perhaps another was Clay's general disinterest in oversight in general, and in the National Archives in particular; his focus then was on the Census, about which, in the 111th Congress alone, he held a dozen hearings.

Our last attempt to publicly examine presidential libraries was scuttled by politics, but not of the foundations' doing. During a long Congressional recess in August, 2010, we planned two field hearings at the Johnson Library. We had to cancel them due to the special session of the House that Speaker Nancy Pelosi called to vote on state-aid legislation passed by the Senate. Those two hearings – scheduled for the same day – got further along in planning than the others. But many leaders of the foundations, including the Johnson Foundation itself, begged off on our invitation to participate, claiming "previous commitments."

A few months later, Republicans retook the House of Representatives, and, therefore, control of committees. On February 28, 2011, the Committee on Oversight and Government Reform and the Committee on Transportation and Infrastructure held a large, joint hearing titled, "America's Presidential Libraries: Their Mission and Their Future." NARA and the foundations willingly, enthusiastically, joined in.

In his opening statement, Transportation Committee Chairman John Mica (R-Florida) said,

> *"I might say at the outset, this isn't one of these hearings where we have a mission of some violation or some problems with the libraries. I think this is a very forward-looking hearing in trying to assess the current status of our Presidential libraries and also their important mission and also their future."*

Later that day, Mica also chaired a friendly, celebratory (and unprecedented) symposium on presidential libraries in the enormous and dramatic Cannon Caucus Room. He began the event by saying,

"This is a rather historic day for our presidential libraries and also for Congress. I think rarely have we had just about representative from every presidential library in town at the same time."

From the mood of the events and the lack of real depth to the issues raised – as well as the fact that, unlike the hearings we tried to hold, NARA and the foundations fully participated in, even welcomed, them – the message was clear: the powerful political organizations that build and utilize the libraries for their own purposes are in charge.

THE RESULTS OF MY FIRST HEARING, ON NARA'S ADVISORY committees, were mixed. On the one hand, the new Archivist of the United States, David Ferriero, who had been sworn in the month after the hearing, made a small but important change. Previously, federal employees who serve as director of a presidential library could also serve, concurrently, as the executive director (or in any position) of the private foundation. In 2009, both R. Duke Blackwood, at the Reagan Library, and Michael Devine, at the Truman, were serving in both positions. Recognizing this as a clear conflict of interest, Ferriero ruled they would have to choose one or the other, and that going forward, no other director could serve within a foundation (both chose to remain federal employees).

However, the agency's response to the serious concerns we raised during that first hearing about membership on the Advisory Committee on Presidential Libraries – that it was only made up of the foundations, and no other stakeholders – was extremely disappointing. And it served us notice that, rather than seeing the foundations as problematic and in need of reform, NARA would instead strengthen their position.

A few months after the hearing, Sharon Fawcett changed the committee's name to the "Advisory Committee on the Presidential Library-Foundation Partnerships." She claimed that, as such, it would be appropriate only to have the library foundation representatives serve on it ("In this way, the diversity within the library system is well-represented"). All of the other relevant presidential library stakeholders still are not welcome on the committee, and are locked out from making any meaningful contributions to improve the system.

CHAPTER 4

PRESIDENTIAL RECORDS

"In these records there are, no doubt, unfavorable remarks made by our political opponents, as well as expressions of appreciation and affection by our friends. We may hope that future students will rely upon our friends."

President Herbert Hoover, at the dedication of his presidential library in West Branch, Iowa, August 10, 1962.

IF THEY'RE LUCKY, YOUR GREAT-GRANDKIDS MAY SEE THE opening of the Barack Obama presidential records; by that time, those of his four predecessors should be open. Probably.

Between now and then, NARA will take responsibility for about eleven more libraries, with their historically-questionable museums open and their historically-valuable records closed. For generations.

Preserving presidential records is a necessity. As a nation, we need to know, and understand, the actions of our presidents, and so we need to have, and see, the president's records. We need to protect and open them, to the greatest extent possible under the law. And we need to understand and learn from them. But do we need presidential libraries – the way we build and operate them today – to do that?

The libraries preserve, protect, and make available the records of chief executives from Herbert Hoover through George W. Bush (and, beginning in 2017, Barack Obama). Because of changes in the 1970s to the laws governing the libraries, the records of the most recent presidents will not be fully available to the public for a hundred years – possibly longer. Without significant reform, taxpayers will continue to support the newer libraries' legacy-burnishing museum functions and public (often partisan) events while historians, journalists, writers, students, and the rest of the public are locked out of the records for as long as they live.

Other writers have done admirable jobs exploring and explaining at length the history of presidential records, legislation, and case law. I will simply point out that it can be roughly oversimplified into three eras: George Washington through Calvin Coolidge; Herbert Hoover through Lyndon Johnson; and Richard Nixon to the present (and, absent reform, the future).

It was only during that brief middle period when the records were generally available and predominately open. While the first was rife with lost, stolen, rotted, sold, or burned documents, our current risks include poorly-designed and poorly-administered laws, inadequate regulations, recalcitrant private foundations, timid federal officials, insufficient resources – and lack of will to demand better.

Franklin Roosevelt's genius in creating his library wasn't in the form and substance of the building, and the way we commemorate presidents. It was in the establishment of the principle that presidential records should be preserved, by the government, and made available to the people. But his deeding of his papers didn't settle the matter, and it didn't change the fact that a president's papers were his personal property (which didn't change for forty-seven years, until Congress decided that the records were the property of the people).

During the last three years of President Harry Truman's presidency, he and his aides explored the question of what to do with his papers. They did not automatically assume that Truman would do as Franklin Roosevelt had done. Conventional wisdom says that Roosevelt began the presidential library system, but I believe Truman deserves the credit. The unique nature of Roosevelt's case – the unprecedented length of his presidency, enormity and scope of his collections, the personal act of his deeding his own land – makes it a special one, and not necessarily a precedent for other presidents to have followed. In fact, Roosevelt did not seek to pass legislation providing for presidential libraries, but simply a law for the acceptance of the Roosevelt Library.

Truman, on the other hand, did support such legislation, allowing the Archivist of the United States to accept presidential papers under access restrictions that presidents would decide (and which was enacted as the Federal Records Act of 1950).

When White House aide George Elsey suggested to the president that only a "very small proportion" of his papers should go to the Truman Library in Missouri – with the bulk being handed over to the National Archives, to be housed in Washington, D.C. – Truman was "delighted" with the idea and instructed Elsey to continue thinking and discussing along those lines. Elsey's argument included not only the fact that a smaller building would be needed, but that scholars would desire to have the "vast bulk of the White House papers in Washington, where they could be consulted in proximity to other official government documents."

This reasoning, echoed by scholars for decades, was (and is) dismissed by National Archives officials, who saw (and see) their clout as a relatively small, independent federal agency increased by operating an ever-expanded system of high-stakes, high-profile presidential libraries.

Whether or not this was the original intent, NARA's claim that presidential libraries need to continue to be spread out around the country so that more people may access the records has become a cover to secure continuing taxpayer subsidies for the private history at the library museums – since the records aren't, and won't be, available.

And as more and more records in the libraries are digitized, and records move from paper to born-digital, the "We Can't Centralize" argument will become moot; if the records are electronic and available online, why have physical locations scattered around the country? The number of pages of paper records in presidential libraries peaked with the Clinton Administration, and have decreased since; digital will out soon outpace paper records altogether.

But more than *where* presidential records are located, or *how* we access them, the greater problem is *whether* we can see them. Laws intended to provide greater, and faster, access have accomplished just the opposite. Today, presidential records are less open, less accessible, than at any time since Franklin Roosevelt dedicated his library. That should be unacceptable, but for NARA, and Congress, it appears to be fine.

THERE ARE FIVE MAIN LAWS THAT GOVERN PRESIDENTIAL libraries, enacted over thirty-one years, and not substantially updated or amended in twenty-nine years. For a time, Congress was responsive – even proactive – in overseeing the system, making changes that would try both to lower the cost and speed access to records in the libraries. But their attention has waned, the foundations have become more aggressive and creative in their attempts to circumvent the letter and spirit of the laws, and the system has become too difficult for NARA to manage. Unless something – or someone – radically changes our course, we will continue to see increasing costs, decreasing access, and the ascendancy of the private political foundations using the libraries to further their own goals. We've come a long way in the last sixty years; a long way away from our original intentions.

Two and a half years after Truman left office, Dwight Eisenhower signed into law the Presidential Libraries Act of 1955, which set out the means by which former presidents could deed a building, and their papers, to the government, and for the operation and maintenance of those buildings. Three decades later, alarmed over rising costs and increasing size of what had been simple archives, Congress passed, and Ronald Reagan signed, the Presidential Libraries Act Amendments of 1986, which sought to limit the size of the libraries, set standards for their construction, and defray the cost of their operation and maintenance.

During that time, three other laws changed the way we preserve and open (or keep closed) government and presidential records, and tried to change the way we build and operate the libraries. In 1966, Johnson unenthusiastically signed the Freedom of Information Act (FOIA), which fundamentally transformed the nature of federal records, declaring that the public had a basic right to, and creating a means to request to, access them, unless the records fell under one of a series of specific and carefully-designed exemptions. The bill began a brief but important era when transparency – the public's right to know what our government is doing – was seen as crucial to democracy.

Eight years later, Congress passed the Presidential Recordings and Materials Preservation Act of 1974 (PRMPA), to prevent Nixon from destroying his records. The bill led to the passage four years later of the Presidential Records Act of 1978 (PRA), which declared that presidential records are the property not of the president, but of the people. That era of transparency – when "sunshine laws" brought the promise of disinfecting the government, throwing open records and holding officials accountable – would not last long; it would end with a succession of presidents who valued secrecy over openness, and saw transparency as something to fight against rather that support.

We are still in that era today.

It falls to us, citizens, and not the powerful, not those in the best position to rectify the situation, to call for and implement reform. Congress has demonstrated for decades no real interest in doing so. And no president has supported the PRA, nor the FOIA. Not truly. Each has tried to weaken the law, have reforms apply only to their successors, or find ways around it. Or they've simply ignored the law.

THROUGHOUT THE HISTORY OF PRESIDENTIAL LIBRARIES, researchers have leveled charges of favoritism, excessive limitations, and withholding of documents. Most were not nefarious plots to keep records hidden inappropriately. They were often the result of a complicated mix of laws, regulations, and the strongly asserted self-interest of former presidents. The majority of these claims have been made against the libraries that were established before the Presidential Records Act (PRA) of 1978, which held that official presidential records created or received after January 20, 1981 were public, rather than private, property.

Access to the papers in pre-PRA libraries is governed by deeds of gift, whose terms can vary widely. In some controversial cases, researchers sought access to papers years before the deed allowed them to be opened. In others, approval for access was granted by the deed to a committee or an individual, whose decisions could be influenced by their relationship to the donor. In certain circumstances, individual researchers were singled out for special access or specific exclusion. One of the goals of the PRA was to eliminate these barriers and create reasonable restrictions and methods of access. It built on the premise of the Freedom of Information Act, which is that the public has a right to access to records of the federal government, subject to certain restrictions such as those related to national security and individual privacy.

In all of these cases, the NARA archivists working in the pre-PRA libraries had to strike a delicate balance between meeting the needs of researchers – a prime responsibility of NARA – and adhering to the deeds of gift (and the expressed or implied desires of former presidents and their families). Most archivists and researchers were uncomfortable with the restrictions, and looked forward to what were hoped to be the significant changes under the PRA. Unforeseen by those who fought for the legislation were the ways that implementation of the act would slow, rather than speed, access. Under the PRA, presidential records were to be made available subject to certain restrictions, dependent on their sensitivity and a president's desire to withhold them for a period of years. These restrictions by and large would no longer apply after twelve years following the end of the administration, when most of the unclassified records could be made available through FOIA requests.

The law works like this: for five years after a president leaves office, no presidential records are available except to Congress, the courts, and the current and former president. At least in part, this period where the records are closed was created to allow NARA to properly arrange, describe, and process much of the records. However, the incredible growth in the number of presidential records as well as the relative lengths of each presidential term were not foreseen by the law's drafters. Eisenhower's eight-year presidency resulted in twenty-six million pages of documents; forty years later, the eight-year presidency of George W. Bush resulted in seventy million pages of documents and eighty terabytes of electronic records, including more than 200 million emails and almost four million photographs. The five presidents immediately preceding the passage of the PRA served an average of four years; including Obama, four of the five presidents subject to the law served two four-year terms.

In pre-PRA libraries, archivists processed and opened entire series according to a schedule sometimes set by the former president or his advisors (President Johnson, for example, directed that his education papers be opened first). Under the PRA, which began with the Reagan Library, archivists must open papers according to FOIA requests, and for the most part, in the order in which they are received. This process quickly became so overwhelming for archivists at the Reagan Library that they abandoned their processing schedule to respond to FOIA requests. This created a backlog of hundreds of requests and a wait time of many years. Similar problems have occurred at the three other PRA libraries (Bush, Clinton, and Bush). Consequently, researchers have two choices: wait years – even decades – for the records they want or examine the few records that have been made available through FOIA requests and the relatively small amount of systematic processing.

The Reagan Library began accepting FOIA requests on January 20, 1994; twenty years later, by January, 2014, the library had made just under forty-five percent of its "traditional holdings" available to the public. The George W. Bush Library began accepting FOIA requests on January 20, 2014; twenty days later, the FOIA backlog had grown to 234 requests. Both libraries, in 2014, assigned one archivist to process records systematically, while their other archivists (eight at the Reagan, and eleven at the George W. Bush) respond to FOIA requests.

The final restrictions for the first presidential records to be covered by the PRA were supposed to have been lifted on January 20, 2001 – twelve years after the end of the Reagan presidency. President George W. Bush delayed the openings for several months, and then issued Executive Order (EO) 13233, titled "Further Implementation of the Presidential Records Act," on November 5, 2001. Rather than easing implementation, the order's effect was to halt implementation, and cause alarm throughout the relevant communities and professions. It reversed the legislation, granting former presidents and their representatives executive privilege in perpetuity. It mandated that the sitting president support claims of privilege by former presidents in the courts. Former presidents could have also overruled sitting presidents on the release of their records. Further, it tilted the burden from the government, who had to provide reasons for withholding records, to the citizen, who had to prove their need for access.

A federal judge invalidated the part of the order granting executive privilege to former presidents in 2007, but the rest remained in effect until President Obama, on his first full day in office, reversed it with Executive Order 13489. In 2014, Congress passed, and President Obama signed, the Presidential and Federal Records Act Amendments of 2014, which limits the amount of time a former president could make a claim of privilege against the archivist's release of a record, and created a formal process for release of a record about which such as claim has been made.

WE FIGHT OVER PRESIDENTIAL RECORDS BECAUSE THEY TELL us, dispassionately, accurately (though not always thoroughly) what presidents do. We grant presidents and their administrations enormous power, not only to act, but, for the period of their terms of office, keep much of what they do secret. For decades, while the public maintained a high degree of respect for the presidency, that secrecy was acceptable to most. As we began to suspect, and then have our suspicions confirmed, that presidents were taking advantage of such secrecy, we began to demand more access to their records. And that's when presidents began to try to hide their records even more.

Do we place too much emphasis on what presidents do (and, therefore, on presidential records)? Perhaps. Judging from the best-seller lists and the PBS NewsHour and basic cable channel specials, what was once the broad expanse known as American history has been narrowed to not much more than presidential history. Even though it's limited, and doesn't begin to reflect the complexity of this nation. Even though it's overrated. We still yearn for presidential history books and presidential history documentaries and we watch and read and cheer celebrity "presidential historians." And we allow presidents to build ever-larger monuments to themselves while keeping their records unprocessed and unavailable.

THE BEGINNING OF PRESIDENT OBAMA'S FIRST TERM WAS A time of hope for many people, on many issues. For those in the freedom of information/open government communities, expectations for a more transparent administration were reinforced by early action on the part of the president and Attorney General Eric Holder.

On his first full day in office, Obama signed a Memorandum on the FOIA. In it, he cautioned agencies that they should not withhold records "merely because public officials might be embarrassed by disclosure, because errors and failures might be revealed, or because of speculative or abstract fears." He also urged affirmative disclosure of information, instructing agencies not to wait for requests from the public. (The same day, the president also, not incidentally, issued the related EO 13489, reversing George W. Bush's infamous EO 13233.)

A few weeks later, Holder issued his own FOIA memo, echoing the president's words and specifying a significant change: the Department of Justice would defend a denial of a FOIA request only if:

> *(1) the agency reasonably foresees that disclosure would harm an interest protected by one of the statutory exemptions, or*
>
> *(2) disclosure is prohibited by law.*

Holder also stated clearly that "agencies should readily and systematically post information online in advance of any public request." Open government advocates weren't hoping that agency officials who were anti-FOIA would suddenly change their minds because of this new direction; they were hoping that all of the FOIA officials who had been claiming to support the law, to support disclosure, to support the public's right to access government information, would, well, act that way.

To some extent, if and when they did, they were thwarted by those above them. But that's an easy out: blame the appointees. That doesn't quite add up, as those are the people who are most sensitive to the politics of whatever current administration is calling the shots.

At some point, we have to come to terms with the fact that, at virtually every agency, there are career federal employees who are doing their best to "protect" their agency by not cooperating with FOIA requesters, withholding too much, and not proactively disclosing information. Regardless of what the president or the attorney general say. NARA is one such agency; the Center for Effective Government, a transparency and accountability nonprofit organization, gave the agency the grade of "F" in their 2014 Access to Information Scorecard.

But more important is the fact that, other than those memos, the president and the attorney general haven't done much to change the culture either. Where are the people who've lost jobs for stonewalling? Where are the reprimands for inappropriate withholdings? Where are the consequences for not fulfilling the spirit of those memos – or the law?

Journalists, requesters, attorneys, activists and others point out that the Obama Administration has been more restrictive, less disclosing, and involved in more lawsuits than the previous administration. It may be worse than any administration in the forty-nine year history of the FOIA.

More and more, journalists, historians, attorneys, advocates, researchers and others are clamoring for significant changes to law. One of the main problems is the government's apparently indiscriminate and often inappropriate use of the (b)(5) exemption, protecting from release those documents that are "inter-agency or intra-agency memorandum or letters" and which would be privileged in civil litigation. In practice, agencies frequently use this exemption to withhold records that contain recommendations and advice – the so-called "deliberative process." Any FOIA requester has their own (and probably several) examples of the patently incorrect application of this exemption in order to withhold a record that clearly should be released, but which may cause embarrassment to the creator or the agency. The specific kind of thing, in other words, that the current president, in one of his first official acts, clearly ordered should not be used as an excuse to withhold a document.

FOIA plays an important role in access to presidential records. The PRA specifies a five-year period after the end of a presidential administration when no records may be released; at the expiration of that period, the public may file FOIA requests for access to most records. Some records, however, may still be withheld under the PRA for an additional seven years, but the president must have signed, while still in office, a document indicating what records are to be restricted, and under which of seven categories those records fall. Because of the potential for politicization, NARA cannot administer these laws effectively without being seen as strictly nonpartisan. And since the 1980s, that's been a problem.

DON WILSON BADLY NEEDED AN EXIT STRATEGY. AFTER working at two Republican presidential libraries – one as director – the former history professor had been nominated by President Ronald Reagan and confirmed by the Senate in 1987 as the seventh Archivist of the United States. Instead of being the rewarding capstone to his career, his tenure at the National Archives had been controversial. From his clashes with Congress and dysfunctional management style to his improper handling of the hiring and supervision of NARA's inspector general and his favoring of presidents in disputes over records, Wilson generated more controversy and problems within and for the agency than perhaps all of his predecessors combined. After just a few years on the job, he needed a way out. He found that the answer was something with which he already was quite familiar: he would do a political favor for a powerful figure.

By the fall of 1992, Wilson's time in the job was running short. Congress, the Federal Bureau of Investigation (FBI), the Justice Department, the Office of Special Counsel (OSC), the President's Council on Integrity and Efficiency in Government (PCIE), the Office of Personnel Management (OPM), and federal courts had investigated and were investigating him. His most recent (and highest-ranking) Republican patron had been defeated in the 1992 presidential election. A new president, from a different party – different from not only the incumbent president's, but from

Wilson's as well – would soon take office and likely clean house. Don Wilson really needed a way out. With a soft landing, if possible.

As archivist, he was found by government investigations to have failed. He was found to have failed in his managerial, administrative, supervisory legislative, regulatory, financial, and ethical responsibilities. In some cases, investigators determined he had acted inappropriately; in others, they found he had improperly delegated responsibility and authority to his subordinates, and then failed to supervise their actions. His term was deemed to have been such a failure and he himself so missing from responsibility and accountability that a Senate committee looking into his activities dubbed him "the Absentee Archivist."

In 1991, the Committee on Governmental Affairs began an investigation of NARA's management practices. The probe took a year, and included the work of the FBI, the OSC, and other offices. On the eve of the 1992 election, the committee issued its report, "Serious Management Problems at the National Archives and Records Administration."

The report concluded, "Archivist Don Wilson failed to exercise care and diligence in fulfilling his responsibilities" and recommended,

> *"The President of the United States should undertake a review of the actions of the Archivist of the United States in connection with the activities detailed in this report, including but not limited to questions concerning compliance with the Inspector General Act (as amended) and the exercise of administrative and management responsibilities."*

So why, if Don Wilson didn't have the experience, skills, and judgment to handle the job of Archivist of the United States, did President George H.W. Bush give him the job of running his private presidential library foundation at Texas A&M University? Perhaps it was because of the one thing Don Wilson did have: the legal authority to declare important records as personal, and not presidential. Wilson had the power to make damaging information about President Bush disappear. And right after he exercised that authority, and benefitted President Bush, Wilson got his reward. And hightailed it down to Texas.

On top of that authority, Wilson was someone Republican presidents could count on. Even though the National Archives is supposed to be strictly nonpartisan – including the position of archivist – Wilson had made it known that he was a loyal member of the GOP.

When he applied to lead the then soon-to-be dedicated Gerald Ford Presidential Library in late 1980, Wilson was serving as Associate Director of the State Historical Society of Wisconsin. With a Ph.D. in history from the University of Cincinnati; a few years of teaching experience; nine years at the Eisenhower Library (three as deputy director, one as acting director); and good references from the history profession, Wilson made it to the short list of three candidates for the job. His chief rival was William Stewart, who, technically, already had the job; he was acting director of the Ford Materials Project, which is what a presidential library is called between the time the president leaves office and the library building is formally dedicated.

Stewart had been in the job for three and a half years, preparing the library and museum to be opened. Before that, he had been assistant director of the Roosevelt Library for seven years. At the time he applied for the formal appointment as director of the Ford Library, he had worked for the National Archives for twenty-one years. He, too, had good references from the profession – including a former Archivist of the United States. In terms of the technical requirements, ability to manage, and experience in the system, Stewart was clearly the frontrunner. He just didn't have Don Wilson's political clout.

The job description for a presidential library director doesn't mention politics. But for years, the National Archives had been taking it into consideration in at least one specific way: presidents were consulted on the choice of director – the first one, particularly, who works most closely with the president and the foundation in planning and preparing the library. That's just what Stewart had spent the previous three and half years doing: working with the architects, builders, university, local officials, foundation, and the former president and his staff, "developing the archival, museum, and public education programs for the Library."

Don Wilson wasn't nearly as experienced, and, at the time he applied, had been out of the agency for two and a half years; Stewart was running – had been building – the library for more than three years. And President Ford had "affection" for Stewart. But in the summer of 1981, Don Wilson got the job. There are strong clues in his application, just four years later, to become Archivist of the United States, that politics made the difference.

RONALD REAGAN WAS HAVING A HARD TIME NOMINATING A new archivist. In early 1983, rumors started circulating that he would replace Robert Warner with a political appointee. Warner, a former president of the Society of American Archivists and respected historian, had become archivist just four months before Reagan defeated Jimmy Carter in the 1980 presidential election. In February, the White House recalled Richard F. Staar, the chief U.S. negotiator to the Mutual and Balanced Force Reductions talks in Vienna. As word spread that Staar soon would be the next archivist, concerns grew that the position would become politicized. Individuals and professional organizations wrote to the White House to protest Warner's removal and urge the president not to propose a political nominee. In the end, Reagan never put forth Staar's name, but he didn't drop the idea of naming his own archivist.

Warner retired in April, 1985, when the National Archives split from the General Services Administration (GSA). The nomination for the first archivist to lead the newly-independent agency garnered a lot of attention, and possible candidates received added scrutiny due to the earlier worries. With NARA finally out from under the GSA, stakeholders were concerned that the post, with its important, nonpartisan responsibilities, not become politicized.

Reagan had signed the National Archives and Records Administration Act of 1984, the law that separated the Archives from GSA. The act required the archivist "shall be appointed without regard to political affiliations and solely on the basis of the professional qualifications required to perform the duties and responsibilities of the office."

The administration's first choice, Peter Duignan, a foreign policy expert at the conservative Hoover Institution for the Study of War, Revolution and Peace, was seen by many as too political even before he was formally nominated (which he never would be, due to concerns about a rocky confirmation process).

It wasn't until May 1, 1986, more than a year after Warner retired, that Reagan nominated John Agresto, a protégé of National Endowment for the Humanities Chairman William Bennett. Professional organizations publicly challenged the nomination, protesting what to them clearly was a political appointment. The Society for History in the Federal Government warned that his confirmation would "decisively impede the aura of impartiality and professional detachment required for such a position of national trust."

The avalanche against Agresto was considerable. His contentious confirmation hearing in the Senate lasted three days. When the Committee on Governmental Affairs met in October to vote, with his rejection the likely outcome, not enough Republican senators were present for a quorum, and the nomination was not considered before the Senate adjourned for the midterm elections. While the White House vowed to resubmit his name, and even considered a recess appointment, Agresto was done. The next choice would have to be non-political, or, at least, be viewed as such. The administration wanted someone they could trust, someone on whom they could count as much as they knew they could count on Agresto, but Reagan couldn't afford another nomination scuttled due to the appearance of partisanship. He turned to another candidate who had applied for the job the previous fall: Don Wilson.

His application had, along with the standard resume, cover letter, and professional references, three additions: a note reassuring the White House about his Republican politics; a list of political references; and a number of letters of strong recommendations from politicians. In contrast to what was publicly known, he couldn't have been more political.

Wilson had initially applied for the position of archivist before the Agresto nomination imploded. But apparently he knew how important politics were to that White House. In a letter to the Office of Presidential Personnel dated October 31, 1985, after touting his work as director of the Ford Library – and pointing out his previous successful experience working with "institutions operated through a combination of public and private funds along with affiliated foundations or boards" – Wilson wrote,

> "What does not precisely appear in the accompanying material are my interests and activities in the political sector. As a college student, I became actively involved in then Republican Congressman William Avery's campaign for the governorship of Kansas (successful). My father served a [sic] Governor Avery's regional campaign manager for North Central Kansas.
>
> "While on the staff of the Eisenhower Library, I was elected to the Abilene City Commission with strong local Republican party support. Although this was a non-partisan election, I was endorsed by the Republican leaders in Abilene and led all candidates in votes received. I served on the five member governing commission until moving to Wisconsin in 1978. Also, in late 1977 and 1978, I was an advisor and volunteer for Deryl

Scheuster [sic] in his unsuccessful bid for the Republican nomination in Kansas for the United States Senate.

"I have enclosed a substantial list of references who may be contacted and who are knowledgeable about my skills and background. I would anticipate no difficulty in receiving Senate confirmation. A number of members of Congress have already indicated support if I were to be nominated."

Wilson's two lists of ten references each were titled "Personal/Professional" and "Political." The latter included two former U.S. Senators, three U.S. Senators, two U.S. Representatives, one lobbyist, and one pollster – all Republicans.

On August 14, 1987, Reagan formally nominated Wilson as Archivist of the United States, and the Senate confirmed him without incident a few months later. Some hailed the political independence of the new archivist. In early December, at his swearing-in ceremony in the Rotunda of the National Archives Building in Washington, Wilson's predecessor, Robert Warner, said, "The installation today of a worthy candidate who fully meets the terms of the law marks the true conclusion of the Archives independence movement."

Congressman Dick Cheney (R-Wyoming) swears in Archivist Don Wilson, December 4, 1987. Patsy Wilson and President Ronald Reagan look on.

President Reagan spoke at the ceremony, but Wilson chose a different politician to swear him in; a former White House Chief of Staff, one of the Members of Congress who appeared on his "Political" reference list: five-term Republican Representative from Wyoming Dick Cheney.

I DO NOT USE THE WORD "LIE" EASILY, NOR HAPPILY. I AM NOT settling a score. I am not sensationalizing. I am simply relating a story, one of the turning points in my research. If this book is about the length to which presidents will go to construct their legacy, this story is about the length to which some NARA officials will go to enable presidents to do so with ease, and without consequence. It is one of several stories in these pages about the same NARA official, enabling and accommodating presidents and their families and surrogates.

In the course of my research, I discovered something major. Something about a president. Something that had never been reported. Something negative, about a president and his choice of a site for his library. A violation of the law and a cover-up. That story is the subject of Chapter 6.

I found this major story in records. Documents. Not in interviews or by trolling social media or through Google searches. In my search for more information, I sought more records about how presidents choose the location for their libraries. Records that I strongly believed would be found within NARA. Records that instead I could not find, even with the help of archivists, who also believed they would be found in NARA.

Such records would be interesting to me not just because they might detail how presidents make the complex and crucial site selection decision. They also were interesting to me because they would detail the level of involvement of the National Archives, a federal – and, purportedly, independent – agency, in the site selection process.

I had heard rumors about that process. About how one archivist in particular had been deeply involved in helping a president select the site for his library. This would be cause for examination regardless of the context; the story always has been that no federal money is spent on presidential libraries before they are built, and then turned over to the government, by private organizations. The National Archives – charged with impartially administering the laws governing ownership of and access to presidential records – maintains that it is not involved in that private, and often political, process.

But I was interested for a more specific reason. This particular archivist had resigned his office under a cloud of suspicion. Amid allegations that he had broken the law – the law governing ownership of and access to presidential records. Allegations that he had made a deal to declare that what clearly were presidential records – and which therefore should go to the National Archives, for their care and processing (and, within the confines of the law, eventual release to the public) – were not in fact presidential records. That these highly sensitive records were in fact the personal property of the president, to dispose of as he saw fit.

The rumors had it that the archivist had done so in return for a job. A soft landing: a lucrative and prestigious job. And that the person with whom he had made this deal was the president of the United States.

So one may imagine the level of my interest in obtaining records held by the National Archives pertaining to that archivist's efforts in regard to the site selection of that president's library.

And one may imagine my surprise when, after being denied access to such records through Freedom of Information requests, a high-ranking National Archives official told me that such records did not exist, because the National Archives did not, and does not, play any role in the site selection process ("we find out where the library will be the same day you do").

One may further imagine my puzzlement when, just a few days later, I received a document – an internal NARA memorandum – detailing the ways in which the National Archives, and in particular the archivist, plays a key role in helping the president select the site for his library.

Finally, one may imagine my shock as I took note of the fact that the author of the memorandum about the archivist playing the key role in the site selection process was the same official who, days earlier, had told me that NARA plays absolutely no role whatsoever in the site selection process. As her explanation for denying my FOIA request for records. About the site selection process. In which the archivist, in fact, plays the key role.

Which brings me back to the word I reluctantly, though accurately, now use: lie. I gained access to National Archives records about the site selection process for three presidential libraries because of what I believe to have been a lie. A lie told to me by Sharon Fawcett, then NARA's Assistant Archivist for Presidential Libraries. Before she made the statement in question, my FOIA requests for the records had been denied on the grounds that NARA held no such records; after Fawcett made the statement – and after I found her memorandum contradicting herself, and shared it with other NARA officials – the records mysteriously, miraculously appeared. Within the records were those about Don Wilson.

IT WAS THIS DON WILSON – PARTISAN, POLITICAL DON Wilson – who, late on the night of January 19, 1993, signed away important presidential records. For decades, the National Archives had provided assistance to presidents and their foundations in planning their libraries. But more than any archivist since the first, R.D.W. Connor, helped FDR plan his library, Wilson sought to aid President Bush in building his. Wilson received and evaluated all candidate proposals, including site visits to the three finalists, and strongly influenced the final choice of Texas A&M University. In fact, during the final phases of the process, Wilson provided the school with more detailed information on Bush's selection criteria than he did the other finalists, the University of Houston and Rice University.

Once the decision had been made, Wilson even offered to inform the losing candidates, so that Bush wouldn't have to make those calls himself.

For several years, Wilson had worked closely with the Bush White House, influencing the planning and steering the site selection process. So it was perhaps not a stretch for the administration to reach out to him, shortly before Bush left office, to ask for one more favor. And, given Wilson's dire circumstances – if he remained on the job, he surely would be fired by incoming President Clinton – it's understandable, if not forgivable, that he said yes.

Since the end of the Reagan Administration, journalist Scott Armstrong, the National Security Archive (NSA) at the George Washington University, and other organizations together had been fighting a battle to preserve backup tapes of the White House email system, known as "PROFS." The most important – and controversial – records in that system related to the Iran-Contra affair.

The tapes were important to both the investigations of the scandal and to history in general. At several times between 1989 and 1993, the Reagan and Bush administrations tried to destroy them. It was only because of the ongoing series of legal actions – restraining orders, decisions that the emails were official records and that the backup tapes must be preserved

– that they survived to the end of the Bush presidency. But even in the face of unambiguous court rulings, the White House continued to try to get rid of them – to get rid of the evidence.

With thirteen hours left in George Bush's term, Don Wilson signed a secret agreement granting the outgoing president exclusive legal and physical custody·of the White House email tapes. The agreement was later declared illegal by a federal judge, who called Wilson's actions, "arbitrary, capricious, an abuse of discretion, and contrary to law."

Two weeks later, Don Wilson announced that he would resign the office of Archivist of the United States, and begin his new position as Executive Director of the George Bush Presidential Library Foundation at Texas A&M University. He denied that his appointment to run the foundation, a $129,000 a year position, was the result of a quid pro quo, or had anything to do with the tapes agreement.

Wilson left the National Archives weaker as an agency, its reputation damaged and its credibility as a nonpartisan arbiter of federal and presidential records laws in serious doubt. And he ushered in a new era, one of strong politicization, deference to presidents and their foundations, and acceptance of skewed history in presidential library museums.

Exhibit table, the War in Afghanistan, the George W. Bush Library, Dallas, Texas.

CHAPTER 5

PRESIDENTIAL LIBRARY MUSEUMS

"This year an estimated one and a half million people will visit presidential museums and libraries, exploring the lives of these presidents, passed down, like oral history, from one generation to another...each president is like a finely cut prism with many facets – their achievements and their philosophy, their family and their humanity."

President George Bush, at the dedication of the Richard Nixon Presidential Library in Yorba Linda, California, July 19, 1990.

COMPARED WITH ITS SUCCESSORS, THE FIRST FOUR MUSEUMS betray little partisan slant to visitors (though Libertarians may bristle at how the Roosevelt celebrates the New Deal and true Keynesians might rue the Hoover's description of the causes of the Great Depression).

For the most part, the earlier libraries deal in non-contentious history. They have been open for decades, and a considerable amount of that history already has been evaluated (even re-evaluated). There is some minor spin, but they do not attempt wholesale revision of what has become accepted history. They feel not only like museums, but seem like part of America's past in and of themselves.

Eisenhower Boyhood Home, left/foreground; Eisenhower Museum, right/background, Abilene, Kansas.

Indeed, the first four are those most closely associated with their president's lives, in ways that modern libraries do not replicate. Two are adjacent to a presidential birthplace, and all four locations are deeply associated with each president. In contrast, the main consideration for modern presidential library site selections is economic, not familial. Franklin Roosevelt was born and raised a few hundred feet away from where he built his library, on his family's estate; George H.W. Bush was born more than 1,800 miles from his library, on the campus of a university neither he nor anyone else in his family had attended.

That these earlier libraries offer visitors something more than the latest interactive exhibits and glass-case displays full of treasures – the sense of being present where history happened – makes them feel less like tourist attractions and more like historic sites. Of course, they are both, but only the most sensitive partisan would find fault with these (relatively) modest shrines, and then perhaps with a specific characterization in a single display, or the omission of a minor gaffe or peccadillo.

The next four libraries – the middle group – represent the start of the transition from historic sites with mostly-unobjectionable history to the most recent group, which is the exact opposite. While more partisan and celebratory than the first group, for the most part, these middle museums do not reflect the current trend of wholeheartedly partisan shrines.

Though the Kennedy Library is unabashedly liberal, its adjunct role as a memorial to the assassinated president dampens political reactions to its exhibits. It was not dedicated until sixteen years after his death, and so the Johnson Library, opened in 1971, technically marks the first departure from both the modesty and the inclusive nonpartisanship of earlier libraries. From that point on, to varying degrees, you know which party is represented – and which president was The Greatest – in each library.

The five beginning with the Johnson have been open long enough to have undergone at least one major renovation of their permanent exhibit since their dedications. The Carter museum, in 2009, and the Johnson museum, in 2012, went through multi-million dollar renovations of their permanent exhibits; in 2015 and 2016, the Kennedy, Nixon, and Ford museums will have completed major renovations of their exhibits.

Despite the National Archives' insistence that presidential library exhibits get less partisan and more accurate over time, the opposite can – and does – happen. Depending on whether the president and/or their close family members are still alive, the current relationship of that president to the national party, and the amount of money available through capital campaigns, there can be enormous pressure to ramp up the spin and provide greater visibility and legitimacy not only to the president's legacy but to the relevant national party's agenda.

The changes made to the Johnson Library permanent exhibit in 2012 turned what had been considered by some to be one of the more open and accurate libraries into a "modern" library, in the partisan, legacy-polishing, historically-questionable mold. The exhibit seems almost as if it were a pointed rebuke of the carefully-documented and widely-lauded biography of Pulitzer Prize-winning historian Robert Caro, in the glossing over of inconvenient facts and refusal to acknowledge negative events or aspects of LBJ's character.

The Reagan Library is the next departure point, leaving the middle group's proudly partisan exhibits rooted in documented history and moving to historically-careless mythmaking based not on fact but on political aspirations (both of the administrations and of the private foundations that build the libraries).

Air Force One Pavilion, Ronald Reagan Library, Simi Valley, California.

What matters in these libraries is how presidents saw themselves, and how their families and supporters wish to see them, and not how history has judged them; that's all the more easy to accomplish, since historians are blocked from reading the majority of these presidents' records. Which is somewhat fitting; about the only actual documents on which this kind of "history" is based are press releases, talking points, speeches, and compensated journalistic promotion. Discussion, dissention, and debate; options, plans, and strategies; and roads not taken, opportunities missed, and consequences – just some of what we would learn from the records we're not allowed to see – have no place in the modern museums.

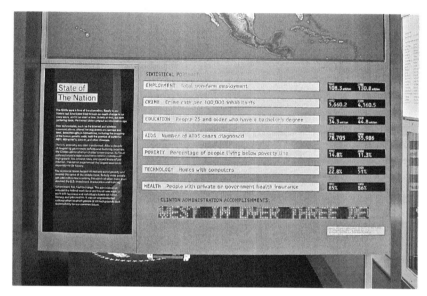

Statistics panel, the William Clinton Library, Little Rock, Arkansas.

It's not simply that only successes are featured in these museums; it's that they contend that the president only *had* successes. And it's not as if the history that is displayed in these museums is the result of standard, accepted practices, simply made more positive. Something different is happening – something that is directly connected to the way in which presidents govern, spending their entire terms in campaign mode.

In the most recent museum, the George W. Bush, a new cycle of history appears to be emerging: during a Republican president's term, the administration announces plans for a new policy; Fox News approves, heavily promoting it; the administration, bolstered by the support, implements the policy; Fox News reports the action, favorably; once opened, the president's museum touts Fox News' judgment, "proving" the president was correct and successful; and, to complete the cycle, Fox News reports positively on the history proudly displayed in the exhibit.

Perhaps once more Democratic presidents are elected and libraries are built for them (remember: four out of the last five libraries accepted by NARA were for Republican presidents), and an enabling media coalesces to support them to the degree that Fox News supports Republicans, we'll see a Democratic equivalent of this "history" cycle.

THE HERBERT HOOVER LIBRARY MUSEUM'S PERMANENT exhibit displays could probably fit within the space occupied by just the entrance rotunda, gift shop, auditorium, and classroom at the George Bush Library. This doesn't reflect simply the change in the scope of commemoration over the thirty-five years that separate the dedications of the libraries; it shows the change in the nature of that commemoration.

While the Bush museum's exhibit space is twice that of the Hoover's, the libraries have grown more grand and impressive over the years. The buildings and locations are part of the exhibit experience for visitors.

The importance of a library's site was most recently demonstrated in the University of Chicago's controversial proposal to build the Obama Library on historic parkland on the city's South Side. But while these factors play a role, the kind of exhibits they contain and the history that they teach are key to how presidents rewrite history.

And rewrite history they do (Bill Clinton was only half joking at the opening of the George W. Bush Library). Through sins of commission and omission, presidents – especially recent ones – tell stories that are often at odds with the truth; spin scandals in the most positive light possible; and outright ignore controversies that would detract from the otherwise success-filled, error-free narratives.

The education programs and invited speakers support this tale, but far more people view the exhibits. And that's where presidents, their families, and their private foundations put the most effort.

If determined by space allocation, subject matter, artifacts, and content (and, admittedly, no benefit of the doubt), the themes of recent presidential permanent exhibits might accurately be described as:

Richard Nixon: *the Misunderstood, Misrepresented, and Misadvised Foreign Policy Genius…Who Also Was Very Good Domestically, Did You Know?*

Ronald Reagan: *the Shrine of Saint Ronald, Who, Through Your Generous Donation to the Reagan Foundation, Could Save Us Again.*

George Bush: *He Had a Long and Distinguished Public Service Career, But Let's Focus Almost Exclusively on the First Gulf War.*

Bill Clinton: *To Distract You From Questions of Character, Here Are Hundreds of Data Points and Statistics to Prove the Eight-Year Peace and Prosperity of the Clinton Administration (Did We Mention Eight Years of Prosperity? Here Are Some More Statistics And Data).*

George W. Bush: *9/11; Freedom; Saddam Hussein, Who Really Did Have Weapons of Mass Destruction; 9/11; the War on Terror, In Response to 9/11; Freedom; and 9/11...And By The Way, Katrina and the Financial Crisis Weren't His Fault. At All. 9/11.*

The George Bush Presidential Library and Museum celebrated their tenth anniversary in 1997 with a grand re-opening after a six-month renovation that cost $8.3 million. The day before, during a media preview, I watched former President Bush stand at the podium in a replica of the White House Briefing Room in the museum, talking with members of the press about the newly-renovated exhibits.

I was struck by how that museum, more than any other in the system, tries to make the visitor a participant, and not just an observer. You can stand behind the famous podium as if you were facing the press corps. In a replica of the Oval Office, you may walk into and around the room, a first for presidential library museums. And – an even bigger "first" – you can sit behind the president's desk, in the president's chair, and have your photo taken as a souvenir.

A replica of the Bush White House Situation Room presents decisions the former president made in the run up to the First Gulf War. Participants sit at the table and receive a briefing, just like the Commander in Chief, and use touch-screen computers to call up relevant information, including dossiers on members of the national security team.

The Gulf War Object Theater, a recreation of a U.S. Army tent in Saudi Arabia during the war, immerses visitors in the sights and sounds of combat, combining first-hand accounts of soldiers with President Bush's televised speeches, network news coverage, and extremely loud and extremely realistic bombs, tanks, missiles and jets. Captions ask the visitor to look at things from President Bush's perspective. Titled "Think of it this way," it tries to make events understandable.

Replicas of the White House Cabinet Room at the Clinton and Ford museums offer a chance to examine in detail a difficult choice the presi-

Gulf War exhibit, the George Bush Library, College Station, Texas.

dents were faced with, and even to make our own choices, given the same information. In both exhibits, regardless of how we choose, we are instructed that the presidents' courses of action were the correct ones.

The "decision" theaters in the Truman and Bush museums go further, and immerse visitors in presidential decision-making. Participants vote on outcomes, learning how the group decided, and how the presidents, did, too (which was, of course, always the correct way).

Are such things relatable? Is it really possible to step into the shoes of the President of the United States and get a sense of the office, the responsibilities, the pressures, with computer simulations, after the fact?

This isn't the point. These exhibits aren't about giving tourists a feel for the office; they're about explaining and excusing decisions that, without the benefit of the museums (and, in the case of George W. Bush, the president himself), we might otherwise have thought to be unwise, imprudent, or, even worse, wrong.

BEFORE I TOOK MY FIRST EXTENDED TRIP IN 2003, I THOUGHT I understood what the libraries meant to people (and to me). I had toured the three that were then closest to where I lived: Kennedy, Roosevelt and Carter. But seeing so many in such a short period of time and paying attention to the exhibits, text, photos and videos, and other visitors, too, my understanding changed, and convinced me to write this book.

At the Reagan museum in Simi Valley, California, one of the exhibits I saw, long since replaced by several updates, was about his campaigns; like most of the other museums' campaign exhibits, this included displays of electoral maps. Particularly for major victories, the contrast between the preponderance of one color and the scarcity of another is shocking.

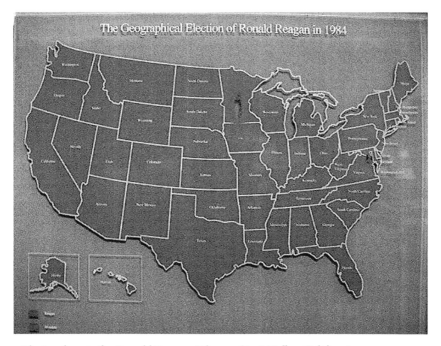

Electoral map, the Ronald Reagan Library, Simi Valley, California.

In the 1984 campaign, President Reagan overwhelmingly won re-election in a landslide against Democratic candidate and former Vice-President Walter Mondale. In that contest, Reagan won 49 states; Mondale, only Washington, D.C. and his home state of Minnesota (the Electoral College count was 525 to 13). In the electoral map displayed in the exhibit, there is a mostly-red state in the middle of the map: Minnesota (this was at a time when Republican states were blue and Democratic red). Unlike artifacts and documents, this map was not in a case, but printed on Plexiglas, where people could touch it. And they did.

So many had, in fact, touched that part of the map – Minnesota – so many had been astonished, surprised, happy, sad, saying to their companions, "Hey, look at this" – that they wore off a patch color. Those visitors were drawn in, had a visceral reaction, and were taught something. I'm sure they were inspired to read more, explore more, find out more about President Reagan, or that election, or U.S. history in general. I had that reaction before I even realized that the color had been worn off.

That experience, seeing people around me do the same thing, showed me I was on the right track and that I had a book in there somewhere.

AFTER PAYING ADMISSION (AND IN MOST PRESIDENTIAL museums, walking past or through the gift shop) visitors view the orientation films, which vary from ten (Carter) to twenty-eight minutes (Nixon); most are under twenty. You might think that planners would take this opportunity to present a full-throated defense of the president, getting in front of controversies to pre-address common questions. Instead, most films, while very positive, aim for a broad overview in their presentation of the life and administration, preparing visitors to tour the museum.

The permanent exhibits tend to have several things in common: an "origin story" relating a president's early life to future achievements ("he saved seventy-seven people from drowning, and later saved the world from Communism"); recreated rooms, including more than just the Oval Office; downplay or erasure of controversy (Monica Lewinsky = the "Republican Fight for Power"); over-emphasis on dubious, spun, or plain inaccurate accomplishments (see "Communism" above); and an area, whose size varies widely among the museums, about the First Lady.

The way a presidential museum commemorates and honors a First Lady depends on several factors, the second-most important being the individual woman's approach to the office. The most important is the assumption of curators that museum visitors are primarily interested – when it comes to the First Ladies – in fancy garments and interior design and what it's like to live and give parties and welcome guests to the White House.

Each of their terms was unique, but society, custom – and even some of their husbands – limited their roles to within a few archetypes. While several broke out to forge new paths for themselves, with one exception (Eleanor Roosevelt) the libraries had traditionally limited these exhibits to "Life in the White House," "State Dinners," "Fashion," and, less often, the policy issue (usually one) most associated with that particular First Lady.

First Lady exhibit gallery, the Lyndon Baines Johnson Library, Austin, Texas.

Perhaps if the earlier exhibits on these remarkable women had reflected the same depth of examination as the multitude of those about their husbands, the focus on clothing and entertaining wouldn't be so jarring to today's audiences.

First Lady exhibit gallery, the Dwight Eisenhower Library, Abilene, Kansas.

Over time, the exhibits changed from self-conscious attempts to make room for a first lady among the large exhibits about her husband to straightforward assessments of the real contributions they make to the administration and the country. As those appraisals have become more serious, away from dresses and china and towards addressing literacy and visiting China – the exhibits have, oddly, decreased in size.

First Lady alcove, the William Clinton Library, Little Rock, Arkansas.

Single exhibit case focusing on personal items related to Hillary Clinton,
the William Clinton Library, Little Rock, Arkansas.

The First Lady with the least square footage/display space allotted to her is Hillary Clinton. After the Clinton Library opened in 2004, some joked this was because she would soon have plenty of space in her own.

About half of the museums recreate the Oval Office and a few others have built partial replicas, or exhibits that suggest the room. I've been to the northwest door of the Oval Office in the West Wing three times; when you walk into that room in a presidential museum (most allow you to travel a few feet in, and two even to walk around and sit down at the desk, for a souvenir photo) the ones that have been staged as near-complete replicas do evoke the "real" one quite well.

The Truman Library was the first to offer an Oval Office replica. Offering a look at where the president works, it was in line with his desire to focus on himself, but to create a "Museum of the Presidency."

Lyndon Johnson also built a replica of the Oval Office in his library. What made his different is that he didn't put it in the museum, in the public area. He made his personal office on the top floor of the library a replica of his presidential office in the White House.

The architect and others were concerned about how this might make the former president look – as if he couldn't give up the trappings of the presidency. Had Johnson lived longer (he died four years after leaving office, and less than two years after opening the library) this might have become a problem. His replica is now part of the public exhibit.

Oval Office, the Lyndon Johnson Library, Austin, Texas.

For some museums, giving visitors the thrill of viewing such an exclusive place – even a copy of a place 2,700 miles away from the original, isn't enough. The experienced must be enhanced. With "facts." For example, docents at the Reagan Library, while standing at the door to the museum's replica of the Oval Office, tell us that President Reagan had such respect for the office of president, and the Oval Office specifically, that he never entered that room in the West Wing without wearing a coat and tie – even though there is photographic evidence that this is not true.

Until the Clinton Library's Oval Office replica, most libraries that featured them placed large backdrops of the White House grounds behind the windows to give the illusion of being in the West Wing.

The Clinton replica was built directly across from exterior windows in the building, allowing natural light to come in. The new George W. Bush Library took this a few steps further, placing its replica on an exterior wall; visitors may not only see it from the outside, they may walk along a replica of the colonnade that adjoins the office, and enjoy the "Texas Rose Garden" built to complement the effect.

While about half of the museums do have some sort of Oval Office replica, more have reproductions of other rooms, such as Herbert Hoover's Waldorf Astoria Hotel suite; George Bush's Camp David office; Nixon's Lincoln Sitting Room; Attorney General Robert Kennedy's Department of Justice office; and the White House Cabinet Room.

An Oval Office replica can be exciting, but including these less-well-known places, where presidents make decisions and history happens, offers a more complete look at the job and the president.

Viewing and interacting with the exhibits in presidential museums, in person, is different from looking at scans, photographs and film clips online (even though, because of conservation and cost, most of the museums only display high-quality document facsimiles, and not originals). The items, the subject matter, and their relevance and importance not only to history but to us today imbue them with a sense of excitement and urgency you cannot get at a distance. In fact, this emotional connection makes it all the more difficult to encounter an exhibit that's easily debunked, or clearly omits salient information; it's all the more dispiriting.

Seeing these items in person in a display is different, for that matter, from viewing the real documents and artifacts while researching in the libraries. I have been thrilled to come across handwritten notes between two presidents and other historical documents that somehow missed the preservationist's review.

But opening a folder in a research room, one does not have the benefit of the curator's expertise, pairing pages with images, explanatory text with illustrative film clips, within a unified vision.

Perhaps the best way to display such items and records is in context: rather than in a simple glass case, why not a re-created room, where visitors feel immersed in what was happening and what it looked – and, perhaps, a bit, felt – like to be there? Such physical context helps visitors to understand the items and their significance.

The trend towards opening up the replica rooms for explanation, souvenir photos, and "selfies" suggests greater opportunities to incorporate more records and objects (and even facsimiles) into the visitor experience.

OTHER THAN THE MUSEUM AT THE FORMER TEXAS SCHOOL Book Depository, the only permanent museum exhibits in the United States that cover the assassination of John F. Kennedy are those at the Kennedy and Johnson libraries. They are very different from one another.

The Kennedy Library has made a point not to commemorate, or even examine, President Kennedy's death. However, near the end of the permanent exhibit is a small area about November 22, 1963. It is austere and solemn; the date is the only exhibit or caption text.

The short, dark corridor has a lowered ceiling. There are five small television screens showing news coverage of the weekend (with no footage of the assassination). Visitors exit through a small, well-lit rotunda commemorating President Kennedy's lasting legacy, showcasing places around the world dedicated to him. Past the rotunda is a warm, wood-paneled corridor that invites visitors to explore, in detail, the Kennedy Legacy, using items in drawers, shelves, and on monitors.

Leaving this corridor, visitors enter a glass pavilion, which, upon entering the building, had appeared to be a dark box, but from within is a beautiful space full of light and hope, with a commanding view of the sky, the harbor and Boston. The effect is dramatic.

The permanent exhibit at the Johnson museum includes a section on President Kennedy's assassination, and contains the perspectives of both Lyndon and Lady Bird Johnson (whose audio recollection, recorded a few days later, plays as visitors enter the gallery).

Naturally, the exhibit marks the tragedy as a transition from Johnson's political career up until 1963 to his presidency. But the difference, in size, scope, content and tenor, from the exhibit at the Kennedy Library, is interesting, as it covers much more about what happened that day in Dallas than does the library dedicated to the president who was assassinated.

WE'RE TAKING IT ON FAITH THAT WHAT WE SEE, HEAR, AND read in these exhibits is an accounting of what happened – fair, accurate and complete. Otherwise, what's the point – particularly after having traveled thousands of miles to visit the museum?

One of the benchmarks I use in evaluating a presidential library museum is to examine a well-known controversy or scandal associated with the president. How is it described, and how completely? From whose point of view is the story told? What artifacts, records and audiovisuals are used to present the issue? Is more than one perspective offered? What conclusions would a reasonable person – knowing nothing more about the subject than this exhibit – draw after viewing it?

If the controversial exhibits (that is, any that exist) cannot handle difficult subjects fairly, the celebratory ones are likely to be...enhanced. An important factor is whether or not the issue even is included; depending upon its importance and level of public awareness, it might be that those who created the exhibit would prefer we not know or think about it at all. As my research at the museums and in the archives, reading the records, developed, three distinct approaches to controversies appeared:

1. Deal with it fairly and fearlessly (the least common).

The Ford museum's Vietnam exhibit contains a powerful artifact: the staircase from the roof of the U.S. Embassy in Saigon. The images of choppers lifting fleeing Foreign Service personnel from the about-to-be-overrun embassy are iconic, and not at all positive for the United States, nor for the Ford Administration. In a meeting during the design process for this new exhibit, others, including former Secretary of State Henry Kissinger, counseled President Ford not to include evidence of defeat in his museum. Ford overruled them, insisting it be part of the exhibit, slapping his hand on the table and saying, "But it's what happened."

Granted, one may argue that in relation to Vietnam, President Ford had the least responsibility of all the presidents – and therefore, it would be easier for his museum to deal with the subject. This point of view is sharpened if one notes that the library for the president most responsible for Vietnam, Lyndon Johnson, does not deal forthrightly with the issue.

The Ford museum deserves credit for dealing with controversy in a straightforward (if not comprehensive) way, as it does with Watergate (another issue for which Ford was not to blame, and about which his exhibit is more balanced than that of the president responsible for it).

The Banning exhibit at the Truman museum displays a letter and Purple Heart that President Truman kept in his desk for two decades, perhaps as a reminder of the grave responsibilities of his office and the consequences of his decisions. The letter is from the father of a soldier killed in Korea, returning the Purple Heart that had been presented posthumously. Holding Truman responsible for his son's death, the understandably upset father returns the medal as a "trophy," writing that he wished the president's daughter Margaret had been able to suffer the same fate. For years, Truman kept the letter and medal in his desk.

It's difficult to imagine a modern president, or a modern presidential library director (though a federal employee, more and more are recruited and vetted by the respective library's private political foundation and charged with the task of "enhancing" the president's standing and "reinterpreting" his place in history) wanting to include this in an exhibit "celebrating" the presidency.

2. Appear to "deal" with it, but actually spin it in the best possible way (the most common).

The Hoover museum handles the Great Depression with an imaginative panel explaining all of the great things the president did to end the Great Depression – including summoning "industrialists to the White House" and winning commitments from the nation's utilities for new construction and repairs – and that "[p]raise for the president's intervention was widespread."

Contrary to critics who years ago predicted otherwise, the Clinton museum does include Monica Lewinsky, and says the president was wrong – but the exhibit is titled "The Fight for Power." It casts the impeachment more as a Republican plot, and not a cautionary tale about his personal behavior. The alcove text includes such subtitles as "A New Culture of Confrontation" and "The Politics of Persecution."

The George W. Bush museum "deals with" the fact that the president approved the torture of detainees by explaining how important it was for the president to have made this important decision – and then by letting Bush off of the hook for his important decision.

In a video, former Secretary of State Condoleezza Rice explains that the president asked the Central Intelligence Agency if torture was necessary and the Department of Justice if it was legal; those two "yes" answers were all the president needed, and he gave the order. As the video progresses, President Bush makes the astonishing (and soundly disproven) assertion that "there can be no debate" that the torture of detainees resulted in "keeping America safe."

The George W. Bush museum also "deals with" the fact that Saddam Hussein had no weapons of mass destruction nor had active methods or means of producing weapons of mass destruction by ignoring that fact and pretending instead that he had them, or was just about to get them. Among the many examples of misleading exhibit text, one panel explains that inspections after the invasion of Iraq "confirmed that Saddam Hussein had the capacity to resume production of WMD."

The Johnson museum renovated their permanent exhibit in 2012, and the room that discusses Vietnam attempts to revise public opinion about Johnson's role in the conflict. A more thorough examination of this particular exhibit will help to illustrate the problems not only of having private political foundations write the history in museums run by (and, therefore, approved by) a federal agency, but of having federally-run presidential museums at all.

Viewing the exhibit, it's as if no time at all has passed. Not in the sense of "boy, this takes me back" or "wow, the Sixties seem like only yesterday." In the sense of whomever created the exhibit ignored much, if not all, of the information that has come to light, and the history that has been written, since the end of the Johnson Administration about this incredibly polarizing conflict.

History that, for the most part, was written from records housed in the Johnson Library. The exhibit creators had access to those records – even more access than do historians – as well as to that history. It does not appear, however, that they availed themselves of all of that information; if they did, it appears they decided that it would be better to stick to a legacy-rescuing narrative rather than provide the public with a full and fair accounting of what actually happened.

In the time-stands-still Vietnam exhibit at the LBJ Library, the Second Gulf of Tonkin incident actually happened (which, in reality, it did not). The Vietnamese presidential election of 1967 was "free and fair" (which, in reality, it was not). And Lyndon Johnson didn't really escalate the war; he didn't really lose the war; and the war didn't really defeat him.

The Johnson Foundation, sponsor of the exhibit, blames his predecessors, the South Vietnamese, his advisors, and the threat of war.

> When he became President, Lyndon Johnson inherited a war already going badly in a tiny nation with a fragile government. The President of South Vietnam was assassinated on November 2, 1963, and a succession of new governments were unstable and corrupt. Amid conflicting advice, President Johnson tried to find a middle way—to win the war without drawing in Communist China or the Soviet Union, or to avoid defeat long enough to negotiate a peace with North Vietnam.

Exhibit panel, Vietnam, the Lyndon Johnson Library, Austin, Texas.

The exhibit provides partial information about events, leaving out what has come to light since, including how Johnson used false information about the Gulf of Tonkin "incidents" as a pretext for escalation despite his assurances to the American people to the contrary.

Rolling Thunder was the largest, longest aerial bombardment campaign in U.S. history, and is generally regarded as a failure in many ways. Airpower expert, retired Air Force Colonel Dennis M. Drew, has described it as having "failed to persuade the North Vietnamese and… failed to destroy their ability to prosecute their war in South Vietnam."

The exhibit suggests that the bombing halts were good-faith efforts to encourage negotiations, while it leaves out any real examination of the bombings; according to the foundation, these were good efforts that were thwarted by the North Vietnamese, who used the lulls to increase their attacks. Message: Johnson = Good; Enemy = Bad.

The crafty use of "Quagmire" in another panel – an apt description for what Johnson created, not inherited, in Vietnam – belies the following text's actual message, which, once again is Johnson = Good; Enemy = Bad. People who view this without the benefit of knowing what actually happened come away with very different views from those who do.

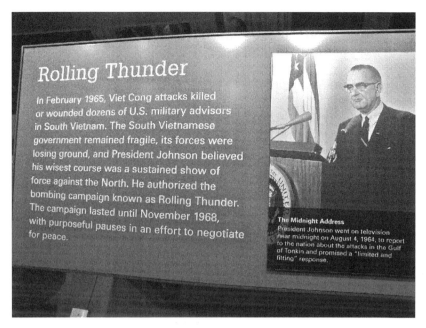

Exhibit panel, Vietnam, the Lyndon Johnson Library, Austin, Texas.

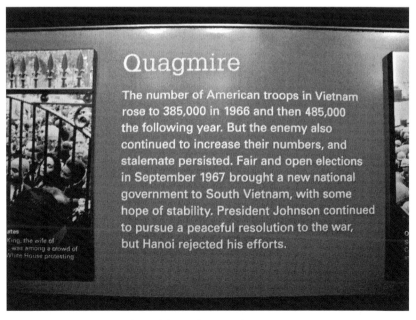

Exhibit panel, Vietnam, the Lyndon Johnson Library, Austin, Texas.

3. Deal with it by not dealing with it (rare, and therefore notable).

One of the most difficult challenges/controversies/scandals faced by President Reagan during his two terms was Iran-Contra (arguably, it was the most important scandal).

Even though others have tried for years to spin, explain or even excuse what occurred, for decades – through multiple revisions – the Reagan Library museum famously handled the issue for twenty years simply by ignoring it completely.

As a result of its most recent (of many) exhibit renovations, however, the Reagan museum does (for now, at least) include a small display about the scandal, ostensibly portraying the "facts" while actually downplaying the most serious issues uncovered by the Tower Commission, and the long-term consequences of the scandal.

It is literally the least they could do in order to claim that the Reagan Library museum no longer ignores the scandal that threatened to bring down his presidency; it is no more than that, and it all but acquits the president of the worst aspects of the crimes.

Of all the elections it has been reported that Lyndon Johnson bought and/or stole outright (including the presidency of the Little Congress, the informal organization of Congressional staffers), none was so important to his political career and its ultimate conclusion as was his second run for the United States Senate, in 1948.

It is a pivotal chapter in Johnson's life. Without winning (rather, buying/stealing) this election, his political career likely would have ended. Yet two small panels – one with the simple text, "November 2, 1948: Johnson wins his first election to the U.S. Senate," one a campaign poster, without comment – comprise the entirety of the discussion of this important campaign in the Johnson museum.

There are many other controversies that are handled forthrightly, spun, or not even mentioned, in presidential museums (including the Nixon Library's Watergate exhibit, which is examined later in this chapter), from mistresses to indictments, policy decisions, personal failings and minor indiscretions.

The preceding are simply some of the more prominent, and illustrative, examples in our system of federally-operated "history" museums. The system we pay for, and explicitly endorse, through our tax dollars.

"WAR CAN BE A HELL OF AN EXCITING PLACE, AND WE NEED TO give visitors that experience," Douglas Menarchik, then director of the George Bush Library in College Station, Texas, told me in his office in 2003. "The sounds, the sights...it needs more 'sizzle.' We're not doing a good enough job of replicating what it's like to be there. But we will."

I had begun the interview by telling him how disappointed I was in the permanent exhibit, but not because I thought it wasn't "exciting" enough. Going through the 17,000 square feet of the museum earlier in the day, I was struck by how prominent a position the First Gulf War had been given – overwhelmingly so. Naval pilot, oilman, congressman, Senate candidate, ambassador to the United Nations, chairman of the Republican National Committee, Chief of the U.S. Liaison Office to the People's Republic of China, director of Central Intelligence, businessman, professor, vice-president, president – not to mention son of prominent parents, husband and father – it seemed that, together, all of these things were not as important as those months in 1990 and 1991 when the U.S. led a coalition to oust Saddam from Kuwait. I was disappointed.

I was disappointed that not only did this relatively minor chapter in an extraordinary life take over the entire exhibit space with its size, it also took over the narrative of his presidency. I was disappointed that the library chose to emphasize a reaction to events (and, given his life story, a relatively minor one at that) over telling a more thorough story about George Bush's life and presidency and his service to this country.

I wanted to tell Menarchik all of these things – and more – but all I got out was "I was disappointed in the permanent exhibit-" before he cut me off, told me how exciting war could be, and promised to do a better job of relating it in the upcoming $10 million renovation that would mark the tenth anniversary of the library's dedication.

The new exhibit, opened in 2007, probably is nothing like being in war: the recordings of bomb sounds, the flashing light bulbs, the television monitors looping CNN reports, the climate-controlled, professionally-lit tents with sandbags and mannequins and plastic-coated caption signs explaining the greatness of the Coalition and the hardships endured by the troops. Hardships we could almost experience, ourselves, thanks to the new and improved *War's A Hell Of An Exciting Place.*

The original George Bush Library permanent exhibit, which ran from the time the library opened in 1997 through the 2007 renovation, contained several displays of presidential campaign electoral maps: 1976, when Bush was chairman of the Republican National Committee; 1980 and 1984, when he was a successful vice-presidential candidate; and 1988, when he ran for, and won, the presidency. These maps illustrate what can be (or what used to be) considerably lopsided contests.

The original exhibit continued, featuring his four years as president and – overwhelmingly the largest part of the exhibit – the First Gulf War. As visitors left the permanent exhibit, almost as an afterthought, there was a small display about the 1992 campaign, which Bush lost, in a three-way race, to Bill Clinton. Because of the flow of the ramp, and the walls, and the exit signs, one's attention was drawn forward, and one had to know to turn 180 degrees at the end of the ramp to see the display, or else walk out of the museum unaware of its existence.

The text described the president's high approval ratings and a "brisk" and "robust" economy, temporarily slowed by what was characterized as a "mild recession" lasting only a few months at the end of 1991 and the beginning of 1992. It informed us that the president's "opponents exploited the theme that America was stalled" and that despite a "last minute Bush/Quayle surge in the polls, Clinton/Gore won."

1997 exhibit, Campaign '92, the George Bush Library, College Station, Texas.

Note the absence of an electoral map. Or any indication of the popular or electoral vote totals. This is how presidential foundations – and, because they accept and operate them on our behalf, NARA – design "history" exhibits: get skewed editorial language in and inconvenient facts out. And if the graphics aren't laudatory, they don't make the cut.

When I saw this, I was disappointed. The 1992 election was unique in our modern history, not least because Clinton won with only 43% of the vote, the fourth-lowest of any presidential election winner. In addition, Ross Perot garnered 19% (the most ever for a third-party candidate, even after quitting, and then rejoining, the campaign). President Bush lost re-election despite having earlier earned overwhelming approval ratings from his initiation of the Gulf War. Of all the political campaigns with which George H.W. Bush was involved to examine in detail in the George H.W. Bush Library, I thought that this should have been the one.

In 2003, I told this to Menarchik (who had been Vice-President Bush's military attaché). He was planning the renovation that would take place in 2007, and I urged him to consider adding a 1992 map, for the reasons above. When I asked him why the first exhibit didn't include this, or examine the campaign in any great detail – particularly since it covered the 1976, 1980, 1984 and 1988 elections – he said, "Well, our guy lost."

[Note to Members of Congress and NARA officials, who have been asleep at the presidential library reform switch for the last thirty-nine years: how about from now on we don't allow anyone who thinks of a former president as "their guy" to have anything to do with running a government presidential archive or designing a government-run exhibit on that president's life?]

Defensively reacting to my comments about some of the other editorial and curatorial choices in the museum, Menarchik had earlier offered his opinion about what likely would or wouldn't be included at the as-yet-unopened Clinton Library (at that point, before the library's 2004 dedication, the most common question asked of me by officials associated with Republican presidential libraries – including Menarchik – when discussing what was left out of their museums was, "Well, will Clinton have the Blue Dress?)."

To emphasize my point about the electoral maps, I asked Menarchik, "Do you want Bill Clinton to have the last word on the 1992 campaign?" He seemed surprised and intrigued, and said that he would think about it. Imagine my own surprise, then, when four and half years later I toured the renovated permanent exhibit and, approaching the exit, saw this:

2007 exhibit, Campaign '92, the George Bush Library, College Station, Texas.

An electoral map of the 1992 presidential campaign, complete with popular and electoral vote totals and the inclusion of the impact of the third-party candidate in the race.

A sensitivity to electoral maps may be familial. Given the contentiousness of the 2000 presidential election and the Bush Campaign's method of resolving it, perhaps it is understandable that the George W. Bush museum's electoral map takes a defensive and unique approach, highlighting the counties won instead of the popular vote total.

As I found out with the Reagan electoral map at the start of my research, much of the "history" in presidential library museums is told through the use of signals and symbols, headlines and graphics and "big picture" items, to try and grab increasingly-distracted and time-crunched visitors, hoping to, at the very least, reinforce the most positive and hide the most negative stereotypes of their respective presidents. Electoral maps, included or removed, are good examples of this practice.

Sometimes, the museum at a presidential library can spin an important part of a president's story to make it sound better, or at least less controversial. At the William Jefferson Clinton Library, Monica Lewinsky is mentioned and the president admits to having acted wrongly, but the exhibit is called, "The Fight for Power" – claiming that the impeachment process was nothing more than Republicans doing what they could not do at the ballot box. Sometimes, the museum at a presidential library can omit an important part of a president's story as if it had never happened. For the first twenty-one years of the Ronald Reagan Library, Iran-Contra was never mentioned. Sometimes, the museum at a presidential library can be wholly inaccurate. The original Watergate exhibit at the Richard Nixon Library used various means – other than the truth – to explain away what the president did (and what the president knew and when he knew it).

And then, at some libraries, there are just plain silly things. For example, at the George Bush Library, near the end of several rooms of exhibits on the First Gulf War, are a series of original framed newspaper front pages. In a world of interactive exhibits, holograms and digital immersion, this is an "old-fashioned" device (and one that I like). It harkens back to a time when the news seemed more straightforward, reported honestly and directly – something we could rely on for accuracy as well as simplicity (or so we thought).

Here's the silly part: when I first visited the library, I was rather surprised to note what appears to be a hint of political censorship (or maybe just partisan prickliness or inadvertent commentary?) in the newspaper section of the exhibit.

There are at least seven front pages from the Washington Times, a conservative newspaper that was very supportive of the war, as well as those from the Houston Chronicle, the Houston Post, the Fort-Worth Star-Telegram, and USA Today. All of those papers, too, had been supportive of the war and of the president generally. Nothing wrong with that, as far as it goes (questions of balance arise, but that's not the point here).

At the end, I came to a newspaper that at first, I couldn't identify; it looked familiar, but it was missing its nameplate. This was odd, for several reasons: first, it didn't look as if the paper had been ripped or otherwise damaged – the nameplate had been removed cleanly. Second, the paper wasn't so old or rare that, given a less-than-ideal partial front page that didn't match the rest (every one of the other newspaper front pages were completely intact broadsheet formats) they couldn't find an alternate, complete version.

But third – and this is the most important – from the way it and all of the others were mounted and framed, one could imagine that the nameplate was removed after being put into the frame, and probably even after being hung in the exhibit; if the decision to remove it had been made earlier, it likely wouldn't have been framed like that, or perhaps not even included in the exhibit, taking up space that could have been used for another, complete paper.

So why do this? Then I looked closely at the article bylines, and discovered that this was not one of the other newspapers that continually had been laudatory of the president: it was the Washington Post.

It seems quite possible that at some point, after the exhibit was ready and complete, someone objected to including that newspaper – *that* newspaper! – but it was too late to do anything other than take it down, cut off the nameplate, and put it back up. Most people wouldn't know.

Warts and all? Perhaps there are some warts that cannot be tolerated.

THE INORDINATE EMPHASIS THE GEORGE BUSH LIBRARY places on the First Gulf War not only detracts from any thorough examination of his term as president, it inappropriately displaces his impressive life prior to his election.

The library does cover those areas, but not as extensively as it does the relatively short period of time between Iraq's invasion of Kuwait and its subsequent expelling by multinational forces.

This "whole-life" approach, documenting and celebrating not just the term(s) in office, is followed by most presidential libraries, save for the William J. Clinton and George W. Bush. With the exception of three small memorabilia cases on a second floor balcony, the Clinton Library focuses exclusively on his two presidential terms; the George W. Bush Library devotes even more exhibit space to his now six-year-long post-presidency than to his *entire life* before the 2000 campaign. Perhaps more than the events and subjects that are celebrated in these museums, the areas of a president's life that are ignored demonstrate the importance to the foundations that use these exhibits to advance their agendas of tending the legacy and carefully controlling the message.

The three greatest crises that George W. Bush faced were, arguably: the September 11th attacks/Afghan War/Iraq War/War on Terror (he combines & conflates these, so I will, too); Hurricane Katrina; and the Financial Crisis. In his library in Dallas, Texas, a significant amount of square footage is devoted to that first crisis (or series of forcibly-related crises). A significant amount. More than to any other issue, theme or event (really, more than to any two or three other issues combined).

Like his father did in his own library, George W. Bush chose a single idea to overwhelm both the specific exhibit space and the general visitor experience. And, like his father, war – and Iraq – are prominent. Unlike the father, though, the son does not have a broad, deep pre-presidential career to exhibit, and so this is not as much of a disappointment in Dallas as it was and is in College Station. Even so, it is, I believe, a mistake – just as it is at his father's library.

The planners of the George W. Bush Library took much of the contemporaneous marketing of the president – "I'm the Decider," "Commander-in-Chief," "I'm a Wartime President," etc. – injected it with the same super-patriotic motifs and imagery as every staged photo-op and *Let's Use the Military As Backdrop* speeches we were presented with over eight years and pumped up…well, just about everything. From the giant, curved panoramic video screen and starkly-labeled panels to startlingly inaccurate and politicized exhibit text to the oversized footprint given it, this combination-of-crises takes over the library.

The other two major crises? Not so much. Together, they get a total of twelve linear feet, in one combined panel/reader rail.

Complete exhibit on both Hurricane Katrina & the Financial Crisis, the George W. Bush Library, Dallas, Texas.

That's it. That's the entire exhibit, for both. Twelve feet. For one of the worst natural disasters our country has ever faced, and the worst financial crisis since the Great Depression. For two of the three issues that, for most, defined the Bush Administration.

It appears, from the…let's call it "content"…that explains the issues and how and why the president acted as he did, the designers believed they had the best case to make with war. Disaster response? Too difficult to avoid blame. Financial collapse? Too complicated to explain. War? Patriotic, multi-media and interactive-display friendly, and utterly spinnable: we can just say we won, and not bother about the facts, nor what's happened since.

And yet, even though they're shoehorned in as afterthoughts, almost at the exit, the designers found ways to spin these two crises. In the small space allotted to Katrina and the Financial Crisis, blame is either nonexistent (no one at the federal level, apparently, was responsible for the failure of disaster response) or directed towards vague "overseas capital" and "financial institutions" and "investors" and "panic." But no mention of "regulators" or "government officials" or "the Decider in Chief" as holding any responsibility whatsoever. Or even playing a role.

Both of these crises, along with "Threat of Saddam Hussein" and "The Surge" are explored in what the Bush Library calls its "Decision Points Theater." After being "briefed" on a crisis and having access to produced video bits of actors playing military officers, government officials and other "advisors" visitors are asked to decide on how to handle the crisis by voting. If the crowd votes down the path the president chose, he appears on the screen to explain why they're wrong (The Daily Show with Jon Stewart dubbed this "Disasterpiece Theater"). The presentation includes real-time displays of the audience's second-by-second evaluation of the advice being presented, much like a focus group.

YOU ENTER THE SEMI-CIRCULAR THEATER AND SELECT A seat. Directly in front of you is a touch screen. At the front of the room is a large, curved screen. The presentation begins, and at once you're astonished. At the slickness of the look of it (that's not a compliment). At the growing unseemliness of it. At the commercial feeling of the whole thing (neither are those). You might not be surprised if someone on the screen reached for a brand-name cola, pointing the logo directly at the camera.

This isn't history, and it's not education. It's a sales pitch. It's a higher-tech version of the free-weekend-at-the-resort, you-too-can-own-a-timeshare lecture. Only instead of Mort and Heather, Condo Sales Associates, we get Andy and Josh, two former White House Chiefs of Staff. And later, the president himself. Which is sort of unprecedented.

The Truman Library Oval Office replica exhibit includes audio of Truman talking about the famous room, recorded for that purpose. Presidents Carter and Nixon videotaped answers to questions that visitors to their libraries could "ask" them as part of exhibits.

President Clinton recorded the narration (ad-libbing late one evening while walking through the exhibit) for the audio tour at his library.

A few other presidential libraries feature snippets of audio and video that their respective presidents produced for exhibits. However, by far the majority of media that visitors can see and hear in a presidential library are contemporaneous clips from their time in office.

The George W. Bush Library is different; the former president appears in longer produced segments (and there is also far more archival footage of him) than any other library. For someone who has spent a lot of time in these institutions, it's a noticeable difference. Earlier presidents have made grand attempts at explaining, spinning and even rewriting history – but in subtler ways, and through third-person exhibit text or by using surrogates; they leave the selling to others.

Decision Points Theater main screen, the George W. Bush Library, Dallas, Texas.

Here, Bush makes his own case strongly, though not unabashedly, as the expensive, aggressive presentation would lead you to believe he might. In fact, throughout the museum, there is, perhaps not surprisingly, a consistent undercurrent of proactive defensiveness and emotion, nowhere more so than when the president speaks. And he does this nowhere more clearly than in the Decision Points Theater. The fact that he appears in order to defend himself, particularly after asking you what you would have done in his shoes, is out of the ordinary. For several years now, these "You Decide" exhibits have been very popular with presidential libraries, but the others use anonymous narrators, and are significantly more modest than the Bush Library theater.

At their core, they all share this notion: that you can present, within the span of a few minutes, information about some of the most important decisions a president has had to make, and museum visitors will be able to make up their own minds about what they would have done.

Or, with hindsight, what the president should have done...which, of course, is one of its flaws: while we may not have the same information the president had when he made the decision – it will be a hundred years before all of the documents are released – we know how it all turned out, which must inform our own present-day decision-making process. In any case, if you end up disagreeing with the president, many of these offer "counter-factuals" – what would have happened had we gone with your idea.

Most of these gently press the belief that the president was right; none, other than the Bush Library, have the president himself come out to explain, in detail, why.

In addition to the Clinton and Ford Cabinet Rooms discussed earlier, the Johnson Library also has a decision exhibit, but not in a theater or room replica; visitors use touch screen tables within the Foreign Affairs room. In a slight twist from the norm, instead of asking you what you would have done, within the scenario you are an advisor, and are asked to make a recommendation to the president.

The Bush Library's version stands alone. The breathless pace of the presentation is quite disconcerting in the room, with a clock counting down. The constant interruptions of "breaking news" and what I believe to be unsuccessful attempts at verisimilitude (actors playing the roles of the advisors). And the focus-group aspect, which is the most odd.

During the briefings – each time you select a kind of advisor (Pentagon, White House, military, etc.) – you get two experts, each opposed to the other. While you are listening, you are asked to move sliders up and down as you agree or disagree with the advice you are receiving. As the Decider, you have to decide between conflicting pieces of advice.

On the main screen, the aggregate scores of how others are agreeing or disagreeing are displayed in real-time, showing which way the audience is leaning as the time to make the decision rapidly approaches.

Instant polling. Instant deciding. Because, when all is said and done (and the sooner, the better), it's about your gut, isn't it?

The Herbert Hoover Presidential Library couldn't possibly have a Great Depression: Decision Points Theater, for one simple reason (other than the technological limits): the library opened thirty-three years after the crash of 1929, and so the history of that era already had been written. Hoover's rejection of significant government intervention, and the consequences of inaction, already had become the conventional wisdom, known to everyone who would visit the Hoover museum.

Had the former president appeared on a screen defensively explaining that such actions "just weren't taken in those days" and that he had had "faith in free markets" it would have made him a laughingstock. It is only the brief time between George W. Bush's actions on Iraq and the Surge – or, in the case of Katrina and the Financial Crisis, his failure to act – and the opening of his library that allowed him to star in the Decision Theater exhibit. By getting a jump on history before others could write it, and by using the same imagery-rich, substance-free, governing-as-campaigning tactics as when we was in office, only partisans and jaded journalists were able to recognize this for the decision experience it is: an exercise in deciding to suspend one's disbelief.

A DEMOCRATIC PLOT TO MAKE SPEAKER ALBERT PRESIDENT. That's how Richard Nixon wanted you to see Watergate when you viewed the exhibit he co-wrote on the scandal that led to his resignation.

Other presidents have been involved in many aspects of their libraries, but perhaps none had such a direct role in the development of an exhibit than did Nixon with the original one on Watergate. And unlike most other presidential museums, which are renovated about every five to ten years, this one lasted for seventeen. Once the library became part of the federal system administered by NARA, the new director removed the exhibit. The saga of that removal, and its replacement (and the controversy that followed) lasted twice as long as Watergate, and ended up the same way: with the leader resigning. A big difference, though, is that the first federal director of the Nixon Library, Dr. Timothy Naftali, resigned not after wrongdoing, but after having succeeded. Among many other accomplishments, Naftali did the seemingly impossible: he told, within the Nixon Library, an accurate and complete story about the Nixon Administration. And he did so against great odds, and in spite of enormous pressure from the Nixon Foundation, former Nixon Administration officials, and even some of his National Archives colleagues and supervisors.

The fallout from Naftali's successful installation of the renovated Watergate exhibit and his subsequent resignation had an impact greater than just correcting one important story. It raised serious questions about NARA's ability to administer a nonpartisan library according to the law. It left the Nixon Library without a director for more than three years. And it appears to have led not to the government asserting greater control over the library, its contents, and its programs, but instead to a deepening of the agency's appeasement of former presidents, their families, and their foundations. While Naftali's tenure demonstrated that carrying out the laws and regulations required of a presidential library director does not necessitate acquiescence to the political demands of presidents, their families, and their foundations, the circumstances surrounding his departure seems to have taught NARA that it does.

During the three years the Nixon Library was without a director, historians, journalists, scholars, and others expressed concern over how that gap allowed the partisan Nixon Foundation to reassert itself in the operation of the library, as well as in plans for renovating the exhibits. In addition, it was reported that the foundation interfered in NARA's process of hiring a new director, including vetoing at least one candidate selected by the agency, a widely-respected historian. To understand what is at stake, particularly in that library, a brief (and incomplete) review is in order. Here is how the Nixon Library became such a battleground for public history, government control of government organizations, and the role of political partisanship in a federally-run museum.

Like his immediate five predecessors, Nixon began planning his library during his time in office; upon resigning the presidency, his plan came to a halt (the story of that plan is examined at length in the next chapter). When he restarted planning for his library, he faced the challenge of finding a host for it. Several locations – including Duke University – rejected him.

One community offered the Nixon Foundation a site on which to build the library, which was the good news; the bad news was that the community is home to the most famous federal penitentiary in the country (insert your own unindicted co-conspirator joke here).

Nixon took sixteen years to find a location, and when finally he opened his library in 1990, he didn't deed it to the government, as every other president since Hoover had done.

Because of the Presidential Recordings and Materials Preservation Act of 1974, a law Congress passed to seize Nixon's records (and that prohibited their removal from the Washington, D.C. area) the private Richard Nixon Library and Birthplace archives only held pre- and post-presidential papers. For several years, Nixon, his family and his close associates were content to operate the private institution on their own, which probably worked out well for NARA; at the time, it was more of a shrine than any other presidential library, and the era of the modern, over-the-top, rhapsodic library had not yet begun.

Since soon after leaving office, Nixon and his estate waged years-long legal battles with the federal government over ownership of his papers, filing lawsuits and appeals challenging the taking of and the administration of access to his records. In 2000 the government settled one of the suits – over compensation for the seized records – for $18 million.

The Nixon was an anomaly among U.S. presidential libraries: it was private. It didn't hold any presidential papers. And it didn't have the cachet of the others: the approval and legitimacy conferred by being operated (and, not incidentally, funded) by the U.S. government.

In 2002, Nixon's daughters, Julie and Tricia, settled an intra-family dispute over a $19 million bequest to the Nixon Library from longtime friend and supporter Charles "Bebe" Rebozo. Even with that bequest, though, the private Nixon Library was struggling financially, and much of the foundation's time was spent fund-raising. In addition, they didn't have the presidential papers to draw scholars; the museum exhibits were widely criticized as factually inaccurate; and many of Nixon's – and the library's – supporters were aging. The future was not bright for the Nixon Library, nor for the family and their supporters. Not, at least, until one day in early 2004, when Congress dropped a surprise into their laps (well, it was a surprise to most, if not to the Nixon camp).

Members of Congress – particularly Rep. Thomas Davis (R-Virginia) – carrying water for the Nixon Foundation inserted a provision in an appropriations bill to repeal the part of the 1974 law that kept the Nixon materials in the Washington, D.C. area. The transfer of the materials to

Yorba Linda, California, though, was not to be accomplished overnight. And the process encountered significant – and valid – opposition.

Many had reasons to be concerned about allowing the materials that Congress had rightly seized from former President Nixon to be moved to the site of the private Nixon Library, for fear he would destroy and/or keep them locked away. NARA sought to ease those concerns by carrying out a formal – and public – negotiation process to bring the private library into the federal system.

A centerpiece of NARA's plan to put critics at ease was a major conference on Vietnam to be hosted at the Nixon Library. The event was supposed to showcase how their much-touted "public-private partnerships" could work between the (ostensibly nonpartisan) government and the (extremely-partisan) private foundation. It didn't go as planned.

John Taylor, executive director of the Nixon Library and Birthplace, claimed that due to low expected turnout, he decided to cancel the conference. Historians and others invited to be part of the event claimed that the foundation grew concerned about the way Nixon and the war would be portrayed. The New York Times quoted Thomas Blanton, director of the National Security Archive, as saying, "Taylor said that with the Vietnam conference, the library was going to turn over a new leaf. Well, it turned out to be a fig leaf."

That the cancellation of the conference confirmed the worst fears about the results of the transfer of Nixon's records cannot be overstated. NARA's assurances that bringing the Nixon Library into the federal system would be positive for all rang hollow. Here was the foundation asserting itself in the most-feared way it would: by distorting, hiding and rewriting history.

Nonetheless, NARA forged ahead – as the agency often does – not heeding the valid criticisms and concerns of stakeholders, who predicted trouble. One cause for cautious optimism was the surprising and welcome choice of Naftali as the first (federal employee) director of what would become the NARA-run library. A respected scholar and writer, with, as they say, no dog in the fight, the selection of Naftali to run a nonpartisan government research center, museum and public events space seemed a step in the right direction to many.

The law governing presidential libraries allows NARA to "consult" with a former president about the appointment of the first director of a presidential library; it does not mention the president's family, supporters, or library foundation officials. Before the Presidential Records Act (PRA) was enacted in 1978, presidents owned their records, and determined when and how to release them.

Under the act, the records belong to the people, and access is administered by the archivist. In order to gain support for the bill, its authors added a provision allowing presidents to withhold certain records for up to ten years (changed to twelve years before final passage) after leaving office.

To put presidents at ease with this new process, Congress included language in the bill permitting the archivist to consult with the president on the appointment of the first – and only the first – director of the library, because that individual would be administering the additional withholding period: "The Archivist is authorized to designate, after consultation with the former President, a director at each depository or facility, who shall be responsible for the care and preservation of such records."

However, for years, NARA granted former presidents and their representatives far more power over who is hired to direct the library than the law allows. Congress never intended to allow presidential library foundations, presidential family members to have ongoing "consultation" rights on the appointment of library directors, much less veto power over such appointments.

In the House Report accompanying the PRA, legislators made this clear:

> "The requirement that the Archivist consult with the former President about the appointment is included to allow the ex-President, as long as he is living, some voice regarding the person who is to administer the access restrictions of his Presidency, particularly during the 10-year maximum period of mandatory Presidential access restrictions. This is not authority for the former President to veto an appointment made or proposed by the Archivist, however."

Unfortunately, this has not prevented NARA from "consulting" presidential families and foundations; in some cases, NARA has allowed them to choose a new director. This means, of course, someone who will put the needs of the foundation, and their political and historical goals, above the needs of their employer – the people of the United States.

In the case of the first federal director of the Nixon Library, however, NARA knew that the selection of a Nixon partisan, openly supportive of the foundation, would spell disaster with stakeholders. Archivist Allen Weinstein's choice of Naftali was not only universally applauded, it had the added bonus – to start off the new relationship on a positive footing – of having already been recommended by John Taylor.

The Naftali appointment allowed the process to continue, but stakeholders were skeptical about the long-term prospects; their concerns turned out to have been warranted.

Even before he began his official tenure, Naftali made it clear that besides the successful transfer of records from College Park, Maryland to Yorba Linda, California, his main priority would be to remove and replace the "factually inaccurate" exhibits in the museum. First to go would be the most egregious: the exhibit on Watergate. That ultimately would take years, bring all of the predicted problems with the Nixon Foundation to a head, lead to Naftali's voluntary-though-pressured departure, and leave us in the situation we now face, with a new director approved by the foundation and family, after having rejected at least one other candidate whom the Archivist of the United States wished to appoint.

Naftali rightly saw his duty as not only to make a partisan shrine into a nonpartisan government facility, but to follow the law; specifically, the 1974 Presidential Recordings and Materials Preservation Act. That legislation required NARA to prioritize the release of "materials relevant to the understanding of Abuse of Governmental Power and Watergate" prior to the release of all other materials. Naftali was given a charge, and a law to abide by, and he expertly rose to the challenge.

Almost immediately, the Nixon Foundation began pushing back. They criticized Naftali to government officials, in private, and in public. When Naftali invited John Dean – whom the president and foundation had blamed for Watergate – to speak at the Nixon Library, the foundation campaigned against Naftali and NARA (at least, those in the agency who weren't cheering on the foundation).

One of the Nixon Foundation's biggest supporters was the NARA official who was supposed to be representing the government's – and the taxpayers' – interests: Sharon Fawcett, Assistant Archivist for Presidential Libraries. Unfortunately, she helped the foundation in many ways, pressuring Naftali to water down the new Watergate exhibit, weakening his position and strengthening the foundation's.

The foundation made considerable efforts – aided by some who, like Fawcett, should have been doing their jobs and supporting Naftali – to prevent the new Watergate exhibit from opening, at least in the form that Naftali planned: factually accurate. In that, the foundation failed.

In their larger scheme to get rid of Naftali, dominate the National Archives, and get their way on what "history" is displayed at the Nixon Library – all while having the U.S. taxpayers foot the bill – the Nixon Foundation did not fail. Naftali resigned, but only after his successful installation of the widely-acclaimed Watergate exhibit.

Naftali later revealed, in a talk at the Miller Center at the University of Virginia, that Sharon Fawcett and another presidential library director, R. Duke Blackwood (who had for years, inexplicably, served concurrently as both the federal head of the Reagan Library and the partisan director of the private Reagan Library Foundation), had told him in 2010 that the only way his Watergate exhibit would be installed and opened would be if Naftali resigned, to placate the Nixon Foundation. Naftali refused, and opened the exhibit as he planned in the spring of 2011.

Eight months later, Naftali left the library – which was then without a director for the next three years.

Finally, in late 2014, NARA announced the appointment of Michael Ellzey as the next director of the library. With no federal government experience, no training or credentials in history, archives, or museums – but with the enthusiastic support of the foundation – his hiring raised new questions. After the troubled history of the library when it had been in private hands, the significant problems Naftali encountered, and the three years that had lapsed, this appointment was seen by stakeholders as crucial: as indicative of which "side" the Archives would come down on: Naftali's vision – supported by the law – of a rigorously nonpartisan federal institution or the appeasement of the private foundation and an inaccurate partisan shrine; apparently, the latter won.

In fact, in a radio interview shortly after he began working at the library, Ellzey said that the Archivist Ferriero had charged him with improving relations with the foundation. He claimed that his first allegiance was to the National Archives, but that his second was "to do whatever I need to do that is consistent with the mission of the archivist in building a relationship with the foundation."

Could Naftali have done a better job in handling relations with the foundation? I don't think that's the question. The issue is whether the foundation should have stayed out of the way of Naftali's – the government's – administration of the library, according to the law. And whether agency officials like Sharon Fawcett should have provided Naftali with support instead of undermining and trying to push him out. Federal responsibilities must take precedence over political, or personal, concerns.

Not only should the Archives not have allowed the Nixon Foundation to veto or approve the appointment, the foundation should not have been allowed to interview the candidates for a federal position prior to the selection. Certainly the foundation may express opinions about the appointment, as a stakeholder, but the archivist should make the appointment on the merits without regard to the wishes of the foundation.

The only ones being allowed to voice concerns or approval are the ones with the most to gain if the director isn't experienced, credentialed, and dedicated to nonpartisan administration of the law. The interview process – and the chance to veto the archivist's decision – gave the foundation the chance to administer at least a political litmus test, if not directly determine the candidate's willingness to assist them in their legacy management. To have appointed someone with no experience or training as an archivist or a historian creates serious questions as to how the library will fulfill its legal responsibilities. To have chosen a director without such credentials but apparently with the strong support of the private Nixon Foundation is very troubling indeed.

This isn't one of those stories about how an organization can't quite find the right person to lead it, nor about the dearth of qualified candidates. It's about the fundamental problem of seriously inappropriate interference by a private organization on the hiring practices of a federal agency (it's happened at other presidential libraries, too). And it's about how that agency, skittish about politics and cowed by power (perceived or otherwise), bows to those private interests instead of protecting the interests of the people of the United States.

Without a leader, the dedicated and talented federal employees who work at the Nixon Library were left to deal with the open hostility of the foundation, which is even more nakedly partisan now than it was when the library was private. NARA officials failed in their responsibility to fulfill their duties, which not only include appointing a nonpartisan director without allowing the foundation to veto – or, worse, insist on – a candidate, but to protect their workers, who only want to do their jobs to the best of their ability.

AFTER CONSIDERABLE THOUGHT, I FIGURED OUT WHAT'S most bothersome to me about presidential library exhibits – even in the museums in which I didn't feel uncomfortable: few presidential administrations (and even fewer presidential lives) deserve full museums to document them. The level of detail about most president's childhoods, education, administrations, and pre- and post-presidential careers is astonishing. And it's inconsistent with most presidents' terms of office, their impact on the country and the world, the amount of public interest, and the considerable sums we spend to operate and maintain them.

I don't mean to suggest that none of the presidents for whom libraries have been dedicated did anything good or noteworthy or of consequence, or that nothing in their presidencies was worth commemorating. But visit all of the libraries and you'll see that much of the exhibit space is taken up by items that feel inserted to fill space, not because of their utmost importance. For the presidents who served since 1929, there certainly are enough documents and artifacts and events important enough to remember and display to fill a single Museum of the Presidency, but most individual presidents do not deserve their own museum.

Spending so much time visiting and revisiting and examining carefully all thirteen presidential museums, it became absurd to see all of the school report cards and belt buckles and letters and clothing and personal items. The "this all makes sense if you just see this one artifact" notion of the designers notwithstanding, little had to do with and shed no light on their presidencies. It would be made only slightly less absurd were the museums completely funded and run by private boosters, but at least taxpayers wouldn't be on the hook for it all.

That the federal government now spends a billion dollars a decade operating and propping up and promoting them is unquestionably wrong. An irony is that the most ardent supporters of a particular presidential library likely would agree on this point – though only about other presidents, especially those from the opposite party – but have readymade excuses why *their* president deserves the full treatment.

The strongest of those supporters, those within NARA, have claimed that without libraries for each president, distributed among the states (as opposed to a single institution to house presidential records in Washington), "Outreach opportunities provided through the Libraries could be lost if future Presidential Libraries are not built in local communities across the country."

And besides how much each president merits a museum, why does presidential history specifically deserve such expenditures, and demand such "outreach" across the country? Surely American history doesn't begin and end with chief executives. And why not other parts of the government? What about the Supreme Court? What about the First Branch?

Far more Senators and Representatives have served this country, and each have come from and worked for "local communities" from across the country. In our form of government, presidents carry out the wishes of the people expressed through the will of Congress, which authorizes and appropriates funds for virtually everything the president does. Civics lessons on Congress are more meaningful than those on the presidency.

The Capitol Visitor Center, opened in 2008, contains a modest museum that does a good job, in a nonpartisan manner, of educating people about the working of Congress. And the White House Visitor Center, reopened in 2014 after a two-year, $12 million renovation, explores the presidency as an institution, not as a religion whose saints, and their relics, deserve veneration. Should we build equivalents of these visitor center museums across the country, bringing, as NARA claims the libraries must do, outreach and education and history to the masses?

In fact, the Edward M. Kennedy Institute for the United States Senate, opening in 2015, plans to do just that, complete with a full-scale model of the Senate chamber; no doubt other Congressional centers, originally built as archives and scholarly resources, are looking into similar ideas.

We already have elevated the presidency far above the other two branches in stature, prestige, and power; we further that inappropriate elevation through our funding and support of presidential museums that add little to our collective wisdom about ourselves and our nation; drain resources and attention away from NARA's core mission; and teach generations not what really happened, but just what presidents and those who benefit from their celebration want us to know, and to think.

It's not just the content of the libraries that illustrates what presidents will do to ensure their legacy. Sometimes, the story of how the presidential library was built – or almost built – is even more illustrative.

CHAPTER 6

THE SECRET NIXON LIBRARY

"...as far as Ronald Reagan's legacy is concerned, it does not need a building to make it live for all of us. Even without a building we always will remember that Ronald Reagan was the president who restored America's military might."

President Richard Nixon, at the dedication of the Ronald Reagan Presidential Library in Simi Valley, California, November 4, 1991.

JUST A FEW MONTHS INTO WHAT WOULD BE RICHARD NIXON'S first, and only full, term as president, he already was planning the way he would enshrine his legacy. The manner in which he – not the historians – would write the great history of the Nixon Administration. The way he always would be remembered.

He wouldn't write this history in a series of books. His memoirs would come later, but he would use something far more politically powerful than a book to tell his life story. The *Age of Nixon*.

As far as he was concerned, Nixon's legacy *did* need a building to make it live for all. It needed an extraordinary building. In an extraordinary location.

And Nixon had a secret plan to create that extraordinary library.

He wouldn't place his monument to himself next to his small birthplace, as had three of his predecessors (Herbert Hoover, Franklin D. Roosevelt, and Dwight Eisenhower). He wouldn't seek out a university campus to give him legitimacy, or rely on bold architecture to add gravitas, as had John F. Kennedy and Lyndon Johnson.

Obsessed with his place in history, Nixon needed to acquire a location that, in and of itself, would command respect – awe, even. He wanted to build his library in a majestic setting, with sweeping vistas and inspiring views. He had the exact spot picked out, and it was spectacular. Its setting alone would trump all past, and likely future, presidential libraries. The only thing preventing Nixon from realizing his vision was something that, in so many other parts of his political life, he never let stop him: it would not be legal.

1971 aerial view, looking south, of original library site (#1); Western White House (#4); freeway entrance (#3); San Clemente Golf Course (#5); Pacific Ocean (top, above #3 and #4). From the Richard Nixon Library.

The Presidential Libraries Act (PLA) of 1955 codified the process by which the Archivist of the United States, on behalf of the American people, lawfully could accept the donation of a presidential library from a former president's foundation. Among the provisions were those concerning the land on which the library sat: it could be deeded to the federal government, or the archivist could make agreements with a "State, political subdivision, university, institution of higher learning, institute, or foundation" to operate the library without receiving transfer of title to the land. It could be pretty much anywhere, as long as the land was provided by a state, local government, school, or private organization.

The only type of land that, under the law, could not be used (and which today still may not be used) for a presidential library is federal. And that presented a problem for Richard Nixon; his perfect presidential library site just happened to be on federal property.

Up until that point, the most expensive presidential library was the one that Johnson was building on a fourteen-acre site on the campus of the University of Texas at Austin, at a total cost – including the land, construction of the building, and all equipment – of $18.6 million ($109 million in 2014 dollars).

In contrast, Nixon would place his library in the middle of more than four thousand acres of prime, impossible-to-acquire real estate worth $160 million – just for the land alone – in 2014 dollars (that figure accounts for simple inflation, and not the increased value of real estate in the intervening forty-five years).

Other presidents, seeking glory, relied on the design of the building or the content of the exhibits; for Nixon, the dramatic site itself would be the major draw. The tract of vast, open, California wilderness contains miles of stunning beaches – including some of the best surfing spots in the United States – and magnificent views of the Pacific Ocean. According to a state resources agency report, the land is comprised of "flat sandy beaches, sheer coastal cliffs, slumping terraces, flat, alluvial floodplains, and rolling foothills. Elevations range from sea level along the coast to 198 meters (650 feet) on the western boundary."

An 1846 description portrayed the site exactly as it remained 124 years later: "a beautiful spot in the centre of an opening in the highlands, extending from the beach to the distant mountains. A small river flowed down the glen towards the sea."

The Richard Nixon Library would be built on this beautiful spot, according to the plan, which was thorough, secret, and perfect – except for two small details: in addition to the fact that it wouldn't be legal to build the library on federal land, the owner didn't want to give it up.

The owner – technically, the *tenant*, as the owner was the United States of America, via the Department of the Navy – was the Marine

Corps. The exclusive parcel was, inconveniently for Nixon (or, actually, inconveniently for the Corps, as it turned out), in the western part of Camp Pendleton, one of the country's largest Marine Corps bases.

Occupying eighteen miles along the Southern California coast and more than a hundred and twenty-five thousand acres between Los Angeles and San Diego, the camp was – and is – the main training base for all West Coast Marines. Vital to the mission and readiness of the Corps – particularly those training to go to southeast Asia – the Marines did not want to give up a single acre or a foot of shoreline. They claimed that losing the land would "severely handicap military functions."

Richard Nixon, however, wanted more than four thousand acres, and six miles – a third – of the camp's beachfront. And he had a secret plan to get it.

It was simple: without attracting any attention, wrest the thousands of acres and miles of coastline from the military, during a time of war; transfer the land from federal control to the state, quietly, even though it needed to be a public process; and ensure that the foundation would be able to use a portion of the site for the library.

Like many of Nixon's plans to circumvent the law, this one included a cover-up. Unlike many of his plans, though, the cover-up had been part of the strategy from the start. Since a large piece of the process could not be secret – the transfer to the state – an alternative reason for removing the parcel from the control of the Marine Corps would be required.

So Richard Nixon simply created an entirely new federal bureaucracy to cover up the land transfer, diverting attention from it and providing a plausible alternative narrative. While the plan wasn't fully successful, the cover-up lasted for more than forty-five years. Until now.

WHEN NIXON LOOKED AT THE CAMP PENDLETON TRACT, HE saw four thousand of the most awe-inspiring – and expensive – acres in the country. The land, a gorgeous mix of ideal California surfing beach, picturesque windswept bluffs and green, untamed shore forest, ran for six miles along the coast and abutted his Western White House, the private home he had purchased in San Clemente upon taking office.

It would make the perfect setting for the future Richard Nixon Presidential Library. A long, winding, drive up a dramatic hill, past thousands of acres of carefully-tended buffer against the outside world, would bring visitors to a prominent memorial fit for a man of his accomplishments – and plans. The problem was, the Corps wasn't giving up without a fight.

Despite the law, Nixon wanted his library right there. Right where Camp Pendleton Marines trained. Right on the land the Department of the Navy said was critical to our nation's readiness. Right where he was looking, longingly, at his future. At History. *Legacy.*

And so Nixon, the hawkish war veteran, and his staff got to work secretly wresting the land away. By the time they were finished, the Marines were out a big chunk of prime federal real estate, the Nixon Library Foundation had drawn up surveys and plans, and he had created a new national bureaucracy just to cover his tracks – and his illegal activity.

Thanks to a carefully-negotiated agreement with the administration of then-Governor Ronald Reagan – a chief executive with a future of his own to fulfill, and who could sympathize with such grand plans – the federal government leased the land to the State of California. Only Watergate and the president's hasty exit from office put a halt to the scheme, which never was fully realized.

Just the first part went into effect, and the land is now a state park. Visitors enjoy year-round camping at the San Mateo campground – near the planned site for the library – and surfers from all around the world come to one of the finest places to hang ten, San Onofre State Beach.

While he encountered some bumps along the way, today the Nixon Library likely would be located on this beautiful piece of land, on the coast next to La Casa Pacifica, his Western White House, were it not for the fact that Nixon resigned the presidency in disgrace.

Owing to the difficulties he encountered in the aftermath, it took Nixon sixteen more years, and no fewer than five rejected locations, for him finally to open his presidential library on a compact, nine-acre site next to his boyhood home, just like three of his predecessors. Though, instead of the grand Roosevelt Estate in Hyde Park, the lovely 186-acre National Historic Landmark park in Hoover's West Branch, or the neat, orderly, "main street" campus in Eisenhower's Abilene, the Nixon Library is surrounded by the strip malls, highways, and closely-packed Spanish colonial homes of inland Orange County, California.

The most astonishing part isn't that he tried it, or that he almost got away with it, but that the plan itself – engineered by perhaps the most-scrutinized president in the history of the United States – could have remained secret for so long. The story of the plan and the cover-up, while known to the Nixon Administration officials who participated in it and a few loyal supporters, has never been told publicly.

This story may seem fantastic to many. As the Nixon presidency has been studied so meticulously for more than forty years, it would be almost unthinkable that this would not have come to light earlier. Or that not even Nixon would have tried to do this. Or that it could be just a misunderstanding.

```
The President's schedule
  -Meeting with Bush
     -Location

Ehrlichman left at an unknown time before 11:16 am.

Nixon Foundation
  -Jo Anne Haldeman
     -Volunteer job
     -Pay
     -Purpose
  -[Yorba Linda] property sale
     -Plans
           -Ehrlichman
           -F. Edward Hebert
           -Timing
                -Congress
        -Standards of Official Conduct Committee
           -Hebert
           -The President's schedule
                -California
                     -Christmas
           -Tour
                -House
     -Possible donation
           -[Julie Nixon Eisenhower and Tricia Nixon Cox]
     -Mrs. Nixon
```

Tape Subject Log, Conversation No. 228-1. Courtesy the Richard Nixon Library.

That the president tried to illegally appropriate federal land for his library would have been inconceivable even to the National Archives staff who, years later, were processing the White House tapes, and preparing logs of the discussions and their participants.

In one tape subject log, the president and others discuss plans for building the library at Camp Pendleton, strategizing on how to get the House committee to go along.

One idea they have is whether or not to bring the Members out to California for a tour of the property, and also to see Nixon's nearby house – La Casa Pacifica – which would be donated or sold to the foundation.

The archives staff creating the tape log after the fact assumed the group was talking about the president's Yorba Linda boyhood home (which, though now part of the library, was not included in the plans until many years later) and think that, because of one of the Members of

Congress mentioned (Rep. F. Edward Hébert), the committee referenced is the Standards of Official Conduct, and not Armed Services – which was the one he was talking about, and the one he needed to convince in order to build his library on the base.

In fact, this all did happen. It didn't come to light earlier because Nixon never was able to see it through all the way. And because it was such a secret plan. And because of the trials and tribulations of his records. And because Richard Nixon told a story to cover it all up.

THE STORY THE PUBLIC WAS TOLD WAS THIS: IN THE SUMMER of 1969, as President Nixon walked along the beautiful surfing beach near his San Clemente home, he noticed that it was empty – a result not only of the Secret Service protections for him and his family, but of his home's location next to the main Marine Corps training base on the west coast, Camp Pendleton.

For as far as he could see inland, too, there was nothing but wild, unused land.

Frustrated that such pristine natural resources were going to waste, the president ordered his aides to look into the use of all federal land, with an eye toward identifying any parcels that were underutilized, for possible transfer to states and local governments for the purposes of parks and recreation. This led to the establishment of the Legacy of Parks program, "a creative avenue for Federal, State, and local cooperation in achieving two of this Administration's principal domestic aims – bringing government closer to the people and improving our environment."

In just a few years, tens of thousands of acres of federal land, including the Camp Pendleton tract, were transferred, or, less commonly, leased, to states to create more than six hundred new parks. The program, and the associated Federal Property Review Board and its successor, the Federal Property Council, are remembered as keystones in President Nixon's environmental record.

As is often the case with Richard Nixon, the story the public was told contained a small amount of truth and left out large amounts of what actually happened, including the reason the Legacy of Parks program was established: to cover up the land grab to build his library on what he hoped would become a former part of Camp Pendleton.

IT IS AGAINST THE LAW TO BUILD A PRESIDENTIAL LIBRARY on federal property. So what if the site you've selected happens to be federal property? How do you get away with building it there? Through a series of complicated, and, if all goes well, secret, maneuvers.

Under the law, you must first get the land declared "excess" – either unutilized or underutilized – by the agency that controls it. That allows the General Services Administration to offer it to other agencies that may need it. If none do, GSA can declare the property "surplus" and offer it to other entities, such as states, local governments, or private organizations.

Once the land is transferred – either to the state, or, say, your private presidential library foundation – you get the new owner to make arrangements for you to build the library on what is now former federal property, thereby "following" the law.

The illegal part (though moralist sticklers may already have found the preceding to violate, if not the letter, the spirit of the law) would come in if, for instance, the federal agency that controls the land refuses to declare it unutilized or underutilized, and instead insists that it is vital to their mission.

If the land is not deemed to be "excess," it could not be declared "surplus," and therefore may not be transferred from federal control. Also, if Congress stepped in and, for example, passed legislation specifically prohibiting that exact land from being transferred, sold, leased, or otherwise disposed of, it would be illegal to go ahead and do so anyway. If that wasn't a problem for you, then you could build your library on federal property.

As early as two weeks before his first inauguration, Richard Nixon was considering building a house on Camp Pendleton. Alternatively, should that "present insurmountable legal problems" he explored the possibility of having the Marine Corps provide him with a "good swimming beach" while he would purchase a "house which is not too far from away it."

Within six months of becoming president, he had incorporated the Richard Nixon Foundation to raise money for and build his library and purchased (in a complicated and controversial financial transaction) La Casa Pacifica, the "Western White House" in San Clemente, adjacent to Camp Pendleton.

The secret plan to build the library on the Marine Corps base followed soon after.

REVIEWING THE PRESIDENT'S DAILY DIARY AND READING THE
White House tape subject logs, at first I was surprised at how often Nixon
and his advisors would meet and talk about the plan for the library at
Camp Pendleton on the same day – sometimes at the same time – as they
discussed major subjects and momentous events, such as the Watergate
break-in, the Pentagon Papers, and the war in Vietnam.

But then I realized that the president wasn't switching back and forth
between serious matters and a trivial one; he constantly returned to his
plans for the library while in the midst of these historic events because
that's the way he constantly viewed them, in real time: how he would be
seen by history, and how his actions would contribute to his legacy.

In eight years as vice-president, and another eight in the "wilderness,"
Richard Nixon had had plenty of time to prepare for not only how he
would conduct his presidency, but how he would memorialize it. Only
weeks after winning the 1968 election, Nixon began work on where and
how he would donate his papers (and how he would deduct the value of
them from his income taxes) and build his library.

In that library, in that dramatic setting, he would tell his story of his
administration: the story that was unfolding even as he was planning to
tell it.

Upon taking office, Nixon began immediately to plan his presidential
library. In itself, that is not unique, or surprising; although they do it quietly, presidents tend to begin working on their library soon after they win
election. What is unique, though, is that, right from the start, the manner
in which he and his staff went about planning to build his library was se-
cretive, and contrary to federal law.

DESPITE THE FACT THAT HE HAD SERVED FOR DECADES AS A
national figure, Nixon did not easily participate in public celebrations.
And his record with presidential libraries was not good.

When President Roosevelt opened his library in June, 1941, Nixon
had not yet entered politics (he was then a partner at the Whittier, California law firm of Wingert and Bewley); and so, as an unknown member
of the public, he was not invited to the celebration.

By July, 1957, when former President Harry Truman opened his library in Independence, Missouri, along with former President Herbert
Hoover, former First Lady Eleanor Roosevelt, Chief Justice Earl Warren,

and President Dwight Eisenhower, Nixon was vice president of the United States, but he did not attend the ceremonies.

He was a candidate for the Republican nomination for governor of California in May, 1962, when former President Eisenhower, the man he served for eight years as vice president, opened his library in Abilene, Kansas; Vice President Lyndon Johnson was among those present for the ceremonies, but Richard Nixon was not.

He had earned his party's nomination for governor by August, 1962, when Hoover opened his library in West Branch, Iowa with Truman present, but Nixon did not attend the ceremonies.

Statesmen like Truman and Hoover dismissed him as a lightweight – a political hatchet man – and did not have him speak at their celebrations. And the presidents who served before him and who knew him rarely had good things to say about Nixon, in public or private.

It was not until the Johnson Library opened, on May 22, 1971, that Nixon finally attended his first presidential library dedication.

Although he desperately wanted to be, Nixon had never been a part of Eisenhower's inner circle. Even though Ike's wariness of him waned, and the men did become somewhat closer when the families were joined in 1968 by the marriage of Nixon's daughter Julie to Eisenhower's grandson David, the first function Nixon attended in Abilene, the site of Eisenhower's boyhood home, library and museum, and Place of Meditation (his final resting place), was Eisenhower's burial, in 1969.

A reporter asked President Eisenhower, weeks before the 1960 election, when a ringing endorsement of his vice-president would have boosted Nixon's campaign, for an example of a major idea of Nixon's that Eisenhower had adopted as president. He answered, "If you give me a week, I might think of one. I don't remember." On the eve of the election, Eisenhower privately told friends, "We nominated the wrong man."

When Herbert Hoover addressed the 1960 Republican National Convention in a sixteen-minute speech, he failed to mention Richard Nixon – the unopposed Republican presidential nominee – even once.

By the time he was inaugurated for the first time in 1969, the presidential libraries of these men were looming large for Nixon. The limestone behemoth that some called Johnson's "pyramid" was under construction, and would come with a School of Politics to help rehabilitate his standing. FDR, Truman, and Ike all had libraries that welcomed historians and tourists alike to review the records of their presidencies.

Kennedy soon would be memorialized in the most beautiful library in the system – next to that *Ivy League* school, of all places (plans had not yet been scrapped to build what then was called the John F. Kennedy Memorial Library in Cambridge, Massachusetts).

Even the dour Herbert Hoover, chased out of the presidency by the Great Depression and FDR's 1932 landslide victory, had *two* libraries.

The Nixon Library needed something that would set him apart from all of its predecessors: a dramatic location. If he had been able to complete the plan, visitors might have been welcomed to the Nixon Library at Camp Pendleton as early as 1976.

That it took sixteen years for him to open his library in Yorba Linda, California (the average is now about four years) illustrates the unique difficulties he faced, owing both to his status and to the considerable efforts he already had expended to put the library on land he took from the Corps. Having resigned the presidency, Nixon lost the clout that former presidents can wield, soliciting donations and having their choice of locations from among many eager aspirants.

In addition, his shameful exit severely limited his initial ability to raise funds and to make his own selection for the perfect site.

After several other possibilities, including Duke University and the city of San Clemente, fell through or turned him down (and a few less-than-ideal locations, such as the city that already hosted the Eisenhower Presidential Library, and Leavenworth, Kansas, home to the federal penitentiary, offered sites that he declined), Nixon chose Yorba Linda.

He purchased his former family home to create what, when opened in 1990 (and for the next seventeen years) would be the privately-run Richard Nixon Library and Birthplace, with none of his presidential papers and no government support.

IN MARCH, 1969, TWO YEARS BEFORE HE ANNOUNCED THE land transfer, Nixon visited the San Mateo Canyon area of Camp Pendleton, and walked along the beach adjacent to the Cotton Estate, the home he would purchase that summer. He had planned for several months to find a house in the immediate vicinity, both as a vacation property and as a retirement home.

But on this trip, he saw the site he would spend the next five and a half years trying to secure for his library.

Just a few weeks later, the organizational meeting to form the Richard Nixon Foundation was held, and articles of incorporation were filed with the California Secretary of State. Over the next few months, the foundation moved quickly. Early on, the group had decided to return unsolicited donations to the library, meeting minimal operating costs through trustees' contributions. If this over concern about how it might look to be collecting money is unknown; however, the foundation was exploring an innovative way to cover building costs.

Representatives of the foundation visited several presidential libraries that fall, and in December met with the General Services Administration – the parent agency for what was then known as the National Archives and Records Service, or NARS – for a two-day briefing.

After the meeting, Archivist of the United States James B. Rhoads told GSA Administrator Robert Kunzig that they had asked several questions about financing, including raising the possibility of a "partnership" in which the federal government would construct the Nixon Library building, rather than the foundation. Reporting to White House Chief of Staff H.R. Haldeman about the meeting, Kunzig noted that the foundation's inquiry about acquiring matching federal funds would have negative political implications; Haldeman agreed. It wouldn't be the last political consideration the library plan raised.

The Nixon Foundation was made up of wealthy donors, local supporters, and others. However, unlike previous foundations, which made attempts to appear distinct from the administration, Haldeman was chairman of the foundation's board of executive trustees, White House Counsel John Ehrlichman was vice chairman – and both directed the work of the foundation. Attorney General John Mitchell, Secretary of Health, Education, and Welfare (HEW) Robert Finch, Assistant Secretary of HEW Patricia Hitt, and Special Consultant to the President Leonard Garment all were board members.

During this time period, "the Nixon Foundation" is interchangeable with "the White House."

In November, the foundation engaged Economics Research Associates (ERA), the consulting company that had determined the sites of many major institutions and events such as World's Fairs and Walt Disney World in Florida, to create a "locational analysis" for the library in southern California. ERA also evaluated the first formal proposal to host the library, from the president's home town of Whittier, California.

With the foundation established and working on financing and scope of the project, the president and his staff turned their attention to the location. That part of the plan developed rapidly. By early 1970, plans were well underway to take the property away from the Marines, secretly; on top of overcoming objections, it required a new bureaucracy for cover.

Map of proposed Nixon Library site at Camp Pendleton (circled); Western White House (large arrow); and larger parcel to be transferred (outlined in black, with smaller arrows). From the Richard Nixon Library.

ON FEBRUARY 10, 1970, PRESIDENT NIXON SIGNED EXECUTIVE Order 11508, "Providing for the Identification of Unneeded Federal Real Property." The order established the Federal Property Review Board, for the "identification of real property that is not utilized, is underutilized, or is not being put to its optimum use" and to make recommendations to the president "regarding the use or disposal of such property." Members included high-level officials such as the directors of the Bureau of the Budget, the Council of Economic Advisors, the Council on Environmental Quality, the GSA, and "other such officers and employees of the Executive branch as the President may from time to time designate."

The board – Bryce Harlow, George Shultz, Paul McCracken, Russell Train, Robert Kunzig, John Ehrlichman, and Donald Rumsfeld – first met on June 24 and began to establish its authority and role in reviewing federal property.

Just one month later, frustrated with the paucity of properties that had been identified to date, President Nixon sent a memorandum to the heads of departments and agencies, telling them that their reports pursuant to his executive order to identify property that was not utilized, underutilized, or not being put to optimum use were "unsatisfactory." He required them to submit new reports by August 21; and to identify the ten percent of their property which was the least utilized, ranking the rest of the ninety percent according to priority for their retention.

In this memo, Nixon does not ask them to identify properties that are legitimately unused, and therefore eligible for transfer; with this ranking system, he orders each agency and department to describe at least ten percent of their property as unused, even if all of it is being utilized. This characterization would help him force the Marines to give up the tract.

The White House submitted Camp Pendleton as a candidate. In October, the GSA surveyed the property, finding – against the opinion of the Corps, the Navy, and the Department of Defense (DoD) – that "775 acres of beach frontage and 3,400 acres of interior lands are underutilized or not utilized…and [that] the 775 and 3,400 parcels be reported excess." GSA concluded the "highest and best use" of the land, where tens of thousand Marines trained, and when there were more than 300,000 U.S. troops still in Vietnam, was as public parks and residential development.

Meanwhile, the White House was working on other strategies to secure the property, in case they couldn't successfully have it declared excess. For example, if the property remained in federal hands, the law would have to be amended to allow it to be used for the library.

On October 22 1970, the president signed S. 1708, the Parks and Recreation Act of 1970, introduced by Senator Henry Jackson (D-Washington). The bill authorized the Administrator to assign to the Secretary of the Interior surplus property for use as a park or recreation area.

At the Property Review Board's second meeting in November, the members discussed draft legislation from the General Services Administration to authorize revenue-producing and other activities on surplus property conveyed to any state for historic-monument purposes. Among other important considerations, this bill would have allowed a presidential library – which charges admission, operates a gift shop, and hosts public events – to be built on such land.

Ostensibly, the Property Review Board examined locations from all across the country that were candidates to be transferred from federal control. But from the very beginning, the Camp Pendleton land was their primary concern. Between the first and second board meetings – and after the president's "unsatisfactory" memo – Ehrlichman reminded board members that the president desired to move Camp Pendleton "into the hands of local government and the private sector." He told them that Nixon proposed the board establish a "long-range plan for this transfer and that all further steps be taken with regard to the property be consistent with that plan of disposal. He suggests that we consider the retention of professional assistance in the development of this plan."

Out of hundreds of proposed transfers, Camp Pendleton was the only one discussed at each board meeting. It was the only one identified as having been initiated by the president himself. The only time that the president made a strategy recommendation to the board was about this property. It was the only transfer about which the board was advised to engage outside experts. The only time that the president attended a meeting of the Property Review Board was one held solely to discuss the concerns and reservations of the Members of the House Committee on Armed Services about the transfer of Camp Pendleton property.

At the second Property Review Board meeting, members discussed Camp Pendleton land as a "problem." Unique to this property, GSA Commissioner Daniel T. Kingsley gave a slide presentation of the field survey of the base – a survey that was initiated at the president's request (the only property reviewed that the president requested be surveyed).

Kingsley, while noting that his study had not included an "expert review of the need for military training at the base" told the board that if the Marines no longer need an amphibious training base on the west coast (the Marines would continue to insist that they did need such a base), Camp Pendleton would "accommodate numerous land uses." He recommended excessing six miles and 775 acres of beach, and 3,400 acres of land. Ehrlichman commented that "the presentation and recommendation for excessing and utilizing limited areas at the base…were fully responsive to the President's request." The board agreed to carry out the recommendations with the Department of Defense.

The number of members of the Property Review Board who were fully aware of the ultimate plan for the tract is unclear, though at least some knew, as subsequent events would prove.

It is notable that the board membership underwent a change before this second meeting. On September 23, 1970, President Nixon issued Executive Order 11560, replacing the Director of the Bureau of the Budget with the Associate Director of the Office of Management and Budget on the Property Review Board. On the surface, this appears to be a "housekeeping" change, as the official name of the agency had changed since the creation of the board. However, the EO had the effect of removing George Shultz, whom some in the White House, including Nixon, did not fully trust (referring to him as a "candy ass") and installing as chairman of the board Arnold Weber, who proved eager to carry out the president's plan; in less than a year, though, the president would replace Weber with an even more eager – and ambitious – chairman.

THE OPINION THAT THE LIBRARY SHOULD BE LOCATED ON A dramatic site was held not only by Nixon and his intimates, but was borne out by subsequent research. Earlier in the year, the foundation had received the locational analysis report from ERA, which noted that "Existing presidential museums generally have not constituted notable visitor attractions...none of the existing presidential museums are elaborate structures designed with a view to attracting large numbers of visitors. On the contrary, they are largely devoted to a static display of various gifts and medals received by recent presidents, and to other artifacts of historical interest...[t]he proposed Nixon Museum...should have a considerably greater attendance potential."

The following month, the architectural firm William L. Pereira Associates presented the foundation with a comprehensive study, "Phase I." In the subject of Site Selection, the first and most important criteria category is "Spirit and Nobility of Site, Character of Landscape and Sense of Place"; the second, interestingly, is "Availability" (of the property).

The minimum area recommended for the complete site – the library and museum, conference center and "Institutes," and "Reserve," is 100 acres; the "optimum" site is 300 acres. Up until that point, the largest site for a presidential library was twenty-two acres.

In order to collect and analyze data for these and other reports, the foundation allowed the public (and even some involved in the project) to believe that Whittier was the main location in contention, all while working almost exclusively on the Camp Pendleton site. Though it was some fifty miles away from the base, the Whittier location allowed for the consideration of many aspects of the plan, and had similar topography (though it was not on the coast).

At the second annual meeting of the trustees of the Richard Nixon Foundation, held at the Western White House in San Clemente, on August 28, 1970, the trustees authorized "additional comparability studies in connection with our site selection activity." This was well after the decision had been made to pursue the Marine Corps property, and a few weeks before Ehrlichman's memo to the board reminding them of the president's desire to transfer the Camp Pendleton land.

During the meeting, Frederick Binder, president of Whittier College, made a presentation "in favor of the Whittier Site" for the Nixon Library.

The White House allowed this process to continue for at least two, and possibly three, reasons: to create additional data needed to evaluate the Camp Pendleton site; to provide a plausible cover for the real location; and to offer an actual alternative site should the secret plan fail.

Concerned that the board was not moving quickly enough to secure the Camp Pendleton transfer, in December a "task force" was formed to develop additional strategies to ensure the success of the plan.

THE PUBLIC COVER-UP BEGAN IN EARNEST IN THE SPRING OF 1971. While the work of the review board had been publicized, its efforts to transfer parcels around the country had deflected attention way from its main purpose. But at some point, the White House would have to specifically address what had been – and what would continue to be – the most contentious of all of the proposed transfers. That point came on the morning of Wednesday, March 31.

President Nixon spoke to reporters in San Clemente, where he announced he had ordered the Secretary of Defense to "report to the House and Senate Committees on Armed Services that 6 miles of beach and 3,400 acres of upland, which presently are part of Camp Pendleton, will be declared excess and will become available for public use."

Nixon went on at length about the genesis of his idea and the reasons for the transfer. He acknowledged – but downplayed – the opposition to the transfer from within Congress and "the bureaus." He did not, however, clarify why, in this instance – as in no others – he had had to "order" a secretary to report the land as excess.

It is worth reading his comments at length, knowing today the real reason he was taking the land:

"I should point out that this action, while it deals with property very close to my home in California...what we are doing here has triggered my thoughts with regard to activities throughout the Nation. Just 2 years ago I was walking along this beach, and I realized that here in southern California there were millions of people who wanted to go to the beach, and that when you go by Santa Monica or Long Beach or any of the other great beaches that I used to go to as a youngster, that they are just too crowded these days, and there is a great need for more beaches where people can go.

"Consequently, I checked and found, and with the cooperation of the Marine Corps, that they did not need the total of 18 miles of beach which they presently occupy. So we have worked out that this 6 miles will be declared excess, and that in the future, millions of particularly young people in California, and older ones as well, that enjoy the beach will have greater access to this property which has been closed since World War II when the Marine Corps took it over for obvious reasons.

"In addition to that, having made that decision 2 years ago with regard to this particular property, I asked that a survey be made of all properties held by the Federal Government, properties held by the Department of Defense, by the GSA, by the Veterans Administration, by the Department of the Interior.

"Over half the land, for example, in the Western States is owned by and controlled by the Federal Government. This is apart from parklands. This is land which is used by, controlled by [the Federal Government], and denied to the public, as far as their use is concerned.

"Much of this use is not proper in terms of the best use. And consequently, this is the first of a series of announcements that will be made over the next few months in which, in all sections of the country, in northern California as well as in southern California, in the East, the North, the South, announcements will be made whereby we will declare excess property that presently is being used by the Federal Government or some agency of the Federal Government, but in a way that we have determined is not the best use.

"That means that then the State, in this case, gets the oppor-

tunity to use this as parkland. In other cases, it may be determined that property, for example, that is in the middle of a city may be turned over to the tax rolls, and the funds that are acquired thereby can then be used to develop parks...

"I say that it probably wouldn't have happened unless I had taken a walk on the beach 2 years ago at San Clemente and walked an extra mile and saw the great possibilities and decided that the time had come for Presidential initiative, Presidential initiative which has overridden, I must say, very deep and understandable bureaucratic opposition and very deep and understandable opposition in some segments of the Congress, only because Members of the Congress at times were reflecting the views of the bureaus. Most Members of the Congress, I am sure, will applaud this decision."

At no point in his remarks – at no point, ever – did he even hint that he planned to build his library on that land (nor, obviously, that this park project, which grew to encompass far more properties, was created to hide the true nature of the Camp Pendleton transfer).

And his characterization that the Marines "did not need" the land is simply not true; the Corps, the Navy, and the DoD fought to keep it. They had explained only six weeks earlier that if the 3,400 acres were declared as excess, "we will severely handicap our military functions at Camp Pendleton," pointing out that during 1970 alone, more than 77,000 Marines trained in the area proposed to be excessed.

After completing his remarks about the Camp Pendleton "park land," Nixon took a helicopter tour of the property with members of the press; they viewed the area that only he, and a small group of aides and associates, knew would be used to build his monument to himself.

In order to help make the controversial transfer successful – and, as a fait accompli, permanent – three days later, Governor Ronald Reagan officially dedicated the first portion of the public park, San Onofre Bluffs State Beach. Nixon had won the first battle over Camp Pendleton.

THE PROPOSED LIBRARY SITE WAS ON THE EXTREME WESTERN border of the base, about 150 acres bordering the Western White House compound. If the library were located there without the other thousands of acres transferred, it would be close – too close – to an active base. And if the entire parcel were transferred to the state of California, it might become difficult to convince state officials to allow the library to be built on that land. The plan to take the land from the Marine Corps didn't include the immediate area where Nixon wanted to build the library; control of that parcel would result from separate, though controversial, legislation.

But how to explain why Nixon wanted to transfer to the state more than four thousand acres of a military base, except for a relatively small portion, and one that was so close to his personal residence?

The president who used – or tried to use – agencies such as the Department of Justice, the Internal Revenue Service, the Federal Bureau of Investigation, and the Central Intelligence Agency for political purposes (to say nothing of the Executive Office of the President), turned to the one organization that was supposed to be above such partisan activity: the Secret Service.

On the afternoon of January 4, 1971 – a year and a half after Nixon made La Casa Pacifica his Western White House, and well after the Secret Service made security determinations for the property – Lilburn Boggs, the Assistant Director of Protective Forces, wrote to Al Toner, in the White House Office of Domestic Affairs, requesting a one-mile "buffer zone" between Nixon's property and Camp Pendleton.

Seven months later, Boggs wrote to White House Counsel John Dean (who was coordinating many aspects of the transfer and cover-up). He reported the Secret Service had re-evaluated their position on the buffer zone due to the "possible conveyance of certain government lands which are now part of Camp Pendleton to the State for use as State Parks."

The Service now wanted to expand the zone, because of the "high ground which overlooks the [presidential] compound from this area."

The high ground to which Boggs referred would not be transferred as part of the park, as the land is where the Nixon Library was planned to be built. To accuse a high-ranking Secret Service official as being complicit in this scheme, though, would require additional documentation.

Such as, for example, a document detailing the plan to have the Secret Service provide the pretext for eliminating the library site from being transferred to the state; advising that they need to proceed cautiously; and admitting the plan is controversial, and therefore should not be made public prior to the president's re-election.

Map of Nixon Library site, Camp Pendleton (circled), with note "To delete approx. 100 acs in this area." From the Richard Nixon Library.

We find exactly that in an "Administratively Confidential/Eyes Only" memo from Dean to Haldeman and Ehrlichman dated July 26, 1971, three weeks before Boggs' second memo. In it, Dean explains that:

> "...the potential library site property must be excluded from that portion of the property to be leased to California. We can make a strong argument that it must be set aside for security reasons. The Secret Service feels that it will create serious security problems if the lands become a public park. Accordingly, this land should be excluded on security grounds, which will keep it available for later acquisition.
>
> "After the land has been quietly set aside for security reasons, I do not think anything should be done until after the election. Obviously, acquiring this land for a Presidential library is going to be very controversial. Accordingly, we should take no action until immediately after the election. In the interim, we should carefully plan each step necessary to make the acquisition."

Dean elaborated in an undated draft memo, likely addressed to the president, written after September 1 and before October 27, 1971:

> "Part of the land originally proposed to be included in this lease, an approximate 150 acre tract of high ground overlooking the Western White House compound, was excluded from the

lease on the basis that the use of the area was incompatible with Secret Service Security requirements. This deletion did not generate any publicity or media speculation...

"It must be assumed that the acquisition of this land for a Presidential library will be very controversial, especially since this land could be used for public parks, the Armed Services Committee and the Marines are most reluctant to permanently give up any of Camp Pendleton, and this would be the first time that federal lands would be made available for a Presidential archival depository. Therefore, no overt action on the project should be taken until after the election...

"...we would, of course, have to get around the theory that this property was needed as a security buffer zone, but presumably this could be done on the basis that the site would not be open to the public until construction was finished, which would be after 1976."

Dean and others appear to be quite candid. Owing to the then legal status of presidential records as being the personal property of the president, rather than public property, Nixon and his advisors had good reason to assume the documents would never be seen. Even so, they use careful language. The White House knew the plan was contentious at best, and outside the bounds of the law at worst.

Detail of undated draft memo from John Dean, September or October, 1971. From the Richard Nixon Library.

1971 BEGAN IN EARLY JANUARY WITH JOHN ERHLICHMAN pressuring Arnold Weber, Chairman of the Property Review Board, to declare, as the president desired, the Camp Pendleton parcel as excess and to make it available for parks and recreation by March 15 (likening Nixon's "Legacy of Parks" to Eisenhower's "legacy of highways").

It ended in late October with Congress passing the Military Construction Authorization Act. The bill, which the president had to sign because of its importance, contained a provision specifically prohibiting the sale, lease, or transfer of lands constituting Camp Pendleton without further Congressional authorization.

Despite that clear proscription (which had been looming most of the year), in the interim – and the months that followed – All the President's Library Men and Women would do everything they could to make the Nixon Library at Camp Pendleton a reality.

For the most part, the president stayed out of the day to day work on the plan. He played his role, though, which was to continue beating the drum in public about his plan to transfer federal land for state and local parks – and to not mention the Nixon Library's part in that plan.

In his 1971 State of the Union address in January, he said, "I will put forward the most extensive program ever proposed by a President of the United States to expand the Nation's parks, recreation areas, open spaces, in a way that truly brings parks to the people where the people are."

For most of the year, the GSA and the DoD fought, debating the Marine Corps' utilization of the base. With the White House not only on its side, but insisting that the GSA successfully effect the land transfer, the GSA would win – but not on the merits of the argument, nor within the confines of the law, but because the White House would insist on it.

The inter-agency fight was only half of battle: whichever path they chose to secure the library land, they would have to deal with Congress.

The president's March 31 announcement about the opening of the Camp Pendleton tract for park land attracted the attention of the chairman of the Real Estate Subcommittee of the House Committee on Armed Services, Rep. Samuel S. Stratton (D-New York). He scheduled hearings on the proposed transfer and sent a document request to the White House. This sent the library planners into full cover-up mode.

Some aides, such as Property Review Board Chairman Arnold Weber, advised that the president invoke executive privilege in order to keep the requested documents hidden. In a May 8 memorandum to John

Dean, Weber expressed an opinion that was not primarily based on the idea that such disclosure would inhibit "candid and free communication" (though he did include that as among his objections).

Weber was convinced releasing the documents would reveal the cover-up, the true story behind Camp Pendleton, and allow the DoD to "reargue their case against the transfer of Pendleton in another forum."

Weber explained that the issue was about covering up facts, not a Constitutional argument about separation of powers, writing:

> "The release of the Presidential decision document could generate a request for the Presidential option paper. Since we probably would not release this document, the question of executive privilege would only be deferred and not avoided.
>
> "Presentation of the material requested by the Subcommittee will not present a balanced case and could bias the Subcommittee thinking in favor of the DOD position. A balanced presentation of a summary of the views of GSA and DOD is the proper vehicle to avoid Presidential embarrassment.
>
> "Release of these documents could impair the President's program of moving excess Federal property into parks or other better uses."

Others disagreed about invoking executive privilege, and argued for release of the records – but not because of a commitment to transparency. Dick Cook, the White House Deputy Assistant for Congressional Relations, took the political strategy angle. He wrote to Dean on May 7 that Chairman Stratton had the "full support" of Armed Services Committee Chairman F. Edward Hébert, and that Stratton was simply "seeking a confrontation to dramatize [the subcommittee's] case against declaration of excess property at Camp Pendleton."

Cook thought that even if the White House released the records, the House wouldn't reverse the president's decision. Most importantly, though, Cook was concerned that not cooperating with the subcommittee would risk losing the chairmen's support for the president on Indochina and the Vietnam War, and on a pending military pay bill (the amount of which the administration wanted decreased).

The most telling opinion came from Assistant GSA Administrator Harold S. Trimmer. On Dean's instructions, he prepared GSA Administrator Robert Kunzig's official response about the request for documents, a memorandum that would be provided to the subcommittee. In an "Administratively Confidential" note, Trimmer told Dean:

> "At your request, the memorandum makes no reference to two items not requested by the Subcommittee, but contained in GSA's files. These items are a September 18, 1970, memo from John Ehrlichman to members of the Property Review Board, and a September 28, 1970, memo from [PRB Executive Secretary] Darrell M. Trent to certain officers of the Executive Branch.
>
> "Please note that no restriction was placed upon circulation of these items, and that, although they were closely held within GSA, they may have been seen in the normal course of events by subordinate staff of this agency.
>
> "I believe that the existence of these items, not requested by the Subcommittee, is itself good reason to comply with the Subcommittee's request for other, less critical materials. In my opinion, compliance with the Subcommittee's request may well avoid a confrontation that may, in turn, lead to further requests, including requests for items such as these."

The two memos Trimmer references, and which the subcommittee did not request – the very existence of which he strongly feels should be hidden – demonstrate the president's direct involvement in the transfer.

That alone – that it was the president who initiated, and pushed for, the land to be taken from the Marine Corps and put into state and/or private hands – was sufficient for these aides to cover up these documents and hide them from Congress. Not only because this would be a political problem on its own, but would lead to questions about why the president insisted on this, and only this, transfer.

A few weeks later, on May 25, the House Committee on Armed Services unanimously voted down the proposal to excess 3,400 acres from Camp Pendleton, but supported the Marines' compromise suggestion that six miles of beach be leased to the state for public use, provided that the Marines always have access to it for amphibious landing exercises.

The next day, during a meeting with Haldeman and National Security Advisor Henry Kissinger, Nixon brought up the committee vote. Haldeman assured him it wouldn't make a difference:

Nixon: "Incidentally, on Pendleton: I hope somebody got on it right away when it was turned down in the House and made a positive out of it. 'The lease goes forward, and everything's just hunky-dory' and so forth. Right?"

Haldeman: "Well..."

Nixon: "The lease does, except for their..."

Haldeman: "The House has no authority..."

Nixon: "Oh, it doesn't, huh?"

Haldeman: "...you just...you took the action and you submit the action to the House committee, uh, for a thirty-day review, and...[unintelligible]...if they don't like it, but now you can do what you want about it."

In July, Nixon made a rare personal appearance at a Property Review Board meeting in the West Wing with Armed Services Members to discuss Camp Pendleton. The chairman and representatives indicated their dissatisfaction with how the process for that base varied significantly from the board's evaluation of all other proposed military property transfers, and their concern the board was telling the military services what they do and do not need. Both sides stood firm, claiming that their rights and prerogatives would be protected.

In the Oval Office across the hall, Haldeman suggested that the president briefly stop in to the meeting, saying,

Haldeman: "Just stick your head in the Roosevelt Room... Hébert, Arends, Stratton and Bill Grey are over there meeting on the Property Review Board..."

Nixon: "They're there now?"

Haldeman: "Yeah...Hébert, Arends, and Grey, were the, you know, the ones that really did the work on the draft...they're meeting on Pendleton and that kind of stuff, which you don't want to get into. But you just stick your head in and say 'you guys are doing a great job...'"

President Nixon entered the meeting briefly to welcome the Members and call for cooperation between the Executive and Congressional representatives. The contentious meeting adjourned without any agreement being reached. Despite the vote and the Members' views, the White House moved forward with the plan. Instead of attempting to fully transfer the parcel, the strategy became to lease it to the state, with restrictive covenants allowing the land to come back to the federal government.

The DoD would still have to declare the land as excess for the lease to proceed, though, and the rest of the summer was spent trying to maneuver the department to accede to the president's wishes, while fighting calls in Congress to prohibit the land's transfer, sale, or even lease.

Seeking to prevent that from happening, the White House relented and furnished the subcommittee with documents (withholding the most important ones) with the understanding that they not be published.

While Weber was negotiating with Hébert to get the House to support the transfer, others were moving forward with plans for the lease. In late July, the House passed the Military Construction Authorization Act, with the prohibition on any sort of sale, transfer, or lease of the parcel. This caught the White House by surprise; Clark MacGregor, Counsel to the President on Congressional Relations, believed he had made a deal with Hébert and Ranking Member Leslie Arends (R-Illinois) to allow for the lease, and not the transfer, of the land.

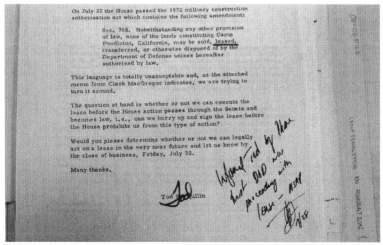

Detail of memo from Tod Hullin to John Dean, July 27, 1971. From the Richard Nixon Presidential Library.

Staff assistant Tod Hullin asked Dean if they could execute the lease before the Senate passes the bill, writing, "can we can we hurry up and sign the lease before the House prohibits us from this type of action?"

Dean noted on the memo that he called Hullin to inform him that despite the pending prohibition the DoD was proceeding, "ASAP."

IT WAS TIME TO WRAP UP EFFORTS TO SECURE THE LAND FOR the Nixon Library at Camp Pendleton. At the end of the summer the president replaced Weber with Donald Rumsfeld as chairman of the Property Review Board.

Concerned the DoD was "less than enthusiastic" about the plan and "given the sensitivity of this issue and the President's strong interest in it and the proposed future use of the property" Dean recommended to Ehrlichman that he (Dean) take over negotiations; Ehrlichman agreed.

It was also at this time that Dean wrote his memo describing the plan as "controversial" and urging "no overt action" until after the election.

No overt action, that is, other than leasing the property to the State of California in spite of Congressional disapproval. Owing to the new leadership of the board and the new negotiator, the governments successfully executed the lease on September 1, 1971; it will expire in 2021.

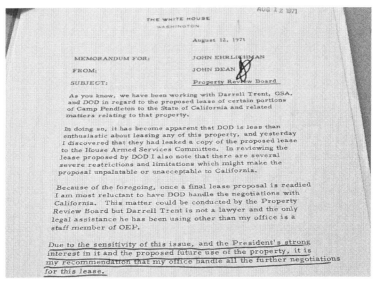

Detail of memo from John Dean to John Ehrlichman, August 12, 1971. From the Richard Nixon Library.

The DoD continued to resist, seeking legislation to require the relevant military service secretary's concurrence if the GSA tried to declare a property as excess, but they lost that fight as well; the White House did not support the legislation, with the president explaining that it would be counter to his executive order establishing the Property Review Board.

And Congress continued to resist, passing the bill to prohibit the "sale, lease, or transfer of lands constituting Camp Pendleton." But the White House already had signed the lease weeks earlier, relying on a legal opinion offered by DoD General Counsel J. Fred Buzhardt, that doing so in spite of pending Congressional prohibition would be lawful.

It was a done deal. The Marines were out their thousands of acres and miles of beach and the president had his dramatic site. All that was left was to find a way to transform those 150 "security buffer" acres next to Nixon's house, which were kept out of the lease, and so still were federal property, into the Nixon Library. For the next eight months, they followed Dean's advice, laying low, and not taking any overt actions on the plan. Besides, they had other things to do.

On January 1, 1972, Nixon announced his intention to seek a second term. In February, he became the first U.S. president to visit the People's Republic of China. In early May, he declared he had ordered North Vietnamese targets bombed and ports mined. In late May, he traveled to the Soviet Union. In June, burglars, acting on orders from the Committee to Re-elect the President, broke into the Democratic National Committee headquarters in the Watergate complex. But instead of that incident and the events of the next fourteen months causing the White House to lay even lower, they made everyone accelerate their work.

ONE MONTH AFTER THE WATERGATE BREAK-IN, NIXON MET with representatives of the Navy, Marine Corps, GSA, the Department of the Interior, and the State of California, to discuss action on the president's request to provide additional facilities to increase public usage of the beach at San Onofre State Park. He wanted to make the case that his transfer of the property resulted in increased usage, and that it was the "highest and best" usage of the land and beach.

A week later, he met with members of the Property Review Board in the Oval Office. With members of the press present, they discussed the Camp Pendleton beach.

One of the questions that Nixon would face, once the library plan was revealed several years later, would be whether that had been a better use of the property than the Corps could have made out of it. With a thriving, popular park surrounding the library, that argument would be easy to make. But it wasn't nearly that popular yet.

Nixon urged the board to find the "best possible uses" for the lands it was transferring. He told the members and reporters, "There's an inertia in government. At all levels…there's bureaucracies in the state governments, and the county governments, and the city governments…I just don't want to have a situation where all we do is to change who's in charge of the property and still not have the property effectively used."

Nixon cited Camp Pendleton as an example. He said he was disappointed when, on July 4, he visited the park that he had created there the previous year – "four miles of the finest beach in America" – and found "at most, *at most*, 200 people on that beach, when there should have been at least 200,000. And there could have been, without despoiling…the beauty of the environment."

Detail, transcript of White House Press Conference, July 25, 1972. From the Richard Nixon Library.

Immediately following the meeting, Chairman Donald Rumsfeld and Executive Secretary Darrell Trent held a press conference in the White House Briefing Room to answer strong questions about the board's transfer of properties. Reporters asked about what are termed as "glaring deficiencies" with the Camp Pendleton parcel, and if any of it had been or would be turned over to "private interests."

Rumsfeld, Trent, and White House Press Secretary Ron Ziegler all denied that any consideration had been given to use the land for anything other than a public park.

As the White House scrambled to contain the fallout from the growing Watergate crisis, it became clear that they wouldn't be able to keep the Camp Pendleton plan secret much longer. The would need to pass legislation both to remove the prohibition on transferring the land and to authorize its use as a presidential archival depository.

The end of 1972 and start of 1973 were inordinately busy, both for the library planners and the White House in general. On October 27, Nixon signed an amendment to the previous year's Military Construction Act, which had prohibited the sale, lease or transfer of the property.

The change allowed that "with respect to said lands [Camp Pendleton] the Secretary of the Navy, or his designee, may grant leases, licenses, or easements pursuant to chapter 159 of title 10, United States Code" – which reads, in relevant part:

> "(a) Lease Authority.— Whenever the Secretary concerned considers it advantageous to the United States, the Secretary concerned may lease to such lessee and upon such terms as the Secretary concerned considers will promote the national defense or to be in the public interest, real or personal property that—
>
> (1) is under the control of the Secretary concerned;
>
> (2) is not for the time needed for public use; and
>
> (3) is not excess property, as defined by section 102 of title 40."

On November 7, Nixon won re-election in one of the largest landslides in history. On December 4, Assistant to the President for Legislative Affairs William Timmons reported to Ehrlichman that the chairmen and ranking members of the House and Senate Armed Services Committees were sympathetic to the idea, and promised fair consideration of the bills (though they did decline an invitation to come to Camp Pendleton, tour the location, and evaluate the library site for themselves).

On December 13, the Vietnam peace talks collapsed; Nixon retaliated with the "Christmas bombings," dropping more than 20,000 tons on Haiphong and Hanoi over eleven days.

In early January 1973, the National Archives proposed a detailed Nixon Library Timetable, anticipating completion by 1976.

On January 8, the Watergate trial began; three days later, break-in leader E. Howard Hunt pleaded guilty to eavesdropping, conspiracy, and burglary.

On January 19, the Planning and Development Committee of the Nixon Foundation met in the Old Executive Office Building to hear a site selection report advocating the Camp Pendleton location by Edward Nixon, the president's brother; the committee approved the site. The next day, Richard Nixon took the oath of office for a second time.

A week later, the parties signed the Paris Peace Accords.

On February 8, H.R. Haldeman, John Ehrlichman, and John Dean met with the directors of the six existing presidential libraries to discuss planning issues for the Nixon Library. Things were moving along nicely.

They had the site chosen and approved. They had fought off the Marines' objections. They had gone around the lease prohibition. They had a smooth path on Capitol Hill. They had a schedule for finishing the library before the president left office (which, of all presidents to have opened libraries to date, only FDR had been able to accomplish).

What they didn't have was a full appreciation of the weight of the freight train that was bearing down on them, and how it would destroy all of their plans – and not just for the library.

The day before the meeting with the six directors, the Senate had passed a resolution establishing the Select Committee on Presidential Campaign Activities – what quickly became known as the Watergate Committee.

THE SPRING AND SUMMER OF 1973 WERE NO LESS BUSY. WORK proceeded on passing the legislation and getting ready for construction, including preparing site and design studies. But the routine administrative work that, in any other administration, would be just that – routine – was far from it.

At the same time that John Dean was considering mundane issues such as road access to the library site and fencing around the property, he began, on April 6, to cooperate with federal Watergate prosecutors; three weeks later, Nixon fired him. Four days after John Ehrlichman negotiated with the city of San Clemente to operate a public golf course on the Camp

Pendleton property, on April 30, he, along with H.R. Haldeman and Attorney General Richard Kleindienst, resigned.

Three days later, on May 3, Rep. Clement J. Zablocki (D-Wisconsin) introduced the War Powers Resolution, limiting the power of the president to commit forces abroad without Congressional approval, in the House of Representatives.

The same day, concerned about how Congress would receive the news that the Camp Pendleton land transfer, all along, secretly had been a plan to build the library, White House Deputy Counsel Fred Fielding wrote a memo to the file describing the project as "on hold for a while."

He suggested that "a requisite congressional cooperation would not be forthcoming" – which he may known at the time would turn out to be a considerable understatement.

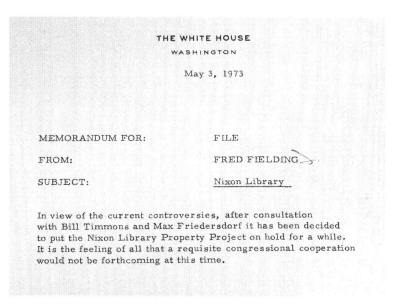

THE WHITE HOUSE
WASHINGTON

May 3, 1973

MEMORANDUM FOR: FILE

FROM: FRED FIELDING

SUBJECT: Nixon Library

In view of the current controversies, after consultation with Bill Timmons and Max Friedersdorf it has been decided to put the Nixon Library Property Project on hold for a while. It is the feeling of all that a requisite congressional cooperation would not be forthcoming at this time.

Memo to the file from Fred Fielding, May 3, 1973. From the Richard Nixon Library.

A week later, the president appointed J. Fred Buzhardt, the DoD General Counsel who had helped to secure the Camp Pendleton land transfer, as Special White House Counsel for Watergate Matters. On May 22, as four of the seven members of the executive board were implicated in the Watergate scandal, the Nixon Foundation announced plans for the library had been put "on the back burner."

But Nixon wasn't giving up. A month later, he issued Executive Order 11724, abolishing the Property Review Board and replacing it with the Federal Property Council, strengthening it and giving the GSA Administrator more authority to declare federal property as excess.

Others involved in planning the library weren't giving up, either. Nixon's firm stances that summer – his refusal to turn over White House tapes subpoenaed by the Senate Watergate Committee, his denial of involvement in the Watergate cover-up – lead Nixon Records Liaison Staff Director Jack Nesbitt to acknowledge to Fred Fielding that the likelihood of Congressional losses in 1974 election would make legislation regarding the Nixon Library at Camp Pendleton more difficult, but that they should plan for activity in 1974. No such activity would take place.

IT ALL BEGAN TO UNRAVEL IN THE FALL OF 1973. ON OCTOBER 10, Vice President Spiro Agnew, under investigation for campaign finance violations and illegal kickbacks while Governor of Maryland, resigned and pleaded "no contest." Two days later, President Nixon nominated House Minority Leader Gerald Ford (R-Michigan) to replace him.

The following weekend, the "Saturday Night Massacre" saw the president order Attorney General Elliot Richardson to fire Watergate Special Prosecutor Archibald Cox, only to have Richardson refuse. Nixon fired him and ordered Deputy Attorney General William Ruckelshaus to fire Cox; Ruckelshaus refused and Nixon fired him. Finally, Solicitor General Robert Bork, the highest-ranking Justice official left, fired Cox.

Over the next few months, Nixon made his famous "I am not a crook" remark to the Associated Press; Gerald Ford was sworn in as vice president; and in his 1974 State of the Union address, Nixon refused to resign, demanding an end to the Watergate investigation.

Six months later, on July 27, while walking along the beach that was to have framed the priceless view of his now-lost library there, Nixon received word that the House Committee on the Judiciary voted 27-11 to approve the first of three articles of impeachment against him.

Perhaps seeking to buck him up, or simply refusing to believe the inevitable, on August 8, during a "hastily-convened" meeting, members of the Nixon Foundation board voted to restart plans for the library.

The next day, Richard Nixon resigned the presidency.

ON A HOT JULY AFTERNOON IN 1990, RICHARD NIXON finally opened his presidential library. After being rejected by Duke University and abandoning a protracted and controversial plan to build it north of La Casa Pacifica in San Clemente, on bluffs overlooking the Pacific (land that is, as of this writing, still empty and in dispute), Nixon gathered with his family, friends, administration officials, and presidents George Bush, Ronald Reagan, and Gerald Ford (Jimmy Carter demurred) to dedicate the building that would make his legacy live for all. Not encircled by four thousand acres of California wilderness. Not with sweeping views of the ocean. Not on the dramatic site he and his advisors worked so diligently, for so long, in secret, to secure. But in Yorba Linda.

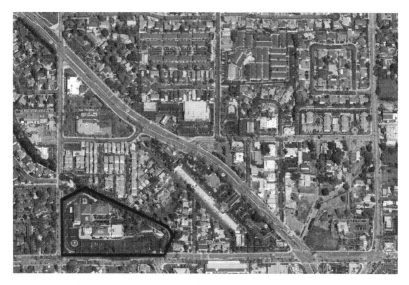

Satellite view of the Nixon Library (outlined), courtesy of Google Maps.

Nixon supporters, especially those now in charge of the Nixon Foundation, complain that Watergate unfairly casts his presidency in negative light, overshadowing his accomplishments (ironically, the Legacy of Parks program is an often-cited example) in favor of a small part of his administration. But Nixon's Secret Library Plan doesn't just show how far presidents will go to ensure and enshrine their legacies. It demonstrates that, no matter what he said he was doing and why he said he was doing it, Nixon likely had far different motives and goals.

There is a lot more for us to learn, buried within the records.

EIGHT MONTHS AFTER NIXON FLED TO SAN CLEMENTE, on April 29, 1975, the first wave of refugees from Vietnam began arriving next door. They later would be resettled, welcomed by communities across the country. Through the end of the year, 50,000 exiles from the war that Richard Nixon had promised to end, but instead escalated and intensified, would come through Camp Pendleton. While there, the men, women, and children who escaped the fall of Saigon with nothing but the clothes on their backs were housed in a tent city on what had been the proposed site for the Nixon Library.

Marine and refugees, Camp Pendleton, 1975. Courtesy of the U.S. Marine Corps.

CHAPTER 7

A WAY FORWARD

"This Library does not say, 'This is how I saw it,' but, 'This is how the documents show it was.'"

President Lyndon Johnson, at the dedication of his presidential library in Austin, Texas, May 22, 1971.

WHERE DO WE GO FROM HERE? HOW DO WE CRAFT CHANGES sufficient to right the ship? How can we make presidential records available in a timely and nonpolitical fashion? How should we reduce the crippling influence of money, politics, and private, partisan organizations in federal presidential libraries? How will we curate balanced, nonpartisan, accurate history exhibits? Must we even be in the business of hosting presidential museums, primary campaign debates, politicians' launching pad speeches, and questionable educational programs – much less square dance lessons, wine tastings, and Remember the '60's parties?

By "we" I mean "the federal government" – which, of course, is us. The presidential libraries are, technically, run by the government: the National Archives, which administers them; the president, who nominates the archivist; and the Congress, which authorizes and appropriates funding for the libraries. But *we* run *them*. We choose our leaders, and therefore our priorities, and we can make our voices heard on these important issues.

Not that it is easy – particularly when contemplating changes in legislation, which is key to reforming the presidential library system. And not the timid, incremental, bites-around-the-edges "reforms" that were passed or considered over the last decade. Those changes benefited primarily the politicians who touted them, and the National Archives, which appears to be "doing something" by embracing the changes, however weak and insufficient.

To fix the presidential library system, we must fix the whole system, in an all-encompassing reform package. The problems with records processing, museum exhibits, money, adherence to existing law, and politicization are not independent of one another. The problems are systemic; the solutions must be as well.

We need systemic reform of the law, regulations, and bureaucracy governing presidential libraries.

As anyone who ever has tried to pass a law – or even to get one introduced – without a ton of money behind them knows, there is a considerable difference between logically, rationally, and systematically devising a solution to a public policy problem, and working with the United States Congress.

But try we must. We cannot continue along our current path. Without external intervention – without the voice of the people – former presidents and library foundations and Members of Congress and NARA officials, all of whom seem quite content with the status quo, will, simply put, do nothing. Too many interests are too closely aligned now for them voluntarily to change. Change must be brought to them.

And therein lies the real problem. For though we should expect NARA leadership to do just that – to lead – decades of inaction and acquiescence to the wishes of presidents and former presidents and presidential families has created a culture of risk-averse, fawning, finger-in-the-air administrators who simply will not lead.

That means, sadly, working with Congress. And the administration. Whichever Congress and administration are in power.

Sadly, because representatives and senators have vested interests in maintaining presidential prerogatives, high secrecy, low access, and closed government. And presidents have even more. Working against those odds will be difficult, but not impossible.

The best solutions are the simplest ones. And the simplest solution is to get the National Archives out of the legacy-management business altogether. That means no more presidential museums. At least not government-operated ones. The Nixon Library proved for seventeen years that a private organization could maintain a presidential museum without government assistance.

Some may point out that the driving forces for the Nixon Foundation and family to seek entrance into the federal system were decreasing financial resources and increasing challenges of operating on their own. But that just underscores a hard truth: for the most part, interest in presidential museums declines over time. They are not self-sustaining institutions. Foundations need the government far more than the government needs foundations (or, for that matter, the responsibility of running presidential museums).

NARA tries to make it seem as if the libraries are self-sustaining because the agency believes that without the public aspects – the museums, and the museum visitors, and the museum gift shop customers, and the public program participants, and the event rentals, and the media attention for all of it – there would be very little reason for presidents to build, and Congress to spend so much money on, just an archival library.

But that's the core mission, approved by Congress: an archival library. Not a tourist attraction. Not a political entity. Certainly not a shrine.

The Library of Congress, which houses the papers of far more presidents, doesn't celebrate or memorialize them, much less "promote understanding of the presidency and the American experience" as NARA touts (and their collections are considerably more open). The Smithsonian Institution, the world's largest museum and research complex, hosts a single exhibit about all of the presidents (and the National Portrait Gallery includes the Hall of Presidents).

We, as taxpayers, as a government, as a nation, should get out of the business of operating anything other than archival institutions dedicated to preserving and making presidential records available as quickly and as thoroughly as possible. But we won't. Not for the foreseeable future. The stakes are too high and interest in wholesale change is too low.

So how do we fix the worst problems until we can get back to the original purpose of presidential libraries? Through changes in the law, certainly. But money is the key. We need to simultaneously get money out of, and money into, the system.

GETTING MONEY OUT OF PRESIDENTIAL LIBRARIES WILL BE like ending concussions in the National Football League. In both cases, the people who run things are not only convinced that they're inherent parts of the system, but they cannot imagine any other way.

Presidents see libraries as their right, having earned them through their time in office and the hundreds of millions of dollars they raise for them. Foundations see the libraries as "theirs" even after they deed, lease, or transfer control to the government, to use them as they see fit. Presidents' families see the libraries as their best (and sometimes last) hope to keep the flame alive, to keep themselves relevant, and, more and more, to further their own political careers.

Processing millions of textual records is expensive, time-consuming, painstaking work, and does not attract the kind of financial attention and star power that, say, an internationally-televised presidential primary debate might. And telling former presidents and their foundations only should they not spend millions on unnecessary museum renovations but that they might consider using the money to make their records available more quickly won't win the National Archives any political support.

NARA sees the libraries as the jewels in their crown, a base of political power, and their entrée to a world that normally would be well beyond their reach. And they know that, under current law, if a president forgoes building a library, the agency would have to provide a place to preserve the tens of millions of records and tens of thousands of artifacts and all the rest of the treasures normally housed in the libraries.

The money has to go. At least, the private money does. And with it, the private organizations. Out. Out of presidential libraries. Out of decisions on what history is told, how it is told, if it is told. Out of the choices of who gets to speak and what they get to say. Out of the way of what is supposed to be an impartial, nonpartisan, professional agency. And out of the business of using government institutions to raise political money.

So does that mean no private presidential foundations? Of course not. Former presidents should be free to establish private organizations. Think tanks. Policy centers. Freedom Institutes. They should be free to build and operate private museums, even. But no more presidential libraries. Not as we know them now.

The presidents and the foundations and the National Archives aren't the only ones who bear responsibility for the current state of the system. In fact, they don't really bear any responsibility; they're working within the boundaries (and, at times, outside of the boundaries) set by Congress. That's who's responsible.

Congress, which each year gives the National Archives a too-small budget, has them spend almost a quarter of it on presidential libraries, and does not require – does not demand – that presidential records are prioritized. Almost one hundred million dollars a year, and yet the records are unprocessed. FOIA wait times exceed a decade. Electronic records are lost. Congress could change this. Overnight.

Even though it appears that the Executive Branch agencies run the government, by law they may not take any actions nor spend any money without the authorization and appropriation of Congress. Each year, Congress gives NARA hundreds of millions of dollars. And each year, Congress does not require NARA to fulfill its mission.

So, yes, NARA is at fault for choosing to reduce critical space for researchers in favor of a gift shop; replacing the inordinately valuable National Archives Library with a trendy and ill-defined "Innovation Hub"; and putting exhibits and public programs over processing records and making them available.

But Congress can change that.

Here is how we get private money and the negative influences it brings out of presidential libraries: by *funding* presidential libraries. We spend a lot of money on them already, but Congress isn't spending it on the right things. Not on the things that will ensure that records are preserved and the public has timely access to them.

Appropriations will only take care of part of the problem, though; the rest will have to come through Congress' power to authorize (and to prohibit). And it's not just NARA that Congress has to regulate; we need to change what presidents may and may not do.

We limit contributions to presidential candidates because we believe that large donations may be seen as influence peddling; what would a donor contributing $50,000 to a candidate expect in return once he or she took office? What about a million dollar benefactor? For politicians used to receiving far lower contributions, thanks to campaign finance limits, what is the effect on six, and even seven, figure contributions?

And if individuals and organizations are willing to take financial risks in elections on challengers – who are not guaranteed success – what does a large contribution to an incumbent president say about that donor's expectations?

The role and purpose of limits on campaign contributions can and have been and will continue to be debated. There seems to be, however, a consensus that some sort of limitation on campaign contributions, or at the very least, disclosure of them – to prevent the outright purchasing of influence – is a good thing.

Why, then, do we allow unlimited, undisclosed contributions to a sitting president's library foundation?

Or to a presidential candidate's brother's, father's, or husband's library foundation?

IT IS A GIVEN THAT WITHOUT AN EFFECTIVE LEGISLATIVE strategy, reform will go nowhere. But before any plans are made to pass legislation, we need to know exactly what needs to be fixed, and how.

Here is a list of changes that desperately are needed. Any Member of the House of Representatives or Senator can send this list to their Office Legislative Counsel, which will turn it into legislative language, identify problems and areas for improvement, suggest ways to strengthen it, and produce a discussion draft of a Presidential Records and Libraries Reform Act in no time (please note that "presidential archival depository" is the legal term for a presidential library):

No president may solicit, accept, nor enter into any agreements for any monetary donations, land, buildings, equipment, or anything of value, for the purposes of establishing a presidential archival depository, nor establish a private organization for the purposes of planning, raising money for, or otherwise establishing a presidential archival depository, until their term of office expires.

It is unlawful for any foreign national to contribute, donate, or spend funds, or anything of value, in connection with the construction and maintenance of any presidential archival depository.

The Archivist may not accept a new presidential archival depository without the express consent of Congress (under current law, the archivist is pre-authorized, unless Congress acts), and after submitting a report on the proposed depository to the relevant committee chairs.

The archivist may not accept a new presidential archival depository until 75% of the nonclassified and 50% of the releasable classified records to be deposited in that presidential archival depository have been reviewed and opened.

The archivist may not accept a material change to an existing presidential archival depository (other than emergency repairs) or any substantial update to a permanent exhibit until 95% of the nonclassified and 75% of the releasable classified records that have been deposited in that presidential archival depository have been reviewed and opened.

The archivist may not accept a new presidential archival depository prior to the review and acceptance of the content of all public exhibits, audio-visual components, and educational programs by an independently-appointed, balanced panel of museum curators, historians, journalists, researchers, archival professionals, and representatives of the immediate predecessor and successor presidents.

The archivist may not accept a material change to an existing presidential archival depository's public exhibits, audio-visual components, or educational programs prior to their review and acceptance by an independently-appointed balanced panel of museum curators, historians, journalists, researchers, archival professionals, and representatives of the immediate predecessor and successor presidents.

The archivist shall not accept, take title to, or enter into any agreement to use any land, facility, or equipment for the purpose of creating a presidential archival depository unless the archivist determines that the purpose of the depository will be solely for the operation of the depository; and any land, facility, or equipment owned by a library support organization and located within or near the depository is limited in purpose to providing direct support to the depository, such as retail or food services.

The archivist shall not accept, take title to, or enter into any agreement to use any land, facility, or equipment for the purpose of creating a presidential archival depository unless the archivist determines that there is available by gift or bequest an endowment amount equal to $20,000,000, for the purpose of providing public and educational programs, and maintaining museum exhibits, at such depository.

If a proposed physical or material change or addition to a presidential archival depository would result in an increase in the costs of operations, the archivist may not accept any gift for the purpose of making such a change or addition, or may not implement any provision of law requiring the making of such a change or addition, unless the archivist determines that: the purpose of the change or addition will be solely for the operation of the depository; any land, facility, or equipment owned by a library support organization and located within or near the change or addition must be limited in purpose to providing direct support to the depository, such as retail or food services; and unless the archivist determines that there is available by gift or bequest an endowment amount equal to $20,000,000, for the purpose of providing public and educational programs, and maintaining museum exhibits, at such depository.

In calculating the endowment amount with respect to any presidential archival depository to which the archivist takes title or enters into an agreement for the creation of the depository, the archivist shall determine the total cost of the land, facility, and equipment of the depository by taking into account all costs of such land, facility, and equipment, including support space and nonusable space, regardless of whether title is or will be vested in the United States; and the total cost to research, design, build, equip, and install all museum exhibits and public spaces, including but not limited to entrance halls, rotundas, and foyers; admission areas; auditoriums, theaters, and classrooms; public exhibit spaces; and private event spaces.

In calculating the additional endowment amount with respect to any physical or material change or addition to a Presidential archival depository, the archivist shall determine the total cost of the land, facility, and equipment of the depository by taking into account all costs of such land, facility, and equipment, including support space and nonusable space, regardless of whether title is vested in the United States; and the total cost to research, design, build, equip, and install all new or updated museum exhibits.

The archivist may not accept any nonfederal records for deposit in a presidential archival depository without a deed of gift transferring immediate legal and physical custody to the United States, and unless the archivist receives an endowment sufficient to cover the cost of arrangement, description, and preservation of said records.

Reiterating the will of Congress expressed in the Presidential Libraries Act Amendments of 1986, the archivist may offer the privilege of consultation to a president on the appointment of the first director of that president's archival depository, but appointment authority will be vested solely in the archivist; under no circumstances will the archivist offer a consultation privilege to presidential spouses, representatives, family members, foundations, or any other persons or organizations.

Said presidential consultation will only occur with the appointment of the first director of a presidential archival depository, and not with any successor directors. Such appointments must be made without regard to political affiliation or potential to support or contradict a president, presidential family member, or presidential library foundation.

No federal employee shall serve in a position, compensated, uncompensated, or ex-officio, in a foundation, university, or private organization established to build or support a presidential archival depository.

Other than for the proper arrangement, description, and preservation of presidential records and gifts, no federal employee may work on any issues relating to the establishment of a presidential archival facility for a president currently serving a term in office, including the development of or coordination with a presidential library foundation.

The authority granted to the archivist by the National Archives and Records Administration Efficiency Act of 2004 (44 U.S. Code § 2119) to transfer funds from NARA to foundations or institutes organized to support NARA or presidential archival depositories operated by it for the public purpose of carrying out NARA programs is hereby rescinded.

In charging and collecting a fee for admission to a presidential archival depository, the archivist may not collect any additional amount with the fee if the additional amount is to be transferred to any other entity, such as a library support organization.

No library support organization, university, or any nonfederal entity may use, for any purpose, government-owned or government-controlled space, offices, equipment, or information systems.

No presidential archival depository accepted and maintained by the archivist may contain presidential office suites, presidential family suites, private apartments or offices, or other personal, off-limits spaces.

As for the records, new legislation would help. But for a start, mandating that presidents can't open new libraries, or make changes to existing libraries, before a large portion of the records are open should spur lots of creative ways to speed up the process.

While presidents want to "celebrate" their presidencies and support their party's next nominee (who, more and more, seem to be related to presidents with libraries) as soon as possible after they leave office, there's no valid reason to open a presidential library museum decades and decades before the records are open.

And since it's a choice we can make, we should prioritize opening records. And if we're still in the museum business, that can come second. Records should come first; it's the National Archives, after all.

THE PUBLIC PHASE OF THE SITE SELECTION PROCESS FOR THE
Barack Obama Presidential Library was the shortest on record. While
behind-the-scenes work is expected (and likely), President Obama
waited until well into his second term even to announce the incorporation of his foundation and the opening of the process; by that time in their
terms, each of his thirteen predecessors already had announced the final
choice for the location of their libraries (though, as it turned out, some of
those choices were less final than others).

The president who began planning his library the earliest was Jimmy
Carter, who established the Carter Foundation for Governmental Affairs
on December 6, 1976 – one month after winning the presidential election. He asked John Dunn, the Georgia state archivist, to begin planning
for the eventual transfer of his papers to the National Archives, and a library to be built in his home state.

Perhaps having learned from the mistakes and tribulations of his
predecessors, the Obama Foundation released a request for proposals
that was the most detailed and thorough of any such document yet made
available to the public. Even so, not every candidate site the foundation
chose to be one of the finalists met all of the requirements at first.

The University of Chicago's bid included land for the library that they
did not own or control, which did not sit well with the foundation. In
December 2014, the foundation informed the university that they would
need to resolve control of any proposed sites in order to remain in the
competition.

And in early February, 2015, the foundation leaked the story that the
president had ceded the site decision to First Lady Michelle Obama, who
was leaning towards choosing Columbia University, in New York.

This political move forced the university, along with Chicago Mayor
Rahm Emmanuel, into high gear; they pressed the city's Park District
board and Plan Commission to approve the transfer of city property;
rounded up aldermanic votes; staged rallies to demonstrate what they
described as a high degree of local desire for the library; and leaked a
push poll showing overwhelming support.

But opposition came from two different groups: community organizers who demanded the university fulfill an earlier promise to create a
trauma center in an urgently-needed area, and conservationists who objected to using historic park land for the library, when other university-
owned land was available right across the street.

No presidential foundation would want to announce the site of the library without being absolutely certain the land is available and locked in. It's happened several times before. Groups have opposed potential sites for earlier libraries; it wasn't always about the president's politics.

Universities and communities have rejected, or have tried to reject, presidential libraries for Nixon at Duke University, Reagan at Stanford University, Kennedy in Cambridge, Massachusetts, Carter in Atlanta, and George W. Bush at Southern Methodist University. Harry Truman and his brother and sister disagreed over the use of the family farm in Grandview, Missouri.

Land acquisition troubles even go back to the first federal presidential library, for Franklin Roosevelt. When he deeded the property for the library to the government at a ceremony in 1939, the Archivist of the United States had to fake signing the deed, because FDR's mother Sara Delano Roosevelt, who owned the property, sailed for Europe without signing it over – which eventually she did a few weeks later.

From my reading of the media stories about the Chicago and Honolulu bids for the Obama Library, it seems as if not many truly understand what a presidential library is, what it could mean for the location, and what it won't (or can't) do for a community. In terms of high expectations for the library to be transformative, Chicago (and to a lesser extent, Hawaii) represents an order of magnitude greater than those for any other presidential library.

Granted, the Obama Foundation's Request for Proposals and Request for Qualifications contained indications that this presidential center will seek to be more transformative with their programs and effect on the community than had earlier library proposals, but not by a considerable amount. For earlier ones, what had been grand designs for international symposia and community outreach have ended up, just a few years later, as movie nights, book signings, proms, weddings, and political events.

In almost every prior library example, both the touted benefits and the dire warnings have been overstated. With the exception of the Clinton Library, which was built in a derelict industrial warehouse district that has become the popular "River Market" area, the promised economic benefits of libraries have, for the most part, failed to meet expectations, particularly when it comes to the long-term effect.

No matter how popular a president is upon leaving office, years go by, administration officials move on, principals pass away, and interest wanes. It's hard to imagine, but the library that holds the (most credible) annual attendance record is the Eisenhower – 765,000 – achieved in the year after his death, 1969-1970. No other library (including the Eisenhower, since then) has come within 200,000 visitors of equaling that mark; it took the most recent library (as of this writing) fourteen months to reach 500,000 visitors. And while President Obama will be a young ex-president, if he follows the pattern of engagement set by Carter and Clinton, the library soon will be a relative afterthought to his work.

Journalist Jonathan Alter wrote of President Obama (in 2009), "to the extent that he had thought about a library, he mused to a friend that maybe it should be an 'online library,' not bricks-and-mortar."

In fact, Obama doesn't have to build a presidential museum. He can – and should – build a presidential library; an archive where the textual and electronic records and other materials of his presidency may be preserved and made available to the public as quickly and as thoroughly as possible – but not a museum. And the library doesn't have to be a spectacular building on historic parkland that, just a few years after opening, becomes a less and less visited institution in a city filled with them.

Imagine raising hundreds of millions of dollars but not building a "presidential center." Imagine the impact that a digital Obama Library – with online access to records, photographs, videos, lesson plans, exhibits, tutorials, oral and video histories, with cutting-edge design and state-of-the-art search and retrieval technology – would have on education, journalism, history, and communities and individuals all across the world.

If he must build a museum, I hope that he doesn't follow recent precedent and build a self-congratulatory, anti-historical temple that ignores inconvenient facts and overemphasizes his achievements.

And if he must build a museum like that, like his immediate predecessors, I hope that he does not donate it to the people of the United States, for us to operate in perpetuity – especially if he does nothing legislatively to fix the way libraries are funded and maintained. Neither the Presidential Libraries Act nor the Presidential Records Act require a president to build anything; nor, if they do, to donate it to the government.

Think of the impact to Obama's legacy – to posterity – if, instead of the largest or the most expensive or the most laudatory or the most "architecturally significant," his library became the fastest to process and release all of its records. If he became the one to stop the dangerous and expensive growth of the institution whose founder, Franklin D. Roosevelt, would not recognize. If finally he matched his presidential rhetoric ("the most transparent administration in history") with his actions by building a different kind of presidential library: one with open records and no private history.

If a one-term president, with no other federal experience, such as Carter, or the unelected president, Ford, decided not to build one, the system likely would have lived on. But if a two-term president, the first African-American elected to the office – the candidate who received the most votes in the history of the United States – could forgo building a shrine, his successors would have a hard time restarting the "tradition."

If only Nixon could go to China, only Obama can end the presidential self-memorialization craze.

Certainly, history would record such a deed as great in and of itself. And the emphasis on preserving, opening, and making his records available rapidly would allow for a full and lasting assessment his presidency – which was Roosevelt's original intent for presidential libraries.

DOES ANY OF THIS ULTIMATELY MATTER? DOES THE conduct of presidents past have any relation to the conduct of presidents current and future? Does the record of what they did, what they didn't do, what they ought to do, and why, make any difference in our lives? Does the way we present their history affect our judgment in creating our own future?

If the answer to these questions is no, then we've both wasted a considerable amount of time. And we as a country are wasting a billion dollars a decade. We may as well stop worrying about presidents and how we remember them.

If we do that, though, we may as well stop worrying about presidents and how we elect them, too. If it matters who *is* president, and what he or she is doing, it matters who *was* president, and what he or she did. And if that matters, so do the records, and the history that we pay for and stamp with our approval.

So if the answer is yes – this all matters – there are more specific questions to ask and to answer.

Should we continue to build, operate, and fund presidential libraries? Where – and how – do we make the cutoff? Should we separate the foundations from the government operations? Will presidents before Herbert Hoover receive government-operated libraries? Should each library be maintained by taxpayers indefinitely?

How can we remove the harmful effects that politics, biased exhibits, and private history have on what are purportedly nonpartisan institutions? Will anyone attempt the legislative and regulatory reforms of the previous chapter? At what point in the research and tourist statistics do we send the records back to Washington and let the foundations run the museums on their own?

These are difficult questions, ones that neither the National Archives nor the thirteen existing presidential library foundations seem prepared to answer in any way other than "no…let's just keep doing as we have done." And, for now, they seem to be the only ones saying anything at all. Tourists, for the most part, are blissfully unaware of the inaccuracies, the missing subjects, and the controversies over how history is rewritten inside (and, thanks to educational curricula, outside) the presidential libraries they check off on their road trip lists.

Historians and other researchers, as long as they have access to the records, will be content to pore over them in the research room, ignoring the museums next door. Journalists, if they don't have an internal controversy to write about or a major scandal to uncover, won't summon the energy or expend the capital to pitch their editors to allow them to spend months on long-form think pieces about the future of presidential legacy.

Most of the professional organizations that work closely with the National Archives – on open government, Freedom of Information, digitization, public history, the National Historical Publications and Records Commission, and state and local government records – don't criticize the agency, and don't push for major, meaningful reform, for fear of rocking the boat, and risking NARA's ire and the loss of their own access and clout with the agency. Individual users of the presidential libraries and NARA have no way to act collectively, even if they had the desire and will to get involved.

Leadership in this area will not be forthcoming, I believe, from within the National Archives. As federal budgets shrink, Congressional gridlock worsens, and presidents become more insistent on enshrining their legacy, NARA will continue to cultivate those who are most able to help the agency – and that decidedly does not include run-of-the-mill researchers, much less the average taxpayer.

And Congress? There's an old joke (one that I tell ruefully, now that I know how true it is), that the reason meaningful reform of the laws governing presidential libraries isn't possible is that the United States Senate is made up of 100 individuals who each think that one day they'll have their own presidential library. Ask those Senators to reform the system, and give up the dream of their own taxpayer-funded legacy shrine?

Several years ago, once I decided to include in this book my proposals for reforming the libraries, I imagined I would somehow champion the reforms upon publication. That I would lobby Members of Congress to enact positive changes. That I would exhort the National Archives to resist political pressure from former presidents, their surrogates, their families, and their water-carriers on Capitol Hill; embrace their status as an independent agency; and practice open government (and not, as I believe they currently are doing, simply employ the buzzwords surrounding that movement). That I would urge the White House to issue executive orders and memoranda protecting and prioritizing records. And that I would rally support from among professional organizations, historians, archivists, researchers and other stakeholders.

Then I became a senior Congressional staffer, and I saw how the sausage was made.

It became abundantly clear to me that without broad, balanced representation – in oversight hearings, legislative negotiations, and, most importantly, on NARA's advisory committee – of all relevant stakeholders, the library foundations and those within the agency and Congress that support them will make sure their interests are protected above those of our citizenry. Even with such increased and equitable representation, our task is formidable.

Decisions are made by people who show up, but if the people most affected by decisions about presidential libraries – historians, journalists, researchers, writers, filmmakers, students, and tourists – aren't invited, are blocked from participating, even, then the decisions will be made only by those who are allowed to show up: those who have the most to gain from fact-free exhibits, politicized events, slowly-opened records, and aggressive policing of public history by government employees doing the work of private political organizations.

I am no longer enthusiastic about playing any meaningful role in reform, and not just because I'm no longer in a position to affect Congressional oversight (and not just because, by revealing what I've revealed,

I'm most likely no longer welcome to help improve the presidential libraries). More than that, I'm not optimistic that any kind of reform even is possible, at least not in the current climate – which, from the results of the last two elections, seems likely to remain as-is for a long, long time.

Without millions of dollars and other strong levers, lobbying – particularly grass-roots lobbying for the kinds of issues involved with presidential libraries and public documents – is a complete waste of time. Members of Congress, who are re-elected at a rate exceeding ninety-five percent, vote along party lines more often than nine out of ten times. They are now virtually immune to such anachronisms as reasoned argument and the pleas of those whom, ostensibly, they represent. Patently-obvious problems urgently requiring their concentrated attention fall victim to the six hours a day Members must dial for dollars, and to the requirements of those they truly serve: donors.

As I demonstrated in a 2013 Salon.com article, collecting co-sponsorships for legislation not only does not increase the chance of its passage, it decreases it. In the House of Representatives, legislation is no longer even debated; despite what appear to be deliberations in committee markups or on the Floor (and they're not, actually), bills aren't voted on unless the House leadership knows, in advance, that the outcome they desire is guaranteed.

And if you can't connect an outrageous, unsubstantiated allegation of criminal activity on the part of the president and/or the cabinet to any of these issues, you're not going to get a hearing out of the committees of jurisdiction in the Senate or the House. One cannot "fight the good fight" in those circumstances; there's no longer even any venue for such a fight.

If we can get private money and private foundations out of – and openness and transparency into – presidential libraries, we have a chance to fix things; if we can't, we don't. There's just no other way.

In any event, I trust I have made my case. I have described and documented real problems and provided clear solutions. I hope that others, who may be blessed with optimism – and strong stomachs – will join the ongoing campaign to improve, refocus, and reform our presidential libraries.

"We believe that people ought to work out for themselves, and through their own study, the determination of their best interest rather than accept such so-called information as may be handed out to them by certain types of self-constituted leaders who decide what is best for them."

President Franklin D. Roosevelt, at the dedication of his presidential library in Hyde Park, New York, June 30, 1941.

ACKNOWLEDGMENTS

THE NUMBER OF PEOPLE WHO HAVE CONTRIBUTED TO THIS book is considerable. Traveling around the country over the last twelve years, visiting and re-visiting the presidential libraries and other organizations, I have had the privilege of working with many impressive individuals who went out of their way to be helpful. While it may not be possible to thank each one by name – for their guidance, candor, and thoughtfulness – forgive me as I try, and if I unintentionally omit anyone.

My first NARA experience was not, as it is with most, as a tourist, viewing the Charters of Freedom or attending a public event. It was as a young researcher, while in college: examining records of the Census and the Department of the Navy to explore my family history. My initial visit was at the direction of a history professor; it was the first and last time anyone had to encourage me to go to the National Archives.

I was keen as I walked into the main Archives Building, using the researcher entrance on Pennsylvania Avenue. I was respectful as I entered the quietly beautiful research room on the second floor. But I did not anticipate the combination of awe, reverence, and joy that I felt when an archivist rolled over to me the cart on which lay large, bound volumes wrapped in red cellophane: the deck logs of the ships on which my grandfather, FC1 Michael T. Pavlicin, USN, served in the years just after the First World War. The archivist told me that the wrapping was original, and, as it had yet to be broken, I was the first researcher to work with those particular logs. From that first encounter – with records as well as with archivists – I was hooked, and I kept coming back.

Researching this book, NARA staff members in the Washington, D.C area and at the libraries were professional, thoughtful, and helpful. They treated me with professionalism, courtesy, and respect, and provided me with, to my knowledge, every document, photograph, film, videotape, and audio tape that they were able and authorized to provide. They made themselves available for in-person interviews and follow-up questions.

Before and after my visits, staff responded promptly and thoroughly to my requests, usually within a day or two. Their assistance and encouragement has been important to me, especially over a long period of time and through trying circumstances. The officers and staff of the private foundations with whom I was able to meet were generous with their time and greatly aided my research. I am thankful for the diligent work of all of these fine people. In my opinion, they do not get nearly enough credit and recognition for their outstanding efforts, which are, for dedicated professionals such as they, everyday occurrences.

I would like to thank the following individuals employed by the National Archives: Archivist of the United States David Ferriero, and staff members Sam Anthony, Jay Bosanko, Laurence Brewer, Carmen Colón, David Davis, Laura Diachenko, Sheila Drumheller, Jane Fitzgerald, Matt Fulgham, William Harris, Jefferey Hartley, Walter Hill, Chris Isleib, Diana Johnston, Judy Koucky, Richard Marcus, David McMillen, Shawn Morton, Miriam Nisbet, Jay Olin, Lawrence Patlen, Richard Peuser, John Simms, Vernon Smith, Ashley Smoot, Gary M. Stern, Steve Tilley, Debra Wall, Paul Wester, Kathleen Williams, and Corinna Zarek.

Officials and staff at the libraries were inordinately helpful, and I offer them my thanks: former Herbert Hoover Library Director Timothy Walch and staff members Craig Wright, Matthew Schaefer, Lynn Smith, Mary Evans, Maureen Harding, and Dwight Miller; former Franklin D. Roosevelt Library Directors Lynn Bassanese, Cynthia Koch, and Verne Newton, and staff members Herman Eberhardt, Jeffrey Urbin, Joanne Tammaro, and Clifford Laube; Harry S. Truman Library staff members Pauline Testerman, Mark Adams, Clay Bauske, Sam Rushay, Randy Sowell, John Miller, Liz Safly, Susan Medler, and Ray Geselbracht; Dwight D. Eisenhower Library Director Karl Weissenbach, former Director Dan Holt, and staff members Valoise Armstrong, Chalsea Millner, Stacy Meuli, Kim Barbieri, and Dennis Medina; John F. Kennedy Library Director Thomas Putnam and staff members James Hill, Nancy McCoy, Allan Goodrich, Laurie Austin, Jane Lindsay, Stephen Plotkin, Sharon

Kelly, and Michael Desmond; former Lyndon Baines Johnson Library Directors Harry Middleton and Betty Sue Flowers, and staff members Tina Houston, Anne Wheeler, Marsha Sharp, Claudia Anderson, Sandor Cohen, Michael MacDonald, Judy Allen, and Jennifer Parks; former Richard Nixon Library Director Timothy Naftali and staff members Cary McStay, Jason Schultz, Olivia Anastasiadis, Gregory Cumming, Meghan Lee-Parker, Paul Wormser, Paul Musgrave, Carla Braswell, and Mindy Farmer; Gerald R. Ford Library Director Elaine Didier, Deputy Director James Kratsas and staff members David Horrocks, William McNitt, Stacy Davis, Donald Holloway, Helmi Raaska, Janice Berling, Kristin Mooney, Barbara Packer, and Joshua Cochran; former Jimmy Carter Library Director Jay Hakes, Deputy Director David Stanhope, and staff members James Yancey, Jr., Tony Clark, Robert Bohanan, Albert Nason, Sylvia Naguib, Bettie Brown, and Jennifer Thompson; Ronald Reagan Library Director R. Duke Blackwood, and staff members Mike Duggan, Sherrie Fletcher, John Langellier, Lou Anne Missildine, Shelly Williams, Tony Chauveaux, and Kelly Barton; George Bush Library Director Warren Finch, former Director Douglas Menarchik, and staff members Brian Blake and Christopher Pembelton; William Jefferson Clinton Library Director Terri Garner and staff member Kim Coryat; George W. Bush Library Director Alan Lowe and staff member John Orrell.

My thanks to those at several of the private presidential library foundations for their cooperation and assistance, including former Hoover Association Executive Director Becky Allgood and staff member Patricia Hand; former Roosevelt Institute President Andrew Rich; Truman Library Institute Executive Director Alex Burden and staff members Kim Rausch, Tom Heurtz, and Kim Brown; former Eisenhower Foundation Executive Director Mack Teasley and former President Stewart Etherington; former Johnson Foundation Executive Director Joe Youngblood and Retail Manager Blair Newberry; former Nixon Library and Birthplace Archivist Susan Naulty; Ford Foundation Chairman Emeritus Marty Allen; former Bush Foundation Executive Director Roman Popadiuk and Bush family spokesman Jim McGrath; and Clinton Foundation Museum Store Manager, the kind and generous Connie Fails.

Kickstarter, the web site that enables creative individuals to realize their goals, proved to be an invaluable resource. Books are the second-least successful kind of projects on the site, yet with the help of many individuals – half of whom I did not know when I began – ours succeeded, and I was able to complete my research. I would like to express my thanks to those who took a chance on me, pledging their support as backers, and ensuring we would reach our goal.

I am grateful to those at two other organizations who extended me courtesies: Francis X. Blouin, Jr. and the late Marilyn McNitt at the Bentley Historical Library at the University of Michigan, Ann Arbor, for their kind assistance in locating the relevant papers of former Archivist Robert Warner and of the Ford Library; and Lt. Ryan Finnegan, USMC, Sgt. Valerie Nash, USMC, and Mr. Larry Rannals, aboard United States Marine Corps Base Camp Pendleton, in California, for allowing me to view the areas of the base adjacent to the property referred to in Chapter 6.

In my research I was privileged to have encountered many terrific archivists, all of whom care deeply about improving their profession as well as assisting researchers. I would like to thank Mark Allen Greene, Elizabeth W. Adkins, Barbara Teague, Trudy Huskamp Peterson, and in particular Richard Cox and Bruce Montgomery, who provided crucial, consistent – and public – support and advocacy for my work among their peers and students, as well as wisdom and guidance along the way.

Advocates of open government, freedom of information and open access are some of the most persistent, devoted, and collaborative professionals with whom I have worked. I thank them for their inspiration, especially Pete Daniel, Sean Moulton, Daniel Schuman, Carl Malamud, Thomas Blanton, R. Bruce Craig, Patrice McDermott, Arnita Jones, Page Putnam Miller, Rick Blum, Kevin Goldberg, and the always thoughtful, ever encouraging Heather Joseph.

In my efforts to provide oversight of the libraries – distinctly apart from the writing of this book – I was greatly aided by the talented professionals in the Congressional Research Service of the Library of Congress. They are unsung heroes who, against all reasonable expectations, consistently provide Members and staff with highly detailed, impeccably accurate, reliably nonpartisan research products on shockingly brief deadlines (some of which, admittedly, I imposed). I admire them for their inexhaustible knowledge and I thank them for their limitless forbearance, especially Jared Nagel, Christina Alexander, R. Sam Garrett, Erika K. Lunder, Kevin R. Kosar, Christopher M. Davis, the deservedly-legendary Harold C. Relyea, and the exceptional, unflappable Wendy Ginsberg.

Public libraries are inestimable public goods, and we should vote and act as if we believe this with all of our hearts. I particularly want to thank the dedicated librarians at three Maryland public libraries: the Prince George's County Memorial, the Anne Arundel County, and the Charles County, for their efforts on my behalf. I sincerely apologize to them for depleting much of their limited Online Computer Library Center (OCLC) resources in my quest to obtain loans of books and copies of every article ever written about presidential records and libraries (an ambition they ably helped me to meet). I also thank the staff and supporters of two Nassau County, New York, libraries: the Mineola Memorial and the Shelter Rock Public – especially those who served during the years 1969 through 1984, and in particular, Mineola Children's Librarian Lois Catherine Bleimann – all of whom opened worlds to me that, to my astonishment, were contained within the deceptively-limited confines of the most important physical items with which I have ever been presented: books. If my father gave me my love of words, public librarians gave me the means to express that love, and I am in their debt.

Professional colleagues and friends provided much-needed expert advice and backing, including Ken Gormley, Andrew Gumbel, Anna Olswanger, Judy Anna Beck, Allida Mae Black, Charlene Bickford, Ann Schwartz Unitas, Raymond Smock, Yonatan Zamir, and former AP reporter – and great boss – Dick Barnes (who, by combing through campaign records from the General Accounting Office, beat WoodStein to the James McCord/CREEP connection by a day); thank you all.

I wish to thank three historians who were especially important to my work. If Dr. C. David Sutton, Professor Emeritus, Appalachian State University, had not advised me to turn my paper in his graduate course into a book, I very nearly might not have, and I am grateful to him.

Professor Benjamin Hufbauer has seen some of the same records and exhibits and spoken with some of the same individuals and encountered some of the same roadblocks as have I, and so he, perhaps more than anyone else, could empathize; he did, and I thank him. He has produced an excellent analysis of how these libraries and memorials shape our public memory – *Presidential Temples* – and certainly you should read it.

Professor Anna Kasten Nelson, an extraordinarily gifted teacher, writer, and advocate, gave me early and dependably strong encouragement. In addition to her widely-acknowledged expertise as a diplomatic historian, no one knew more about public documents, and making them broadly available, than she. Deeply troubled about the way the National Archives handled their own records about presidential libraries, her urging me to "get to the bottom of this mess" confirmed that I was on the right track. When I told her I had accepted the position on the House subcommittee that oversees NARA, her response that I was now "in the catbird seat" gave me the courage to try to do what was right, against strong odds and powerful interests. I always will be grateful for her sage advice, her kind support, and for the considerable efforts she made throughout her remarkable career to ensure the preservation of, and our continued access to, presidential and other federal records.

Longtime personal friends Mehrdad Maz, Kevin Ryan, Cathy Barry Rio, Raymond Colby, Alexandra Peeler, Janet Timmes Sorel, John Wirenius, and my second parents, the loving, caring, and gracious Achille and Giovanna Marcoccia, all cheerfully offered their support during many conversations, visits, and meals, kindly asking about my progress towards completing this book and sharing with me the wisdom of their experiences. I thank each of them.

By the time I was eighteen, I had spent two-thirds of my life in Catholic schools. Whatever knocks their leaders have deserved, I have no doubt whatsoever that I am the writer, the critical thinker – the moral human being – I am today largely as a result of the mostly thankless efforts of the dedicated Sisters of Charity of Halifax, Marianist brothers and priests, lay teachers, and staff of my elementary school and high school. I thank them for unrelentingly holding me to high standards, strongly challenging me to ask thoughtful questions, quietly encouraging me to answer those questions for myself, and gently pointing me toward truth.

For more than a decade, my three brothers, John, Tommy, and Mike, have had to listen to many versions of my "brief" description of what this book would be about, where I'd just been (or to where I would be going) for more research, what I'd just discovered or uncovered, and how and if and when, finally, the book would come out. Each time, they made it seem as if it was the first they'd heard about it, and they never let up on their insistence that it was an interesting topic. Thanks, guys.

Hannah Beth Grisar traveled with me to visit two presidential libraries; a proposition that, I confess, can try one's patience, given how carefully (and slowly) I would examine each exhibit. In addition, she spent countless hours considerately listening to my ideas, museum critiques, general declamations about the project, and my challenges in finishing it. She has continually and uncomplainingly offered unflagging encouragement and thoughtful advice. I thank her for all of it.

Elizabeth Anne Haynie, whom I met in first grade, provided much-needed friendship and support to me over the last few years as I finished this book, as well as in the various ups and downs I encountered personally. In addition, she dedicated hours to reading and providing insightful, detailed feedback on some early chapters as I completed them. The varieties of ways in which she has helped me are too numerous to list. I simply offer my eternal gratitude to her (as well as to her family, who were patient while she spent so much time listening to and advising me).

Marco J. Marcoccia, my closest friend for thirty-five years – and, really, my fourth brother – is a constructive critic, reliable skeptic, wise counselor, and a damn fine human being. From halfway around the world, he keeps me as honest as he can, and I thank him for that, and for so much more. My estimation of him can be summed up by this exchange from the episode "He Shall, From Time to Time" of the National Broadcasting Company television series *The West Wing*, when the president is advising a cabinet officer as to what to do should he, in a national crisis, assume the presidency:

> *President Bartlet:* *You got a best friend?*
>
> *Secretary Tribbey:* *Yes, sir.*
>
> *President Bartlet:* *Is he smarter than you?*
>
> *Secretary Tribbey:* *Yes, sir.*
>
> *President Bartlet:* *Would you trust him with your life?*
>
> *Secretary Tribbey:* *Yes, sir.*
>
> *President Bartlet:* *That's your chief of staff.*

Thanks, pal.

NOTES

ABBREVIATIONS

AP – the Associated Press
BHL – Bentley Historical Library, the University of Michigan at Ann Arbor
CST – the Chicago Sun-Times
CT – the Chicago Tribune
FDRL – the Franklin D. Roosevelt Library
FOIA – the Freedom of Information Act
JFKL – the John F. Kennedy Library
HSTL – the Harry S. Truman Library
LBJL – the Lyndon Baines Johnson Library
NARA – the National Archives and Records Administration
NYT – the New York Times
OA – Office of the Archivist of the United States
OMB/PRB – Office of Management and Budget; Procurement Policy Division; Property Review Board Records.
PDD – the President's Daily Diary, Richard Nixon Library
PPF – President's Personal Files, Richard Nixon Library
RNL – the Richard Nixon Library
RRL – the Ronald Reagan Library
SMOF – White House Staff Member and Office Files, Richard Nixon Library
WHCF – White House Central Files, Richard Nixon Library
WHSF – White House Special Files, Richard Nixon Library
WP – the Washington Post

INTRODUCTION

PAGE

4   "Franklin D. Roosevelt donated his family's property…" Memorandum, FDR to Sara Delano Roosevelt, July 28, 1939; Memorandum, Assistant Attorney General Norman L. Littell to FDR, July 27, 1939, FDR Library File, Box 1, Folder 7, FDRL.

4   "Harry Truman's brother and sister…" *Harry S. Truman Library,* HSTL web site: https://www.trumanlibrary.org/places/in25.htm

8   "…including, incredibly, denying that…" Sharon K. Fawcett, recorded interview with the author, Washington, DC, April 18, 2008

8   "…finds out where a presidential library…" Ibid.

8   "NARA can play a key role…" Sharon K. Fawcett, "Briefing paper for meeting with the President," Memorandum to John Carlin, Archivist of the United States, and Lewis Bellardo, Deputy Archivist of the United States, January 11, 1997. Document released to the author through FOIA from OA.

11   "We spend close to a hundred million…" FY 2015 Congressional Justification, March 10, 2014, NARA.

14   "…record number of FOIA lawsuits…" "FOIA Lawsuits Increase During Obama Administration" Transactional Records Access Clearinghouse, Syracuse University, December 20, 2012.

CHAPTER 1: THE LAST CAMPAIGN

PAGE

19   "In his final months in office…" "Cheney Is Ordered to Preserve Records," *AP,* September 20, 2008.

19   "…a president pardons an international fugitive…" Alison Leigh Cowan, "Ex-Wife of Pardoned Financier Pledged Money to Clinton Library," *NYT,* February 9, 2001

19   "…change the numbering on the elevator…" Claudia Anderson, Supervisory Archivist, LBJL, interview with the author, April 27, 2007.

19   "…a president signs an unlawful…" "Archivist Gave Bush Control of Tapes, Will Run His Library," *AP,* February 13, 1993.

20   "A small group of people…" Agreement of Association, John F. Kennedy Memorial Library, December 6, 1963. Folder 2, Subject File, Box 16, the Evelyn Lincoln Collection, JFKL

20   "Congress seizes the papers…" "Presidential Recordings and Materials Preservation Act, 1974" (93-526, December 19, 1974).

20   "Also on the last night…" John Markoff, "Computers Challenge Freedom of Information Act," *NYT,* June 18, 1989.

21   "…papers of their presidencies…" Improving Declassification: a Report to the President, Public Interest Declassification Board, December, 2007, 18.

25   "The second honorable mention…" "Presidential Libraries: Designing A Legacy," Chicago Architecture Foundation, February 3, 2015:

http://www.architecture.org/cac-obama-library

25   "Cowdrey and Kirk posit that…" Ibid.

25   "…marshal resources to address…" "A shared destiny," Obama Library
     Foundation Request for Qualifications, March 20, 2014:
     http://www.barackobamafoundation.org/i/ObamaFoundation_RFQ.pdf

32   "During John Roberts' Supreme Court…" Christopher Lee, "The Case of
     Roberts's Missing Papers," WP, May 11, 2006.

34   "…Bush reportedly raised…" Melissa Repko, "Bush library funded by $500
     million in private donations," The Dallas Morning News, April 21, 2013.

34   "In late 2001, he ended…" Executive Order 13233, November 1, 2001.

34   "…Obama reversed that…" Executive Order 13489, January 21, 2009.

CHAPTER 2: PRESIDENTIAL LIBRARIES

PAGE

43   "…a report by the General Accounting Office determined…" "Expenditures
     for Operation and Maintenance of Presidential Libraries," United States
     General Accounting Office, November 6, 1979.

43   "…the National Archives submitted to Congress…" The Presidential Li-
     braries System: A Review. Report to Congress, National Archives and Re-
     cords Service, General Services Administration, January 1979. Brief-
     ing/Orientation Materials, Presidential Libraries (Folder 1/3), Box 2, Robert
     M. Warner papers, BHL.

43   "In May, 1980…" Presidential Libraries Study, the General Services Ad-
     ministration, Office of Plans, Programs and Financial Management, Office of
     Planning and Analysis, May 16, 1980. Briefing/Orientation Materials,
     Presidential Libraries (Folder 3/3), Box 2, Robert M. Warner papers, BHL.

43   "…mandated a study of establishing a central museum…" The Act directed
     NARA to report the findings of the study in the agency's annual report for
     Fiscal Year 1986; they appear on pages 36 to 38 of the report. The lack of en-
     thusiasm for such a centralized facility is evident in the group's findings: "It
     was clear from the start that there would be serious difficulties in establish-
     ing a full-scale museum with permanent collections for research and exhibi-
     tion. The vast majority of historically significant artifacts and memorabilia
     of the American Presidency are already in the care of other museums. It is
     very unlikely that these institutions would willingly donate their Presiden-
     tial items to a new museum. The study team thus abandoned the idea that a
     full-scale museum would be a viable possibility." The majority of said items
     belonged to the National Archives itself, in the presidential libraries, and so
     their centralization would not nearly have posed as much difficulty as the
     group suggested. One positive result from this study was the idea, produced
     as an alternative to the "full-scale museum" Congress asked NARA to study,
     for what became the White House Visitor Center, which is managed by the
     National Park Service (the White House Historical Association operates a
     book and gift shop in the center).

43 "Section 6 of the Presidential…" S.3477, 110th Congress: Presidential Historical Records Preservation Act of 2008, Enacted October 13, 2008. Pub.L. 110-404.

44 "In a 1980 briefing book prepared…" "NL Briefing for the Archivist." Internal document, National Archives and Records Service, General Services Administration, January 1979. Briefing/ Orientation Materials, Presidential Libraries (Folder 2/3), Box 2, Robert M. Warner papers, BHL.

44 "NARA submitted their 'Report…'" "Report on Alternative Models for Presidential Libraries Issued in Response to the Requirements of PL 110-404," NARA, September 25, 2009.

45 "…NARA hires more library…" Martin Wisckol, "Nixon library chief greeted with relief, dismay," *the Orange County Register*, January 3, 2015.

45 "…as well as to appease the foundation's…" Adam Nagourney, "Rescuing a Vietnam Casualty: Johnson's Legacy," *NYT*, February 15, 2014.

48 "They tried a size limit…" Section 3, "Presidential Libraries Act Amendments of 1986" (99-323, May 27, 1986).

48 "Congress tried to require…" Ibid.

49 "In the year following…" 1980 Presidential Libraries Briefing Book, Office of Presidential Libraries, NARA.

51 "The Bush Library notified…" "Bush Library: Ben Carson files," Muckrock.com: https://www.muckrock.com/foi/united-states-of-america-10/bush-library-ben-carson-files-13205/.

53 "In 2014, controversy surrounded…" John Byrne, "House committee OKs $100 million for Obama library," *CT*, April 17, 2014.

53 "…the state of Texas built…" 1980 Presidential Libraries Briefing Book, Office of Presidential Libraries, NARA.

57 "…even that he was reluctant to have one…" Alter, Jonathan. *The Promise: President Obama, Year One* (New York: Simon & Schuster, 2010), 154.

CHAPTER 3: NARA AND THE FOUNDATIONS

PAGE

61 "'As I think the chairman knows'…" Fawcett, Sharon, statement to the House Committee on Oversight and Government Reform. Hearing: "Reform to the Presidential Library Donation Disclosure Process," February 28, 2007.

64 "The revelation that…" "In Using Personal Email, Aide Says Clinton Didn't Break Law," All Things Considered, NPR News, March 3, 2015.

64 "In the 2014 Best Places to Work…" Report, "2014 Best Places to Work in the Federal Government," Partnership for Public Service.

66 "In 2012, the Eisenhower…" 2012 Internal Revenue Service 990 forms, Eisenhower Foundation, Reagan Foundation.

68 "In the Reagan Foundation's fund-raising…" Reagan Presidential Foundation, mass email to author, February 6, 2014.

69 "In 1988, then-Archivist…" Sharon Fawcett, testimony before the House Committee on Oversight and Government Reform. Hearing: National Ar-

chives: Advisory Committees and Their Effectiveness," October 20, 2009.

73   "They found ways around the size limitations…" The endowment formula specified in the 1986 amendments to the Presidential Libraries Act requires the foundation to provide to the Archivist of the United States, at the time a new library is dedicated (or a material change is made to an existing library), an amount equal to: "the total cost of acquiring or constructing such facility and of acquiring and installing such equipment, multiplied by 20 percent; plus, if title to the land is to be vested in the United States, the product of the total cost of acquiring the land upon which such facility is located, or such other measure of the value of such land as is mutually agreed upon by the Archivist and the donor, multiplied by 20 percent; or, if title to the land is not to be vested in the United States, the product of the total cost to the donor of any improvements to the land upon which such facility is located (other than such facility and equipment), multiplied by 20 percent." Three new libraries – for George H.W. Bush, Bill Clinton, and George W. Bush – have been accepted into the system since this requirement was enacted; not one of the foundations has provided an endowment anywhere near the required 20%, due to creative accounting and imaginative ways around the law. Beginning with the first to fall under the law – the George Bush Library at Texas A&M – NARA and the foundations (at that time, the Bush Library Foundation was headed by former Archivist Don Wilson) determined that Congress did not in fact intend to include the total cost of acquiring and improving the land and constructing the building (which may come as a surprise to Congress), and so exempted large portions of those costs from the endowment formula. In order to avoid an endowment penalty the law required for any building constructed larger than 70,000 square feet, the foundations now create buildings significantly larger, but only deed or transfer control of a maximum of 69,999 square feet. This creates the very real problem, twenty or thirty years after it opens (and therefore its foundation possibly, even likely, in financial straits), of an inordinately large presidential library building for which NARA must assume operational control – without the full endowment required by Congress to offset costs.

73   "…and speculate about 'foreign money'…" Some readers may wonder why more attention is not paid in this book to fundraising by presidents and their foundations. To the greatest extent possible, I have avoided speculation. I have attempted to document assertions of fact with records from presidential libraries, the National Archives, and (as infrequently as possible, books, newspapers, and magazines. Where I offer my opinions, I base them on my extensive experience visiting, reviewing, researching in, and trying to reform presidential libraries. The laws governing presidential libraries are woefully inadequate; a great example of this is the lack of limits, prohibitions, disclosure requirements (or oversight of any kind) with regard to donations for a presidential library. Many others have speculated as to the reasons why some presidents have accepted foreign donations; the specific ex-

pectations of donors who bestow enormous amounts of money on sitting presidents; the likelihood of a quid-pro-quo, such as with presidential pardons; and the motives of presidents and their foundations for keeping all of this secret. Without real documentation, anyone making such speculations is guessing – and badly. I decline to participate in such exercises. Unless and until donations to presidential libraries are disclosed – even after a president leaves office – I see no point in blindly accusing anyone without basis in fact.

73 "Ferriero was calling with…" Darryl Piggee, conversation with author, April 26, 2010.

76 "This is a rather historic day…" Symposium on Presidential Libraries, February 28, 2011. Transcript provided by C-SPAN.

76 "In this way, the diversity…" Advisory Committee on the Presidential Library-Foundation Partnerships Justification filed with the General Services Administration, July 16, 2010.

CHAPTER 4: PRESIDENTIAL RECORDS

PAGE

77 "By that time…" Blanton, Thomas, National Security Archive, statement to the Senate Committee on Homeland Security & Governmental Affairs. Hearing: "National Archives Oversight: Protecting Our Nation's History for Future Generations," May 14, 2008.

79 "When White House aide…" Memorandum for the file, George M. Elsey, August 2, 1950. George M. Elsey papers, HSTL.

80 "…Johnson unenthusiastically signed…" Statement by the President Upon Signing S. 1160, July 4, 1966. Courtesy LBJL.

82 "This created a backlog…" Mike Duggan, Supervisory Archivist, RWRL, email to author, February 21, 2014.

83 "The George W. Bush Library began…" John Orrell, Public Affairs Officer, GBWL, telephone interview with author, February 5, 2014.

83 "…and cause alarm…" "ALA raises red flag on recent Bush executive order." Press release, American Library Association, March 1, 2002.

83 "A federal judge invalidated…" Memorandum opinion, American Historical Association v. National Archives and Records Administration, Civil Action No. 01-2447 (CKK), October 1, 2007. United States District Judge Colleen Kollar-Kotelly wrote, "The Archivist's reliance on § 3(b) of Executive Order 13,233 is arbitrary, capricious, an abuse of discretion, and not in accordance with law and accordingly in violation of the [Administrative Procedures Act]."

84 "On his first full day…" Obama, Barack. Memorandum to the Heads of Executive Departments and Agencies on the Freedom of Information Act, January 21, 2009.

84 "A few weeks later…" Holder, Eric. Memorandum to the Heads of Executive Departments and Agencies on the Freedom of Information Act, March 19, 2009.

85 "Holder also clearly stated..." Ibid.
86 "By the fall of 1992..." "Serious Management Problems at the National Archives and Records Administration." Report by the Senate Committee on Governmental Affairs, October, 1992, iv.
87 "...the Absentee Archivist..." Senator John Glenn (D-Ohio), opening statement, hearing before the Senate Committee on Governmental Affairs, May 23, 1995.
87 "The report concluded..." "Serious Management Problems," xi.
88 "...and good references from..." Application for the position of Director, Gerald R. Ford Presidential Library, Don W. Wilson, December 9, 1980. Ford Presidential Library Folder, Box 3, Robert M. Warner papers, BHL.
88 "...Wilson made it to the..." Memorandum, James O'Neill, Assistant Archivist for Presidential Libraries, to Robert Warner, Archivist, June 29, 1981. Ford Presidential Library Folder, Box 3, Robert M. Warner papers, BHL.
88 "He, too, had good references..." Application for the position of Director, Gerald R. Ford Presidential Library, William J. Stewart, undated (1980). Ford Presidential Library Folder, Box 3, Robert M. Warner papers, BHL.
88 "...Ford had 'affection'..." Handwritten note, Warner, Robert, undated. Ford Presidential Library Folder, Box 3, Robert M. Warner papers, BHL.
89 "...wrote to the White House to protest..." The folder titled "Correspondence re: Replacement of Archivist of U.S., February 1983-July 1983" in Box 2 of the Robert M. Warner papers, BHL, contain these letters, which were sent to the White House but referred to Administrator of General Services Gerald Carman, for response on behalf of the president. The content of the letters, from both individuals and professional organizations, strongly suggests a coordinated effort to support Warner.
89 "...the White House recalled..." Phil Gailey and Warren Weaver, Jr., "Briefing: Of Archives and Politics," NYT, February 5, 1983.
89 "As word spread that he would soon..." Ibid.
89 "The administration's first choice..." Colin Campbell, "Reported Choice of G.O.P. Adviser As Archivist Is Protested," NYT, June 22, 1985.
89 "...Reagan nominated John Agresto..." Ronald Reagan: "Nomination of John Thomas Agresto To Be Archivist of the United States ," May 1, 1986. Online by Gerhard Peters and John T. Woolley, The American Presidency Project. http://www.presidency.ucsb.edu/ws/?pid=37198.
89 "Professional organizations publicly opposed..." Leslie Maitland Werner, "Scholarly Groups Oppose Archives Nominee," NYT, August 19, 1986.
89 "The Society for History..." Leslie Maitland Werner, "National Archives; Some Historians Worry About Access In Future," NYT, May 20, 1986.
90 "'What does not precisely'..." Cover letter, Don Wilson to Eric Vauter, application for the position of Archivist of the United States, October 31, 1985. Topical Files, Appointment of Archivist of United States, Box 4, Robert M. Warner papers, BHL.
91 "Wilson's two lists of ten..." Attachment to cover letter ("References"), Don

Wilson, application for the position of Archivist of the United States, October 31, 1985. Topical Files, Appointment of Archivist of United States, Box 4, Robert M. Warner papers, BHL.

91 "...Reagan formally nominated Wilson..." Ronald Reagan: "Nomination of Don W. Wilson To Be Archivist of the United States ," August 14, 1987. Online by Gerhard Peters and John T. Woolley, The American Presidency Project. http://www.presidency.ucsb.edu/ws/?pid=34700.

91 "Wilson's predecessor, Robert Warner..." W. Dale Nelson, "New Chief of National Archives Pledges 'Expanded Mission'," *AP*, December 4, 1987.

93 "...'we find out where the library will be'..." Sharon Fawcett interview, April 18, 2008.

94 "...and strongly influenced..." Letter, Don Wilson to President George Bush, reporting candidate site evaluations and final recommendation for selection for presidential library, March 5, 1991. Document released to the author through FOIA from OA. Wilson reports that Rice and the University of Houston sites are "satisfactory" while Texas A&M is the "most pleasing," describing it in glowing terms. He counters the claim that an urban setting guarantees higher visitor attendance (praising Texas A&M for being "aggressive in addressing the issue of museum attendance"). Wilson writes that "[T]he patriotic values and military traditions which give TAMU its unique personality virtually guarantee a perpetual compatibility between the university and the Library. The George Bush Library would always be the 'crown jewel' of the TAMU campus...In my opinion, the tradition and character of the TAMU alumni now, and in the future, would sustain a strong financials support base for private giving to the Library that will enhance its public programs...if your personal choice is one of the other two sites, I have no doubt either could be developed into an outstanding Presidential Library." In a letter later that month to William Mobley, the president of Texas A&M, Wilson thanked him for the "wonderful hospitality" when he and his wife visited the university the week prior. He wrote, "Needless to say, Patsy joined ranks with me as one your growing number of boosters. It's too bad we can't move the entire Archives to College Station so we could enjoy the university and your company on a more frequent basis....Working with you has proven to be among the highlights of my tenure." Three years later, Wilson would move to College Station to lead the Bush Library Foundation.

94 "...Wilson provided the school with more..." Texas A&M University, "Additional Ten Questions from Don Wilson Received March 19, 1990, Regarding the Bush Presidential Library." Document released to the author through FOIA from OA.

94 "...than he did other finalists..." Rice University, "Answers to Specific Questions on Bush Library Proposal," April 20, 1990; University of Houston, "George Bush Presidential Library [Proposal], Responses to the Questionnaire from the Archivist of the United States." Documents released to the author through FOIA from OA.

94 "Once the decision had been..." Talking Points, "the Presidents [sic] Discussion with the University of Houston Officials"; Talking Points, "the Presidents [sic] Discussion with Rice University Officials." Documents released to the author through FOIA from OA.

94 "Since the end of the Reagan..." For an excellent examination of the PROFS case, see Blanton, Tom (Ed.), *White House E-Mail: The Top-Secret Computer Messages the Reagan/Bush White House Tried to Destroy* (New York: The New Press, 1995).

95 "With thirteen hours left..." Pete Yost, "Archivist Who Signed Records Agreement Will Head Bush Library Center," *AP*, February 12, 1993.

95 "...who called Wilson's actions..." "Judge Rules Against Effort By Bush to Control His Records," *NYT*, February 28, 1995.

95 "He denied that his..." "Archivist Says He Did No Wrong on Bush Records," *AP*, February 18, 1993.

95 "...a $129,000 a year position..." Editorial, "Wrong Candidate for the Archives," *NYT*, March 29, 1994.

CHAPTER 5: PRESIDENTIAL LIBRARY MUSEUMS

PAGE

111 "In a meeting during the design..." Martin Allen, Chairman Emeritus of the Gerald R. Ford Presidential Foundation. Interview with the author, November 5, 2007.

112 "...President Truman kept in his desk..." *President Truman and the Banning letter*, HSTL web site: http://www.trumanlibrary.org/banning.htm

114 "...failed to persuade the North Vietnamese..." Drew, Col Dennis M. "Rolling Thunder 1965: Anatomy of a Failure" CADRE Paper, Report No. AU-ARI-CP-86-3, Air University Press, October 1986.

115 "...including the presidency of the Little Congress..." Caro, Robert A., *Master of the Senate: The Years of Lyndon Johnson* (New York: Alfred A. Knopf Inc., 2002), 115.

117 "War can be a hell..." Douglas Menarchik, Director, George Bush Presidential Library. Interview with the author, June 3, 2003.

118 "...mild recession..." Reminding fans of the 1993 Kevin Kline film *Dave* that Bill Mitchell's presidential library likely would characterize his first, massive cerebral hemorrhage – the one that completely incapacitates the president – as a "mild stroke" and, downplaying it further, a "slight circulatory problem of the head."

119 "'Well, our guy lost.'" Menarchik interview.

127 "A Democratic plot to make..." The original Watergate exhibit depicted the events as attempts by Democrats who "wanted Nixon out." One panel read, "With the vice presidency vacant as a result of Spiro Agnew's resignation on unrelated charges, the Speaker of the House Carl Albert, a Democrat from Oklahoma, was next in line for the Presidency until a new Vice President could be confirmed. Bella Abzug, a left-wing congresswoman from New

York was quoted by Albert as saying, 'Get off your goddamned ass, and we can take the Presidency.' Another prominent Democrat, former JFK speech writer Ted Sorenson, had asked Albert for permission to write a secret 'comprehensive contingency plan so that the Democrats could swiftly seize control of the White House should Nixon be forced out.' Evidently, more than a few Democrats were hoping to win through Watergate what they had failed to win at the polls." The Clinton Library's original exhibit on Monica Lewinsky and the impeachment– still on display more than ten years after opening – makes the same exact argument about Republicans.

128 "…the foundation interfered…" Jeffrey Frank, "Who Owns Richard Nixon?," *The New Yorker,* May 20, 2014.

128 "…including Duke University…" "Duke Faculty Unit Votes Against a Nixon Library," *NYT,* September 4, 1981.

128 "One community offered…" "Leavenworth Endorses Nixon Library Campaign," *AP,* November 11 1982.

129 "In 2000 the government settled…" "Nixon estate to get $18-million for seized papers, tapes," *AP,* June 13, 2000.

129 "In 2002, Nixon's daughters…" James Sterngold, "Nixon's daughters end rift over gift/Presidential library gains access to $19 million bequest from family friend," *San Francisco Chronicle,* August 9, 2002.

129 "…inserted a provision…" Ben Pershing, "Congress Frees Nixon Papers," *Roll Call,* January 26, 2004.

130 "John Taylor, executive director…" "Nixon's Library Cancels Conference, Drawing Protests," *AP,* March 6, 2005.

130 "Well, it turned out to be a fig leaf." Scott Shane, "Nixon Library Stirs Anger by Canceling Conference," *NYT,* March 11, 2005.

130 "…surprising and welcome choice of…" "National Archives Names Director of the Richard Nixon Presidential Library and Museum," NARA press release, April 10, 2006.

131 "In the House Report…" House Report 95-1487, Part I, to accompany H.R. 135000, the Presidential Records Act of 1978. August 14, 1978, 13.

132 "…having already been recommended…" John H. Taylor, Letter to the Editor, *Journal of American History* (2012) 99 (2): 700.

132 "…Naftali made it clear…" Timothy Naftali, email to author, April 25, 2007.

132 "When Naftali invited John Dean…" Michael Isikoff, "A New Fight Over Nixon and Watergate," *Newsweek*, June 12, 2009.

132 "One of the Nixon Foundation's biggest supporters…" Andrew Gumbel, "Nixon's Presidential Library: The Last Battle of Watergate," *Pacific Standard*, December 8, 2011.

133 "…aided by some, who, like Fawcett…" Ibid.

133 "Naftali later revealed…" Timothy Naftali, "Watergate in Nixonland: The Challenge of Presenting Public History in a Presidential Library," Forum, Miller Center, Charlottesville, Virginia, April 30, 2012. Video: http://millercenter.org/public/forum/detail/5997

133 "Finally, in late 2014..." "Archivist of the United States Appoints Director of the Richard Nixon Presidential Library and Museum," Press Release, NARA, December 15, 2014.

133 "With no federal government experience..." "Nixon library chief greeted with relief, dismay" Martin Wisckol OC Register January 3, 2015

133 "...this appointment was seen..." The Nixon Library Needs a New Director, Now The Nation Jon Wiener May 13, 2014

133 "...in a radio interview..." "Conflict over the Nixon Presidential Library," *Which Way, LA?* KCRW, February 17, 2015. audio: http://blogs.kcrw.com/ whichwayla/2015/02/how-to-remember-richard-nixon

135 "Outreach opportunities provided..." Report on Alternative Models, 8.

136 "And the White House Visitor Center..." White House Visitor Center Re-opens after $12.6 Million Revitalization Joint Press Release, National Park Service and White House Historical Association, September 10, 2014.

136 "In fact, the Edward..." About the Institute brochure, Edward M. Kennedy Institute for the United States Senate, 2014. http://emkinstitute.org/page/-/FINAL%20_about_EMKI_university13%20%284%29.pdf

CHAPTER 6: THE SECRET NIXON LIBRARY
PAGE

139 "...the most expensive presidential library..." Presidential Library statistics, Briefing/Orientation Materials, Presidential Libraries (Folder 1/3), Box 2, Robert M. Warner papers, BHL.

139 "According to a state resources agency report..." San Onofre State Beach Revised General Plan State of California – the Resources Agency, Department of Parks and Recreation June 1984

139 "An 1846 description portrayed the site..." Life in California During a residence of several years in that territory Alfred Robinson New York: Published by Wiley and Putnam 1846.

139 "...'severely handicap military functions.'" Letter, Shillito, Barry, Assistant Secretary of Defense for Installations and Logistics, to Arnold Weber, February 21, 1971. OMB/PRB, NARA.

140 "...cover-up lasted for more than..." While the land transfer was made public at the time – though with the cover of the Legacy of Parks – the rest has remained secret, and almost unreported. Interestingly, on two different occasions since 1974, one individual spoke publicly, and briefly, about the plan, but no one at the time followed up on his remarks to uncover the story. The first was in testimony in March, 1999, during Nixon's lawsuit seeking compensation for his papers and materials that Congress ordered seized under the PRMPA (and reported by George Lardner, Jr., in the Washington Post – "Nixon Aide Testifies Against Boss," March 29, 1999). The second was for an oral history recorded July 30, 2007, by Timothy Naftali, and available at the Nixon Library. That individual is John Dean.

143 "...Legacy of Parks program..." Richard Nixon: "Statement About a Report

of the Property Review Board," July 25, 1972. Online by Gerhard Peters and John T. Woolley, The American Presidency Project. http://www.presidency.ucsb.edu/ws/?pid=3503.

143 "...tens of thousands of acres..." Ibid.

144 "Under the law..." Federal Management Regulation, Subchapter C—Real Property, Part 102-75—Real Property Disposal.

144 "As early as two weeks before.." Dictated memo, Nixon, Richard to John Ehrlichman, January 4, 1969. WHSF, RNL.

144 "...'insurmountable legal problems'..." Ibid.

145 "Only weeks after winning..." Chattel deed from Richard Nixon to the United States of America, December 30, 1968. Archives and Library Folder, Rosemary Woods Name/Subject File, PPF, RNL.

146 "A reporter asked President Eisenhower..." Dwight D. Eisenhower: "The President's News Conference," August 24, 1960. Online by Gerhard Peters and John T. Woolley, The American Presidency Project. http://www.presidency.ucsb.edu/ws/?pid=11915.

146 "On the eve of the election..." Geoffrey Perret, *Eisenhower* (New York: Random House,)1999, 597.

146 "When Herbert Hoover addressed..." Hoover, Herbert, Republican National Convention Address, July 25, 1960. http://www.c-span.org/video/?280721-1/1960-republican-national-convention-address

146 "...that some called Johnson's 'pyramid'..." Letter, Warner, Robert to Jane Isaac, March 16, 1973. Correspondence with University of Michigan, 1958-1980 Folder, Box 1, Robert M. Warner papers, BHL; Martin Waldron, "Nixon Hails Johnson Library at Dedication," *NYT*, May 23, 1971.

147 "After several other possibilities..." "Leavenworth CC Helps Woo Nixon," *AP*, November 11, 1982.

147 "...Nixon visited the San Mateo Canyon..." 10:01 am – 10:49 am, Saturday, March 22, 1969. PDD, RNL.

148 "...the organizational meeting to form..." Minutes of the Organizational Meeting of the Board of Executive Trustees of the Richard Nixon Foundation, June 2, 1969. Garment, Leonard Subject Files, SMOF, RNL.

148 "...the group had decided to..." Statement by Counsel to the President, John D. Ehrlichman, Review of events leading up to the formation of The Richard Nixon Foundation, undated. 553xx [Richard Nixon Foundation] Box 180 Folder, PPF, RNL.

148 "...for a two-day briefing." Memorandum, Kunzig, Robert L. to Peter M. Flanigan and H.R. Haldeman re: Visit of Richard Nixon Foundation Representatives, December 17, 1969. 553xx [Richard Nixon Foundation] Folder, President's Financial and Family Papers, PPF, RNL.

148 "...the possibility of a 'partnership'..." Memorandum, Rhoads, James to Robert Kunzig re: Visit of the Richard Nixon Foundation to Washington, December 16, 1969. 553xx [Richard Nixon Foundation] Folder, President's Financial and Family Papers, PPF, RNL.

148 "…have negative political…" Kunzig to Flanigan and Haldeman.

148 "…Haldeman agreed." Ibid.

148 "…the foundation engaged Economics Research…" Letter, Haldeman, H.R. to Harrison Price, ERA, November 10, 1969. Pres. Nixon Museum Folder, H.R. Haldeman SMOF, RNL.

148 "…the site of many major…" Letter, Price, Harrison to H.R. Haldeman, October 31, 1969. Pres. Nixon Museum Folder, H.R. Haldeman SMOF, RNL.

150 "…met on June 24…" Memorandum, Trent, Darrell to Property Review Board, November 18, 1970. Property Review Task Force Meetings Folder #1, OMB/PRB, NARA.

150 "…frustrated with the paucity…" Memorandum, Nixon, Richard to the Heads of Departments and Agencies, July 24, 1970. Property Review Task Force Meetings Folder #1, OMB/PRB, NARA.

150 "…GSA surveyed the property…" Administratively Confidential Report, U.S. Marine Corps Base Camp Pendleton, General Services Administration, October 23, 1970. J. Fred Buzhardt, Office File/Nixon Library Timetable with Attached Surveys of Camp Pendleton 3/3 Folder, SMOF, RNL.

150 "…'highest and best use'…" Ibid.

150 "…the members discussed draft legislation…" Minutes of PRB Meeting, November 18, 1970. Property Review Task Force Meetings Folder #2, OMB/PRB, NARA.

151 "…Ehrlichman reminded board members…" Memorandum, Ehrlichman, John to Property Review Board, September 14, 1970. Property Review Task Force Meetings Folder #2, OMB/PRB, NARA.

151 "…all further steps to be taken…" Ibid.

151 "…discussed Camp Pendleton land as a 'problem'…" Minutes of November 18, 1970 PRB Meeting.

151 "…gave a slide presentation…" Ibid.

151 "…initiated at the president's request…" Ibid.

151 "…'accommodate numerous land uses'…" Ibid.

151 "Ehrlichman commented that…" Ibid.

151 "The board agreed to…" Ibid.

152 "President Nixon issued Executive Order 11560…" Shultz had been named as the first director of the Office of Management and Budget, which had replaced the Bureau of the Budget earlier that year.

152 "…referring to him as a 'candy ass'…" Dean, John. Statement to the House Committee on the Judiciary. Hearings pursuant to H. RES. 803: a resolution authorizing and directing the Committee on the Judiciary to investigate whether sufficient grounds exist for the House of Representatives to exercise its Constitutional power to impeach Richard M. Nixon, President of the United States of America, July 11, 1974.

152 "…locational analysis report from ERA…" "Locational Analysis for the Proposed Nixon Center Prepared for the Richard M. Nixon Foundation," Economics Research Associates, March 9, 1970. The Nixon Library [CFOA

10179] Folder, Garment, Leonard Subject Files, SMOF, RNL.

152 "...foundation with a comprehensive study..." "A Study for the Richard Nixon Foundation, Phase I," Project Number 69104.X, Report Copy Number 12. Nixon Library Planning Material, William L. Pereira Associates Folder, President's Financial and Family Papers, PPF, RNL.

152 "...the first and most important criteria..." Ibid.

152 "The minimum area recommended..." Ibid.

152 "...the largest site for a presidential library..." Ibid.

152 "...the foundation allowed the public..." The White House and the Nixon Foundation needed to move forward with plans for the Nixon Library at Camp Pendleton without making those plans public, and keep the number of people who knew them low. Therefore, the studies prepared by ERA and Pereira were based on locations in the area that met two basic criteria: they were roughly similar to the Pendleton site, and they could plausibly be considered for the Nixon Library. The analyses would have to be updated to reflect the actual conditions at Pendleton, but only after the White House made the plan to build the library there public – which they never were able to do.

153 "...the trustees authorized..." Letter, Firestone, Leonard K., president, the Richard Nixon Foundation, to Leonard Garment, December 23, 1970. The Nixon Library [CFOA 10179] Folder, Garment, Leonard, Subject Files, SMOF, RNL.

153 "...made a presentation..." Presentation before the Nixon Foundation in Favor of the Whittier Site by Frederick M. Binder, Ph.D., President of Whittier College, August 28, 1970. Folder 3:1, Box 3, WHSF, RNL.

153 "...in December a 'task force'..." Minutes, Federal Real Property Review Task Force Meeting, December 16, 1970. Property Review Task Force Meetings Folder #1, OMB/PRB, NARA.

153 "President Nixon spoke to reporters..." 10:50 am – 10:58 am, Wednesday, March 31, 1991. PDD, RNL.

154 "...comments at length..." Richard Nixon: "Remarks Announcing Plans To Make Land in Camp Pendleton, California, Available for Public Recreational Use.," March 31, 1971. Online by Gerhard Peters and John T. Woolley, *The American Presidency Project.*
http://www.presidency.ucsb.edu/ws/?pid=2957.

155 "They had explained only six...", Letter, Shillito, Barry, February 27, 1971.

155 "...Nixon took a helicopter tour..." 11:09 am – 11:22 am, Wednesday, March 31, 1991. PDD, RNL.

155 "...Governor Ronald Reagan..." Helen Thomas, "Nixon seeks work for 65,000 who lost space jobs," United Press International, April 1, 1971.

156 "...Lilburn Boggs the Assistant Director..." Memorandum, Boggs, Lilburn to Al Toner, January 4, 1971. Property Review Task Force Meetings Part 2 Folder #1, OMB/PRB, NARA.

156 "...Boggs wrote to White House Counsel..." Memorandum, Boggs, Lilburn, re: Conveyance of Property – San Clemente, California, August 17,

1971. J. Fred Buzhardt Office file [Loose Materials Concerning Camp Pendleton 3 of 3] Folder, SMOF, RNL.

157 "…memo from Dean to Haldeman…" Administratively Confidential/Eyes Only Memorandum, Dean, John to H.R. Haldeman and John Ehrlichman, re: Nixon Library, July 26, 1971. J. Fred Buzhardt, Accordion File: RN Library at Camp Pendleton, Camp Pendleton-RN Foundation Folder, SMOF, RNL.

157 "Dean elaborated in an undated…" Memorandum, Dean, John, undated. J. Fred Buzhardt, Accordion File: RN Library at Camp Pendleton, Camp Pendleton Folder, SMOF, RNL.

159 "…Ehrlichman pressuring Weber…" Memorandum, Ehrlichman, John to Arnold Weber, January 14, 1971. Property Review Task Force Meetings Part 2 Folder #1, OMB/PRB, NARA.

159 "…Eisenhower's 'legacy of highways'…" Ibid.

159 "…late October with Congress passing…" "Military Construction Authorization Act, 1972" (92-145, October 27, 1971).

159 "…specifically prohibiting the sale…" Section 709, "Military Construction Authorization Act, 1972" (92-145, October 27, 1971): "Notwithstanding any other provision of law, none of the lands constituting Camp Pendleton, California, may be sold, leased, transferred, or otherwise disposed of by the Department of Defense unless hereafter authorized by law."

159 "In his 1971 State of the Union…" Nixon, Richard M. "Annual Message to Congress on the State of the Union," January 22, 1971.

159 "…hearings on the proposed…" Memorandum, Trent, Darrell to John Ehrlichman, May 19, 1971. J. Fred Buzhardt, Accordion File: RN Library at Camp Pendleton, Camp Pendleton-RN Foundation Folder, SMOF, RNL.

160 "…Weber expressed an opinion…" Memorandum, Weber, Arnold to John Dean, re: Release of documents relating to Camp Pendleton to House Armed Services Committee, May 8, 1971. Office file, Camp Pendleton (3/5) [Maps and Surveys] Folder, J. Fred Buzhardt, SMOF, RNL.

160 "..Weber explained that the issue…" Ibid.

160 "…and that Stratton was simply…" Memorandum, Cook, Dick to John Dean, re: Camp Pendleton, May 7, 1971. J. Fred Buzhardt, Office File/Nixon Library Timetable with Attached Surveys of Camp Pendleton 2/3 Folder, SMOF, RNL.

160 "…Cook was concerned…" Ibid.

161 "…Trimmer told Dean…" Administratively Confidential Letter, Trimmer, Harold to John Dean, May 7, 1971. J. Fred Buzhardt, Office File/Nixon Library Timetable with Attached Surveys of Camp Pendleton 2/3 Folder, SMOF, RNL.

161 "…unanimously voted down the proposal…" Wire service report, United Press International, May 25, 1971. J. Fred Buzhardt, Accordion File: RN Library at Camp Pendleton, Camp Pendleton Folder, SMOF, RNL.

162 "'Incidentally, on Pendleton'…" EOB, 253-13; May 26, 1971; White House Tapes; RNL.

162 "...indicated their dissatisfaction..." Minutes, Property Review Board Meeting, July 1, 1971. Property Review Task Force Meetings Folder #3, OMB/PRB, NARA.

162 "...both sides stood firm..." Ibid.

162 "In the Oval Office across the hall..." OVAL, 534-12; July 1, 1971; White House Tapes; RNL.

162 "...Nixon entered the meeting..." Minutes, Property Review Board Meeting, July 1, 1971.

163 "...the White House relented..." Minutes, Property Review Board Meeting, July 21, 1971. Property Review Task Force Meetings Folder #3, OMB/PRB, NARA.

163 "...Weber was negotiating..." Ibid.

163 "...the House passed..." Memorandum, MacGregor, Clark to William Timmons and Kenneth BeLieu, re: Camp Pendleton, July 24, 1971. J. Fred Buzhardt, Accordion File: RN Library at Camp Pendleton, Camp Pendleton – 50 Year Lease Folder, SMOF, RNL.

163 "...believed he had made a deal..." Ibid.

163 "...can we hurry up and sign..." Memorandum, Hullin, Tod to John Dean, re: Camp Pendleton, July 27, 1971. J. Fred Buzhardt, Office File, at Camp Pendleton : RN Foundation 2/2 Folder, SMOF, RNL.

164 "Dean noted on the memo..." Ibid.

164 "...with Donald Rumsfeld..." Memorandum, Trent, Darrell to John Ehrlichman, August 27, 1971. OMB/PRB, NARA.

164 "...less than enthusiastic..." Memorandum, Dean, John to John Ehrlichman, re: Property Review Board, August 12, 1971. J. Fred Buzhardt, Office File [Loose Material Concerning Camp Pendleton] 3/3 Folder, SMOF, RNL.

164 "...no overt action..." Memorandum, Dean, John, undated. J. Fred Buzhardt, Accordion File: RN Library at Camp Pendleton, Camp Pendleton Folder, SMOF, RNL.

164 "...executed the lease..." Memorandum, Fielding, Fred to Darrell Trent re: Camp Pendleton Lease, September 4, 1971. Box No. 4, Accordion File Folder, F. Buzhardt's Office/R.N. Library at Camp Pendleton, SMOF, RNL.

164 "...seeking legislation to require..." ..." Memorandum, Nixon, Richard to Secretary of Defense Melvin Laird, December 11, 1970. OMB/PRB, NARA.

165 "...with the president explaining..." Ibid

165 "...relying on a legal opinion..." Memorandum, Buzhardt, J. Fred to Darrell Trent, August 3, 1971. Accordion File Folder, F. Buzhardt's Office/R.N. Library at Camp Pendleton, SMOF, RNL.

165 "...Nixon met with representatives..." OVAL, 752-7; July 25, 1972; White House Tapes; RNL.

165 "...they discussed the Camp Pendleton..." Ibid.

166 "...'There's an inertia'..." Ibid.

166 "...'four miles of the finest beach'..." Ibid.

166 "...Chairman Donald Rumsfeld..." Transcript of Press Conference, Office

of the White House Press Secretary,, July 25, 1972. Real Property Review Task Force, Federal Folder #1, 12/70-72, OMB/PRB, NARA.

167 "The change allowed that..." Section 708, "Military Construction Authorization Act, 1972" (92-545, October 25, 1972): "Section 709 of Public Law 92-145 (85 Stat. 394, 414) is amended to read as follows: 'Notwithstanding any other provision of law, none of the lands constituting Camp Pendleton, California, may be sold, leased, transferred, or otherwise disposed of by the Department of Defense unless hereafter authorized by law: Provided, however, That with respect to said lands the Secretary of the Navy, or his designee, may grant leases, licenses, or easements pursuant to chapter 159 of title 10, United States Code.'"

167 "...Timmons reported to Ehrlichman..." Memorandum, Timmons, William to John Ehrlichman,

168 "...detailed Nixon Library..." Nixon Library Timetable, January 1973. Nixon Foundation Meeting Roosevelt Room Folder, H.R. Haldeman, SMOF, RNL.

168 "...to hear a site selection report..." Memorandum, Higby, Larry to H.R. Haldeman re: Ed Nixon, December 14, 1972. Nixon Foundation/Library/Museum Folder, H.R. Haldeman, SMOF, RNL.

168 "...met with the directors of the six..." Memorandum, Nesbitt, Jack to H.R. Haldeman, February 7, 1973. Nixon Foundation/Library/Museum Folder, H.R. Haldeman, SMOF, RNL.

168 "...the Senate had passed a resolution..." S. Res. 60, 93rd Congress, February 7, 1973.

168 "...such as road access to..." Memorandum, Casselman, William to John Dean, re: Location of Future Presidential Library at Camp Pendleton, April 11, 1973. J. Fred Buzhardt, Office File, Camp Pendleton Folder, SMOF, RNL.

168 "...he began, on April 6..." Carl Bernstein and Bob Woodward, "Dean Alleges Nixon Knew of Cover-up Plan," WP, June 3, 1973.

168 "...after John Ehrlichman negotiated..." Letter, Pressley, Paul, Councilman, City of San Clemente, California, April 26, 1973. J. Fred Buzhardt, Office File, Camp Pendleton Folder, SMOF, RNL.

169 "...the War Powers Resolution..." H.J.Res.542, 93rd Cong. (1973).

169 "...Fielding wrote a memo..." Memorandum to the file, Fielding, Fred, re: Nixon Library, May 3, 1973. J. Fred Buzhardt Office file [Loose Materials Concerning Camp Pendleton 1 of 3] Folder, SMOF, RNL.

169 "...the president appointed..." Organization Authority Record, Office of the Special Counsel for Watergate Matters. OPA, NARA: http://research.archives.gov/organization/1185817

169 "...on the back burner." Everett R. Holles, "Watergate Halts Nixon Library Plan," NYT, May 23, 1973.

170 "...Jack Nesbitt to acknowledge..." "Informal note," Nesbitt, Jack to Fred Fielding, September 18, 1973. J. Fred Buzhardt, Accordion File: RN Library at Camp Pendleton, Camp Pendleton Folder, SMOF, RNL.

170 "…'I am not a crook' remark…" R.W. Apple, Jr., "Nixon Declares He Didn't Profit From Public Life," *NYT*, November 18, 1973.

170 "…while walking along the beach…" "President Plans Own Defense in Full House," United Press International, July 27, 1974.

170 "…Foundation board voted…" Everett R. Holles, "Nixon Foundation Speeds Start on West Coast Library and Museum," *NYT*, August 11, 1974.

171 "…complain that Watergate unfairly casts…" Adam Nagourney, "Watergate Becomes Sore Point at Nixon Library," *NYT*, August 6, 2010.

172 "…the first wave of refugees…" Bill Parsons, "Camp Talega – 1975," *Groundbreaker*, newsletter of the Camp Pendleton Historical Society, Vol.8 No.2, Second Quarter 2014, 1-3.

172 "…50,000 exiles from…Vic Olly, "Pendleton once home for 50,000 war refugees," *Orange County Register*, April 8, 2010.

172 "…on what had been the proposed site for the Nixon Library." Ibid.

CHAPTER 7: A WAY FORWARD

PAGE

182 "…who established the Carter Foundation…" "Carter Owes No Tax But Will Pay Some," *AP*, June 25, 1977.

182 "He asked John Dunn…" Schewe, Donald B. (1982) "Transfers and Trans-formations: Processing the Papers of Jimmy Carter," *Georgia Archive*: Vol. 10: Iss. 2, Article 6.

182 "…informed the university…" Lynn Sweet, "Chicago Obama library bids in trouble; foundation has 'major concerns' with U. of C. proposal," *CST*, December 12, 2014; Julie Bosman, "Chicago No Longer Seems a Lock to Host Obama's Library, and Many Are Alarmed," *NYT*, January 17, 2015.

182 "…February, 2015, they leaked…" Michael Sneed, "Michelle Obama gets to pick library spot — and she favors NYC," *CST*, February 4, 2015.

182 "…they pressed the city's Park District…" Dahleen Glanton, "Chicago Park District approves transfer of parkland for Obama library," *CT*, February 12, 2015; John Byrne, "Aldermen give nod to Obama library land transfer," *CT*, March 11, 2015.

182 "…staged rallies to demonstrate…" Conor Skelding, "Chicago issues could boost Columbia's Obama-library bid," *Capital New York*, January 13, 2015.

182 "…and leaked a push poll…" Lynn Sweet, "Obama Foundation poll shows support for library in South Side parks," *CST*, February 25, 2015.

182 "…community organizers who demanded…" Isaac Stein, "Trauma center activists march on UCMC; Protesters attack University's bid for Obama library but not trauma center," *The Chicago Maroon*, May 28, 2014.

182 "…and conservationists who objected…" Fran Spielman and Lynn Sweet, "Parkland OK'd for Obama library, but site decision on hold until after election," *CST*, March 9, 2015.

183 "…represents an order of magnitude…" Other cities and universities have imagined that landing a library would add to their stature, prestige, and cof-

fers, and enhance their campuses or communities. But the expectations of those most vocal about bringing the Obama Library to Chicago – that the neighborhood, the community, the city, will be transformed, uplifted, rescued from dire economic conditions, and fundamentally changed for the better – have no equal in the history of the presidential library system.

184 "...to reach 500,000 visitors..." Tom Benning, "Bush Library has drawn 500,000 visitors so far," *Dallas Morning News*, June 30, 2014.

184 "Journalist Jonathan Alter wrote..." Alter, 154.

188 "As I demonstrated in a Salon..." Anthony Clark, "Cosponsoring bills," *Salon.com*, August 2, 2013.

INDEX

ABOUT THE AUTHOR

Anthony Clark is a former legislative director, speechwriter and committee professional staff member in the United States House of Representatives. During the 111th Congress, he was responsible for oversight of the National Archives, federal records, the (then) twelve presidential libraries, and federal information policy. Born and raised on Long Island, he graduated from St. Aidan School in Williston Park, New York, and Chaminade High School in Mineola, New York, and earned a Master of Science in Management and Systems from New York University.

He now resides in rural Maryland, where he enjoys the outdoors and misses bagels and pizza.